DO YOU REALLY NEED AN MBA?

THE WAY OF
AN ENTREPRENEUR

DO YOU
REALLY NEED
AN MBA?

DAVID M. CAMPBELL

Douglas & McIntyre
VANCOUVER/TORONTO

Douglas & McIntyre Ltd.
2323 Quebec Street, Suite 201
Vancouver, British Columbia v5t 4s7
www.douglas-mcintyre.com

LIBRARY AND ARCHIVES CANADA CATALOGUING IN PUBLICATION

Campbell, David M. (David Milton), 1920–
Do you really need an m.b.a.?: the way of an entrepreneur / David M. Campbell.

ISBN 1-55365-079-4

1. Businessmen—Canada—Biography. I. Title.

HC112.5.C33A3 2005   338.092   C2004-904846-5

Jacket design by Peter Cocking
Text design by Ingrid Paulson
Printed and bound in Canada by Friesens
Printed on acid-free paper that is forest friendly
(100% post-consumer recycled paper)
and has been processed chlorine free.

We gratefully acknowledge the financial support of the Canada Council for the Arts,
the British Columbia Arts Council, and the Government of Canada through the Book
Publishing Industry Development Program (BPIDP) for our publishing activities.

To Vivian, whose love and devotion made me realize
that life can be very meaningful and fulfilling.

To all young entrepreneurs.
May you have the courage to follow your dreams.

CONTENTS

Acknowledgements

ix

CHAPTER 1: The Type E Personality

1

CHAPTER 2: The First Dollar

14

CHAPTER 3: Life Is a Risky Business

34

CHAPTER 4: Fools Rush In

55

CHAPTER 5: The Next New Thing

77

CHAPTER 6: Matters of Character

90

CHAPTER 7: Other People's Money: Part I

104

CHAPTER 8: Other People's Money: Part II

122

CHAPTER 9: Getting to a Handshake

145

CHAPTER 10: Golden, but Still Handcuffs

168

CHAPTER 11: Top of the Game

184

CHAPTER 12: Life as an Angel

202

CHAPTER 13: Still Crazy (After All These Years)

220

Appendix

233

ACKNOWLEDGEMENTS

IF BY A STRETCH of the imagination the words that follow end up being called a book, it will have come about only through the collaborative effort and encouragement of many people. You were right. I could not have done it myself. Special thanks are owed to the following:

Chris Wood, Editor, who researched and provided all the political and historical content for this book, and who guided me through the pitfalls of the English language and made readable my ramblings about business theory and my recollections about each "crazy new idea."

Morley Torgov, Author/Humorist and winner of the Stephen Leacock Medal for Humour, who when I was discussing the possibility of this book and outlining some of the things I felt should be expressed, threw back at me one of the entrepreneurial phrases I used: "Just do it. Don't keep talking about it. Just do it."

Peter Grant, Lawyer and Specialist in Communication Regulations, who said, "I know the number of things you have started from scratch that challenged the regulators and the establishment. You must document that for future entrepreneurs."

Wendy Fitzgibbons, Editor, made sure I did not inadvertently malign someone and advised that saying things once is sometimes enough.

Professor Paul Perron, Principal of University College at the University of Toronto and author of innumerable books, who took time out of his incredibly busy schedule to comment on the first drafts and some of the rewrites and give me his critical review and suggestions.

John Fraser, Master of Massey College and Journalist, who on reading the draft of the first chapter called to say "Why did you stop? I want to read the rest. For someone without an M.B.A. you appear too intelligent. I did not know you had that many words in your vocabulary."

CHAPTER 1

THE **TYPE E** PERSONALITY

"A person who initiates, organizes, operates, assumes the risk and reaps the potential reward for a new business venture."

SCOTT MCNEALY, CHAIRMAN AND CEO, SUN MICROSYSTEMS

I CROSSED Wellington Street, dodging cabs and delivery trucks. The October afternoon was cool under an overcast sky. Above me, my destination glowed with serene cubist perfection. Somewhere up there was my office, on the twenty-seventh floor of Toronto's Royal Bank Tower. Through its gold-tinted window glass, the outlook was perpetually sunny.

Today, October 18, 1987, that was no optical illusion. Despite the clouds overhead, I had reason to celebrate. I had just completed one of the only significant deals to close in the very uncertain days after the October stock-market crash. A leading international corporation had just taken over the pioneering data network company I had founded and owned until an hour ago. And I had sold it for cash! Financially, I was set and secure and could do anything at all in the world I wanted with the rest of my life.

As I entered the heavy glass doors into the lobby of the bank tower, I had a momentary vision of another time.

THE YEAR IS 1924. A little boy sits on a tricycle on a sidewalk. The day is like this one, cool and grey, and the boy is dressed in short pants and

1

leggings. Suddenly an arched wooden door flies open, releasing a thrilling rush of stamping hooves and rippling horseflesh. Four huge brown animals snort and toss their heads, embodiments of power and spirit. They are pulling the red bulk of a fire engine.

THE SIGH OF elevator doors closing in front of me brought me back to the present. The car started to move, lifting me towards the twenty-seventh floor, farther by the moment from that brief recollection of where it had all begun. But that feeling of disorientation, of a strange detachment from my own identity, stayed with me; it remained long after I had returned to my desk at the company I had envisioned, established, nurtured through crises and opportunities—and now disposed of.

In sixty-seven years of life I had never had this much money, but that satisfactory knowledge was mixed with sadness—and a little confusion. I had exchanged decades of intense personal commitment and effort for a cash fortune. And I wondered if I had lost who I was.

When you create a business from scratch and own it for an extended period of time, that enterprise is who you are. You have an identity. Often you have power as well, commensurate with the size and influence of that business.

The moment you relinquish the business, all of that dissolves. You may walk out of the room with a cheque, but you no longer hold the allegiance of your staff. You may even receive a salary for a little longer, but your decisions no longer matter. You are no longer the one making the calls and taking the falls—or claiming the prizes.

For a bred-in-the bone "Type E" personality, it is a very strange and uncomfortable feeling indeed.

WHAT IS A TYPE E PERSONALITY?

YOU ARE FAMILIAR no doubt with the concept, derived from psychology, of the driven Type A personality. Its more prosaic associate is the common Type B.

Neither comes close to capturing the combination of traits and attributes shared by another of society's "types," perhaps the most vital of all: the individual who sees the possibility of some daring and unprecedented economic undertaking and brings it to reality.

To coin a phrase, this is the Type E personality: the born Entrepreneur.

There are many definitions of the term "entrepreneur." One of the briefest states simply that an entrepreneur is "someone who starts a new business."

Seldom has so much been glossed over in six simple words. In fact, the challenge the entrepreneur "undertakes" (as the word literally means in its French origins) is one of the most complex, courageous and difficult yet necessary adventures in the spectrum of human endeavour.

Consider the scale of the challenge the entrepreneur accepts. His or her idea must first improve on the status quo. It must present distinctly unique benefits. But that spark of innovation is just the beginning.

The product's unique qualities must distinguish it from competitors sufficiently to give consumers a reason to seek it out. Enough people must grasp the benefits of the innovation to constitute a viable market. The new offering must be capable of being sold at a price greater than its cost, or else there will be no profit to sustain a business.

Because the idea is new, the entrepreneur will need to invest time, effort and money in it before he or she can know for certain whether it will work. Usually, he or she must convince not only himself or herself of the value of this unproven idea but also others: customers, suppliers, lenders, employees and investors.

Then that commitment, effort and investment must be maintained—for months and years, in the face of every setback and discouragement and disappointment.

The effort required, the dangers and the ultimate returns mark out a path that bears a close resemblance to biological life cycles. The entrepreneurial cycle is fertilized when someone recognizes an opportunity and develops an idea in response to it. It begins to germinate when an entrepreneur accepts the inevitable risk and assembles the resources to initiate a new business. The enterprise that survives its infancy must explore its environment, discover nourishment and adapt to external threats. If it is able to do this, over time it will grow and reach maturity. The life cycle of a mature entrepreneurial enterprise comes to an end when it is disposed of, wound down or absorbed into some larger business.

> "All kids are inventors. It's because they're not afraid to get their hands filthy. To eat the paste. To use a hammer as a brush. To break something to see how it works. And to start with the impossible, which is where most grown-ups usually stop." **HEWLETT-PACKARD CORPORATION ADVERTISEMENT**

BY THAT OCTOBER afternoon in 1987, I was familiar with all of this. Reviewing my adult life, I could identify more than half a dozen "entrepreneurial cycles." I had founded, expanded, nurtured from start-up to stable profitability and eventually disposed of three substantial businesses and a number of smaller ones.

The latest, a financial markets data network named CMQ Incorporated (originally Combined Market Quotations Incorporated), had 250 employees on the day it was sold, offices across Canada and business contracts around the globe. In the last year under my ownership, its revenue had been in excess of $100 million.

I had been, until that day, a full-time entrepreneur continuously for forty-two years (with a brief period when I was simultaneously an executive of a large international corporation). In all those decades, I had never felt more happily assured, more comfortable or more essentially *myself* than when I had been in complete command of an enterprise, engaged in turning another one of "Dave's crazy ideas" into a profitable reality.

The moment I signed the documents to sell CMQ, I was no longer in command. I was no longer an entrepreneur. I felt like a band leader onstage in the spotlight, all alone.

In the past, whenever one of my enterprises came to the conclusion of its entrepreneurial cycle I had always had another venture ready to move from the back of the stove up onto the hot element at the front. This time would be little different. Within weeks of CMQ's sale, it was apparent to me that I simply could not stop thinking like an entrepreneur. I would not cease spotting business opportunities just because I was no longer "in" business. Besides, there was all this money crying out to be put to productive use—plus the leverage that amount of cash could generate.

There was only one thing to do: start another company.

Previous ventures had involved audio recordings, retail electronics, cable television, telephony and finally global business networking. The new company, Tricaster Holdings, would launch me into still another significantly different arena of entrepreneurship: the role of "angel" investor. From that perspective I would observe the culmination of a remarkable transformation in the culture of Canadian and North American business. In the past, I had always been the quarterback, calling every play in the huddle. Now through Tricaster I was supposed to stand on the sidelines, dispensing investment and coaching advice to younger players in the same technology fields. It wouldn't be easy to become that angel. I am told old habits die hard. I would always want to be a hands-on entrepreneur.

BUSINESS, WHEN I first entered it in 1945, was personal. Most companies I dealt with were run by their owners or major shareholders. The accepted qualifications for management (apart from social or family connections) were acumen, competitiveness and character. Some people had university degrees, but those were in liberal arts, science or engineering, not in business, per se. The modern master of business administration degree, or M.B.A., although it originated in 1908, was not yet ubiquitous.

Beginning in the 1950s, however, management at big corporations became increasingly "professionalized." People who had received academic training in the "principles" of "scientific" management were widely hired in the belief that their credentials qualified them to run virtually any enterprise.

The trend took flight in the 1960s. In the decades since, formally trained "masters" of business administration have come increasingly to dominate executive hiring, especially in certain industries. "The Masters of Business Administration is," *BusinessWeek* observed, "a ticket to the higher reaches of Corporate America."

The celebrity of M.B.A.-type thinking is even more common than the degree itself. Manuals on "management style" and "organizational transformation" have crowded whodunits from the bookshelves.

Through the 1990s, the business press gave its adoration to "imperial" CEOs who assembled the greatest stock-market capitalization, even if it was frequently at the expense of employees and even of customers trying to transact real business. The fictional Gordon Gekko of the movie *Wall Street* was hardly more controversial in his greed than some real-life characters in business.

To judge by lineups for enrolment at business schools, a generation of young Canadians has been raised to believe that an M.B.A. is what you need if you want to go into business. Much worse, a generation of human-resources "professionals" has, in many instances, endorsed that view by requiring a business degree as the price of admission to an interview, never mind a job.

Whether any of this has been good either for aspiring young business people or for the companies that hired them is open to question. A growing body of evidence and argument suggests that the claims made for the superiority of M.B.A.-type thinking are overstated.

In a recent book, McGill University business professor Henry Mintzberg makes the case that many graduates from masters of business administration programs are instead masters of little. Among other evidence he cites in *Managers Not MBAs: A Hard Look at the Soft Practice of Managing and Management Development** is one study that tracked the nineteen graduates of the Harvard Business School class of 1990 who had reached CEO status a decade later. More than half had by 2003 been drummed out of their jobs because their companies had gone bankrupt, become dissatisfied with their performance or been swallowed up by competitors. Only five of the grads had earned good records.

---

* Berrett-Koehler, 2004.

The return on investment may be no greater for the individual who has spent $60,000 to $100,000 to acquire the coveted degree. Stanford University Graduate School of Business professor Jeffrey Pfeffer and a research colleague sifted through four decades' worth of studies and statistics for evidence that people with M.B.A.s earned more as a group than those without the degree. He found essentially none. "Usually it just makes you a couple of years older," Pfeffer has remarked.

Academic business programs in the United States receive their accreditation from an organization called the Association to Advance Collegiate Schools of Business, based in St. Louis, Missouri. In 2002, the association admitted in a report that most of its members' graduates emerge with an "out-of-touch, ivory-tower" view of business that is little help in the real world.

Or, as *BusinessWeek* summarized Mintzberg's case: "B-schools foster an arrogant, 'elitist' class who understand little yet think they can solve any problem."

Despite this criticism, however, mainstream human-resources thinking and a good many young Canadians' career expectations have become ever more tightly focussed on the "professional" M.B.A. as a prerequisite preparation for a life in corporate business.

In fact, the economic reality for most Canadians is going in the other direction. Big corporations since 1988 have more often shrunk their workforces than expanded them. The "in" ideas in management are all about "squeezing out costs." Typically, this means paring people from payrolls in order to focus on a company's "core competency," while "outsourcing" as much as possible of everything else.

Many of those same outsourced services, meanwhile, are now being provided by smaller, often new, companies or by self-employed individuals. "Deconstructing" the corporation, in short, has created vast new opportunities for entrepreneurs.

The portion of all people working for small companies or for themselves has continued to rise. The self-employed—really, just entrepreneurs with staffs of one—accounted for three-quarters of all the new jobs created in Canada during the 1990s. By the turn of the twenty-first century, more than two million Canadians worked for themselves or a business that they owned. (Nearly 60 per cent of those had fewer than five employees.)

Business forecasters predict that these trends will continue and even accelerate as companies become more "atomic" and "virtual." Some futurists already envision a world economy driven by millions of "corporations of one."

In other words, young Canadians with business ambitions who pursue an M.B.A. in expectation of finding employment in a big corporation may not only be preparing themselves poorly but preparing for the wrong future.

Even if Mintzberg, Pfeffer and others are wrong, the academically trained "professional" executive is trained to *manage* a business; that is, to operate within an existing organization as a custodian. Especially in the last decade or so, that has often meant an obsessive interest in cutting costs or, at worst, the kind of accounting sleight of hand at which the likes of Enron and WorldCom excelled.

True entrepreneurial energy casts aside convention and existing practice to conceive an entirely *new* answer to people's needs, and with it creates real new wealth.

This dynamic, replicated again and again over the span of human history, has been the heartbeat of capitalist success—and sometimes the heartbreak. The entrepreneur's spark provides much of the energy that fuels the economy.

Academies are by their nature conservative. Many do extend the frontiers of the known through research, but their first task is to impart the consensus of the day. Rules easily become boxes that limit and discourage speculation beyond their walls.

Entrepreneurs know that in order to get wherever they want to go they will have to fly in the face of consensus and break with old rules. If they do, they may also achieve results that defy the most analytically rigorous expectations of M.B.A.-type thinking. As George Bernard Shaw famously wrote, "All progress depends on the unreasonable man."

"Some people manage by the book, even though they don't know who wrote the book, or even *what* book."   **HARVEY HUTTER & COMPANY, MANUFACTURERS**

THE LITTLE BOY on the tricycle pedalled that day in 1924 to a warm and supportive home, but to little of what most families today would consider the barest of domestic necessities—even less of luxuries.

The fire station with its horses was on King Street in the small town of Fredericton, New Brunswick. My father was a peddler, my mother a farm girl. Neither had more than a very basic schooling. As soon as the Depression struck, my father's income became erratic.

We moved to Montreal, where I finished elementary school. And there, at the age of twelve, I began my "business career": reselling penny scribblers to my classmates.

My first formal job, under the shadow of desperate global conflict, ingrained in me a philosophy of innovation at all costs. I learned to cultivate those occasional inspirations that many of my peers joked were more of "Dave's crazy ideas." And at the age of twenty-three I struck the most important partnership of my life: a marriage that has endured for more than six decades.

A year later, with my bride, I turned one "crazy" idea into our first serious business. It was called Dave Campbell's Melody House. What we began as a simple record store soon became a mini Future Shop of its day, selling the very latest in mid-twentieth-century consumer electronics.

By my thirtieth birthday, a new technology was transforming society: television. Melody House was making money selling television sets, but I was looking ahead. My idea was to adapt for Canada something I had been reading about. I would bring "better than off-air" pictures to those same televisions through a wire from a common antenna. We called the company incorporated in 1952 to introduce this novel concept Cable TV Limited.

A decade later, Cable was generating steady profits but the world was changing again. Computers were transforming communications. Business was going global and round-the-clock. The third major venture at the frontiers of technology created Canada's first—and for twenty-five years its biggest—network distributing financial market information: Combined Market Quotations (CMQ).

With this business now sold, I planned to use the proceeds to fund yet another new enterprise. In my mind, Tricaster Holdings would advance risk capital to companies I would help younger Type Es to run. I would help them to learn how to chase whatever new opportunity technology exposed in its onward march.

THERE IS ONE value in business schools that even their critics concede: It's the idea that a secret network of favouritism lurks behind the "old school tie." "The connections, the networking, the 'being anointed'—all that has value," Jeffrey Pfeffer states. Whatever you may or may not learn in class, spending your evenings with other future Harvard M.B.A.s, for example, does buy the nearest thing to a life membership in the American Establishment.

The halls of elite schools and insiders' habitual preference for other insiders like themselves may favour the socially preconnected. In the world of the entrepreneur, this masks a disadvantage: The narrower the range of views inside the tent of the anointed, the more static, conventional and ingrown their ideas will be—about business or anything else.

The wide-open fields and blue skies of the entrepreneur are open to anyone. More than open: they actively favour the maverick. The outsider, the person not constrained by the learned inhibitions of academic training, is the one who is likely to find it easier to see what is unexpected, to recognize the opportunity contained inside the shell of a problem. When the box was never that rewarding to begin with, it's much easier to think outside it.

Merely to work for yourself does not make you a true Type E individual, any more than wearing a stethoscope is all it takes to make you a doctor. Some companies in recent years have forced former employees to become grudgingly self-employed contractors. Even among those attracted by the cachet of owning their own business, not everyone is suited to the life of an entrepreneur. This is a lesson the founders of "family" companies too often discover only after handing the reins of an enterprise to their offspring.

But for the fortunate individual who commands the right mix of attitude, instincts, reflexes and gifts of character, nothing on earth could be more thrilling than conceiving of an idea that might just make a buck, seizing the moment, assembling the resources, piloting a risky venture into the stratosphere, reaping the rewards that go to the daring— and being able to say: *I* did that.

That person is a born entrepreneur, a true Type E personality.

A HANDFUL OF occupations today earn astronomical compensation. Celebrity entertainers and athletes, superstar CEOs, all these do very well. But those roles are very few and found in a limited number of cities.

A much greater number of "wealthy" people* in North America acquired their money by starting and owning a consistently profitable business. The M.B.A. club may help those who are already rich stay that way; the entrepreneurial cycle is how those who aren't rich yet will get that way tomorrow.

Money isn't nearly all of it, though. There is a potency you feel when an idea comes together, an opportunity is realized and a value you only imagined becomes a reality. The next time the Virgin chain opens another outlet, notice the zest in founder Richard Branson as he makes his trademark dramatic entrance by parachute or water ski. There's an entrepreneur celebrating the moment when an idea acquires a heartbeat.

"Celebration" doesn't describe every day for a Type E, however. Far from it. Take a look at some longer definitions of the type. An entrepreneur is:
- "one who assumes the financial risk of the initiation, operation and management of a given business"
- "a person who assumes the risk to start a business"

---

* By one common definition, anyone with liquid financial assets—investments and savings, not including their home—of more than $1 million can consider himself "wealthy."

- "someone who is willing to assume the responsibility, risk and rewards of starting a business"
- "one who takes on the financial risk"
- "a person who accepts both the risks and the opportunities"
- "one who assumes inherent risk"
- "a person who risks time and money."

One word cannot be overlooked: *risk*. Not every day will be Christmas.

In the corporate world, by contrast, M.B.A.-thinking CEOs seem more interested in asterisks than risks. They have managed to insulate themselves from most of the risk. Many in the last few years have cashed obscenely enormous bonuses even as their companies went down the drain.

The Type E accepts that omnipresent risk is the condition of all life. For him or her, the rule is ironclad and inescapable: no risk, no reward. And risk means *risk*. Sometimes things fail; you lose. The only certainty the entrepreneur can count on is that business life will be the polar opposite of a "job."

Working for someone else may or may not be exactly nine-to-five, but if you are in doubt about something you can always check the "rules"—the corporate policy book or employees' manual. The entrepreneur is at "work" from the moment he or she awakens in the morning. The responsibilities are, as they say these days, "24-7 and 365 days a year." And the entrepreneur writes the manual as he goes.

Some experts describe the entrepreneur's relationship to his business as being like a marriage. Others compare it to that of a parent's obsessive care for a child. Either is apt. And just like success in either parenthood or marriage, successful entrepreneurship has less to do with what you know than with how well you handle what you do *not* know. The trained manager relies on the M.B.A.-thinker's equivalent of a parents' manual. The Type E is an artist of improv.

The F.W. Olin Graduate School of Business at Babson College maintains an entrepreneurial hall of fame of sorts in Boston, Massachusetts. It once asked twenty-one of its all-star Type E inductees to identify the most important factors in their self-made business success. Knowledge of EBITDA ("earnings before interest, taxation, depreciation, amortization"), discounted cash flow and internal rate of return, the kinds of metrics that M.B.A.s pore over, did not figure high on anyone's list.

All, however, identified four personal attributes as necessities:

· they took personal initiative
· they responded positively to, and learned from, mistakes
· they possessed perseverance
· they identified the needed product or improvement.

Qualities like these were consistently far more important to these entrepreneurs than credentials. Their personalities made more of a difference to their later wealth than either their trust-fund portfolios or their financial sophistication.

Knowledge can be learned. Skills can be acquired. But where do you look for those qualities of attitude and personality that make the great entrepreneur? Do *you* have the right stuff? Are *you* a Type E?

"Wherever you see a successful business, someone once made a courageous decision."   PETER F. DRUCKER, *THE BUSINESS WORLD ACCORDING TO PETER F. DRUCKER*

THIS STORY BEGINS in a time of horse-drawn firehose reels but ends in one of digital cam-phones. It covers periods of hot war and Cold War, peace and terror. Some readers will find much of the daily texture it describes strange and unfamiliar; for anyone now at the age I was when I started Melody House, life before the PC is dimly remembered, but even they may have trouble imagining life before radio was everywhere.

The world has been transformed not once but several times since then, and with each transformation Type E personalities have discovered new and profitable opportunities for their creative verve and energy.

Not everything is different today. Little boys still ride tricycles. Canadians are still forever on the lookout for the latest new product. The currents of relentless change that drove the half century just past are undiminished in the present, and we can be quite certain that constant change will drive the future.

CHAPTER 2

THE **FIRST** DOLLAR

"After all is said and done, a hell of a lot more is said than done."

ANON.

NOW AND THEN you hear a board of trade member or a minister of industry extol the economic contributions Type E personalities make, the importance of small business as a generator of jobs or new technology. Those occasional apple-pie endorsements aside, the great majority of young Canadians today grow up expecting to "get" a job, not create one of their own. Top commerce graduates are encouraged to aspire to start somewhere on the corporate ladder. They expect to be inserted partway up an existing corporate chain and move higher still.

It wasn't always so. There was a time, before M.B.A.s were originated, when almost everyone was an entrepreneur of one sort or another, in the sense that they owned and operated the source of their livelihood. As the twentieth century dawned, Lithuania was one such place.

Lithuania was then part of Russia. The region's capital, Vilnius, was a manufacturing centre. Its countryside of lakes, farms and forests was dotted with smaller communities where independent bakers, shop-keepers, shoemakers and blacksmiths served local markets.

By the spring and summer of 1915, however, Lithuania found itself caught between the advancing armies of Germany's kaiser and Russia's czar. First one military force and then the other occupied the strategic gateway between Europe and Russia. As Lithuania descended into anarchy and chaos, historically good relations between the region's Jewish minority and its Christian majority spiralled downward. Mutual suspicion and fear soon spilled over into violence.

In what would come to seem a bitter irony before the new century was half over, a frequent cause of friction was the suspicion that Lithuanians of Jewish background were aiding the German invaders. When Russian Cossacks moved in, "they looked for hidden Germans among the Jews," one eyewitness recorded. Christian peasants joined Russian soldiers in plundering Jewish assets. One old rabbi, records relate, advised his congregation, "Even if we are not deported, it would still be best to leave."*

Among those who turned their backs on Lithuania's descent into violence were three brothers of the Kimmel family. Together, they set off for the beacon of stability and freedom that the New World represented. Their goal was America.

But between Lithuania and America lay Europe, and Europe was at war. In the chaos of a continent in arms, the brothers became separated. Two remained together, eventually finding their way to an Atlantic port and passage on a steamer bound for the west. Those two became citizens of the United States.

The third brother, my father, struggled in an unfamiliar language to find a ship to carry him to opportunity in the New World. In time he found such a ship, buying a one-way passage that entitled him to a dormitory bunk on a lower deck. But this vessel would not carry anyone to Ellis Island in the shadow of the Statue of Liberty; its destination was Canada.

The ship docked in Halifax and Samuel Kimmel stepped ashore and joined the line waiting for a Canadian official to record his arrival. In

---

* So many Lithuanians of Jewish faith heeded this advice that the region's economy promptly collapsed. Three years later, Lithuania achieved a shaky political independence that endured until the Second World War. During that conflict, nearly all of the 160,000 Jews who remained in Lithuania vanished into the Holocaust.

his hand he held identification papers issued in haste and filled out in a variety of European and Slavic languages, as well as in Yiddish.

When his turn came he presented himself to the immigration officer, who asked his name. Samuel provided it, but in the heavy accent of eastern Europe his family name came out sounding more like "Kammel" than anything else.

In Nova Scotia, the most Scottish of all Canadian provinces, it may have been natural enough to hear in the sound of Samuel's last name the phonetics of a common surname. Or perhaps the fellow was hard of hearing, or simply possessed a sense of humour. However it happened, the officer at the desk registered the arrival in Canada of one "Samuel Campbell." That was the name on the identity papers he handed to the young Lithuanian refugee standing in front of him, and it would be the name my father carried to his grave.

Other immigration officers in Halifax wanted to know whether the personable young Lithuanian had a job. When he admitted he did not, they asked, "Well then, what can you do?"

"I can speak several languages," he answered. In dealing with Lithuania's succession of occupiers and administrators, Sam had picked up a working knowledge of Russian, German, Polish and several other Slavic dialects, as well as speaking his native Lithuanian and the Yiddish spoken in the Kimmel home. This knowledge was valuable in a time when Canada was welcoming thousands of new immigrants a month from eastern Europe.

The Immigration Department promptly hired "Sam Campbell" as an interpreter. He was posted to McAdam Junction, a hamlet in central New Brunswick, to recruit construction labour among newly arriving immigrants for Canada's expanding railways.

While the job lasted, my father saved his meagre wages. Eventually he had saved enough money to buy a horse and wagon. With this investment he started a peddling route, his first entrepreneurial venture in his new country, travelling the rough roads of rural New Brunswick, visiting small towns and isolated homesteads with a stock of essential goods and small luxuries.

His route carried him frequently through the town of Woodstock, where he usually stayed with the Meltzer family. Across the street lived one of the town's two other Jewish families, the Isaacsons. Philip Isaacson happened also to be Lithuanian. He had come to North America nearly two decades earlier, at a time when the United States was welcoming anyone who agreed to farm or develop idle land. Philip's three brothers had settled near Rochester, New York, but he chose Maine, settling along the Canadian border.

At the time, the border was still somewhat vaguely defined and formalities for crossing it were loose. People and livestock often wandered from one country into the other without being aware of it. Over the next few years the frontier became more clearly drawn—and the rules were rigorously enforced. For Philip Isaacson it became increasingly risky to "re-enter" America with his wayward herd each time it drifted over the border to its favourite pasture on the Canadian side. After one particularly harrowing day spent chasing his cattle deep into Canada, and with rumours around of new guards on the border, Philip decided it would be easier to follow his cows' apparent wishes and become Canadian than risk further run-ins on the frontier. Rather than go home to Maine, he directed his wife to join him in Woodstock, New Brunswick, with their household belongings and three daughters.

The middle of these daughters was named Ida, and she quickly caught the eye of the significantly older travelling vendor staying across the street with the Meltzers. His interest was returned and soon the two wed.

Sam Kimmel was thirty-one when they married, Ida sixteen. Their wedding picture shows a diminutive bride in a long dress, the groom wearing a stovepipe hat. In due course the couple had a daughter whom they named Dorothy. And then, on May 23, 1920, they had a boy. They named him David. I had entered the world, the second child of a pair of accidental Canadians with a Jewish heritage and a Scottish name.

IN NORTH AMERICA, immigrants and children of immigrants are overrepresented among entrepreneurs. There are reasons for this: If you are smart, ambitious and from an established, mainstream family, it is axiomatic to look for opportunity with a big, established corporation or in the professions. Big corporations, in turn, favour the (perceived) lower risk of hiring someone from within the same predictable and like-minded background. Immigrants and their children are at a disadvantage in this game. The alternative jobs open to them are likely to be in one of those unpleasant and menial occupations traditionally reserved for newcomers with little other choice: sweat labour, such as changing hotel sheets or washing restaurant dishes.

On the other hand, the immigrant's constant insecurity, envy and willingness to do whatever it takes to survive in a new land and be accepted into a strange culture are among the very qualities that drive an entrepreneur towards success. Hardship, that is, may confer an entrepreneurial advantage. Precisely because we were denied the silver spoon at birth, some of us fight all the harder later on.

It is true that we cannot pick our parents. Yet childhood experiences and the values we absorb from our families have a significance in later life that we cannot ignore. That is especially true for the entrepreneur, who operates more by instinct and reflex than according to any book of rules. The entrepreneur more than the salaryman relies on his own judgement, his own vision, his own values; in short, on himself.

How well such self-reliance works for you, however, will depend on *your* own "self": on your inner qualities and resources of character. To create something brand new, you must break whatever rules apply to doing things the old way. This isn't a question of simple rebelliousness. Breaking rules is nothing but random destruction unless, in the process, you also create something new that is better than the old way allowed. And that something had better appeal to more than just *you;* it must be valuable to other people. Then you'll have to get off your backside and make it happen.

A willingness to break the "wrong" rules at the right time; a sincere interest in other people; drive, ambition and optimism, and the willingness to work up a sweat: these are facets of the Type E personality you should possess by the time you reach your teens—or you will likely never possess them at all.

"Youth is not a time of life. It's a state of mind. It's a temper of the will, a quality of the imagination, a vigor of the emotions, a predominance of courage over timidity, of the appetite for adventure over the love of ease."

SAMUEL ULLMAN, BUSINESSMAN AND EDUCATOR

IN SOME MATERIAL WAYS, at least, the 1920s were, as they are often described, a "simpler" time. There was certainly far less to buy than today's vast array of gadgets, conveniences, entertainment devices and appliances. The biggest wish book of the era in Canada, the thick T. Eaton Company department store catalogue, offered a smaller selection than even the smallest Wal-Mart store does today.

Much of what today's readers probably consider "old" was still barely imagined in the 1920s. The hot technology of the time was radio; only the most far-sighted experimental engineers imagined the same thing could be done with pictures. There were no such things as ballpoint pens, frozen dinners, credit cards, dishwashers or pop-top drink cans. The icebox of my childhood was just that: a box with shelves for food and a place above the shelves to put the ice that kept everything cool.

At the same time, a great many things were far *less* simple than today. There was no charging lunch at a restaurant, no popping a ready-to-eat frozen dinner into the microwave, no sending someone a contract or a snapshot by E-mail with a press of the "send" button.

My parents moved into a house on King Street in the New Brunswick capital, Fredericton. The house was next door to the fire station. Routinely, especially on winter nights, the clanging of a loud bell would precede the clattering rush of the horse-drawn fire engine out of the firehouse door. The Fredericton fire department has long since moved on to new technology and other quarters but the old station house is still there, occupied now by a dry cleaner.

In other parts of North America, Model T Fords and the radio craze were fuelling the optimism of the Roaring Twenties. Little of the excitement or novelty reached the idyllic town of roughly 30,000 people on a bend of the Saint John River. Fredericton was home to several shoe factories and a plant that made the world-famous Chestnut canoes. But like other New Brunswick centres, its foundries and other factories had been losing business to competitors farther west in Canada. The Maritime provinces, history would record, had entered a long and painful economic decline.

There was never hunger in the house on King Street. There was much joy, with a great deal of family visiting back and forth of a sort that still goes on more in the Maritimes than in Canada's big cities. Everyone, it seemed, played an instrument or knew a song. But the food was often plain and the clothes were almost always articles someone older and, until recently bigger, had handed down.

My mother's frugality remained with her for life. My sister and I were often frustrated when our gifts to her in later years were waved off with a remark such as, "You shouldn't have. I don't need it." After her death, we were startled to discover many gifts we had given her over the years—but never seen her use—carefully stored in cupboards, still in their original boxes.

The fact that despite our Scottish surname we were Jewish seemed of no great importance. My father was religious and philosophical, but he did not impose his Orthodoxy on his children. In any case, there were only a couple of dozen Jewish families in the capital. If we went to services twice a year, that was a lot. Judaism was more context than content in our lives. It ordered the calendar for high-holiday dinners and the special meals those called for. While Fredericton's other Campbells may have eaten hot scones with their tea, our mouths watered for my mother's European *taglah*—light pastry balls boiled, then baked, then dipped in honey and piled to cool in a sticky pyramid on the block of ice in the icebox.

Our family's faith never became an issue between schoolmates and me. Instead, my physique did. Like many families living on a tight budget, ours relied heavily on starchy staples such as porridge and local potatoes. For a while we shared a roof with one of the new immigrants my father had hired for railroad work, who became a handyman around our house. Stephan Butnack was from Romania and had known famine there. He made it his mission in life to see that I ate enough, with the result that I ate far too much and became overweight.

Children are frequently cruel and the oft-spoken assurance "Sticks and stones can break my bones but names can never hurt me" is a lie. Names *can* hurt. Three or four boys in particular took to following me home from school. They would start by hurling insults such as "Fatty" and "Big Ass" and "Pudgy," but soon they progressed to knocking my books from my hand and, when I bent to retrieve them, kicking me or knocking me down.

The first time this happened, I ran home crying. Mother consoled me. But she also said: "You have to stand up and fight for your right to respect, otherwise you will be picked on all your life. Fight back if you are attacked. Do not start the fight, but make sure you finish it."

A week or so later the same group again trailed me home. Hoping to avoid them, I ducked into an alley. This turned out to be a mistake: they simply followed me and in the privacy of the alley became even more threatening. I had nearly reached the street at the far end when they jumped me.

I don't remember much of what followed—or know where my resolve came from. But instead of cowering I lashed back. I struck out and kicked and punched until the only blood I saw was on my attackers. It wasn't a long fight. The other boys fell back; I grabbed my books and ran for home. I noticed I was bleeding, too. I hurt all over. But I had stood up for myself. The bullies never bothered me again. I enjoyed a new respect, just as my mother had said I would.

My mother's personality was far stronger than her husband's. Mother *did;* Father more often dreamed about doing, or gave up part-way. My father was away most of the time, working his peddling circuit and eventually opening a general store with everything from tea to toques on its shelves in a place called Plaster Rock, east of Fredericton. The lessons I took from him came out of his more reflective temperament. For example, his model of sincere respect for my mother, I believe, influenced my own attitudes towards women for the better.

I remember once witnessing a strong argument between my parents. Father, I thought, had the better case. But in the end he relented and ceded the point to Mother. Later, I asked him why he had given up. "You will learn," he told me, "to pick your battles. You might have to give up a few. But some are not that serious; those you can afford to give up. When you do that, the other side feels they have won—yet they will be vulnerable the next time, because they think they have you on the run. Save your best effort for the battles that really count."

Other lessons I absorbed were unspoken yet powerful. Stephan may have encouraged my bad eating habits, but he also opened my eyes to the idea of opportunities. Borrowing my toy wagon for the purpose, he showed me that empty pop and beer bottles could be collected by the barrelful and turned in at the local bottling plant for money. He demonstrated how to use scissors and a small bottle of rubber cement to turn old letters and envelopes into scratch pads.

But if my parents sometimes struggled to provide for my sister and myself, their struggle soon became that much harder. To a Canadian schoolboy, Tuesday, October 29, 1929, was just a day like any other. To the headline-reading grown-ups of the world it would forever be Black Tuesday: the "Big Board," otherwise known as the New York Stock Exchange, lost 12 per cent of its value, on the heels of a 13-per-cent loss the day before. The worst run on a stock market in history to that time—and for another half century, until it was exceeded in 1987— became known as the Crash of '29. It set off the Great Depression.

I was nine and a half.

THE COLLAPSE OF THE financial world at first made little difference to the Campbells of Fredericton. Our lifestyle had never been lavish to begin with and hadn't far to fall. But it was clear that our parents were working harder, to avoid joining the growing numbers of unemployed queuing at food kitchens. Over the next three years, unemployment in Canada would reach 30 per cent of the workforce.

There were no national welfare standards in those days. "Relief" was mainly left to towns and cities to provide, and it was far from generous. Families of five in Halifax received just $15 a month.* Thank God, our family never found out what the relief rate was in Fredericton, but there were certainly some changes in our lives. My father's general merchandise store in Plaster Rock suffered, and for most of the next decade he would be in and out of work.

My mother, ever the steelier, withdrew some of their small savings to invest in an ambition that became a second income for the household—and at times the only income—as well as an indelible model for me of the entrepreneurial instinct at work. She travelled—by train, of course—to Montreal to earn a hairdressing diploma. Back in New Brunswick, she invested in a recent breakthrough in beauty technology: the electric rollers and hair dryer that made possible the permanent wave. With these she set up a hair salon in our King Street house.

It was never a subject of conversation, but I suspect that for most of the rest of my childhood and adolescence it was Mother who was the family's real breadwinner. Her business thrived to the point that she was able to afford to buy a used car. During the summer, she would bundle her permanent-wave equipment into the back seat and me into the front, and together we would travel a beautician's version of my father's peddling circuit, bringing fashionable hairstyles to the villages and hamlets of the Maritimes.

I discovered in these trips the inspiring summer loveliness of that region. The lush green of the Saint John River valley and glowing seasonal blush of Nova Scotia's Annapolis Valley with its apple and pear orchards fed a sensibility in me that would blossom into a lifelong avocation: the collection of art and other beautiful objects.

---

* Roughly $200 in today's dollars. Here and throughout, where historical dollar figures are converted into present-day values, conversion has been done according to conversion factors available online at http://oregonstate.edu/dept/pol_sci/fac/ sahr/sahr.htm.

From the eager groups of women who welcomed us at every stop, I learned something else: the inestimable value of being the exclusive provider of a desired service. My mother's mobile hair-waving salon was something entirely new to the farmsteads of the Miramichi and Annapolis Valleys. It was different, it was unique, and even in the hardest years of the Depression grateful Maritime women dug into their scarce savings in order to pay for it.

> "Life is a series of moments. They are mundane. They are profound. They are once in a lifetime. They are with your children at bedtime. They are at 5:48 on a Tuesday morning. They are during the final act of a play. They are fleeting. They are yours to make happen."
>
> **AMERICAN EXPRESS CORPORATION ADVERTISEMENT**

THE MARKET CRASH had set off the Depression but it was not its worst moment. In fact, the economy continued to contract for another three years. My father's general merchandise business in Plaster Rock struggled in the hard times and dwindled to nothing. In 1932 my parents made a fateful decision: They would pull up stakes and "emigrate," my father for the second time. That summer we moved to Montreal, then Canada's largest city.

Through the years my father had come to know people in New Brunswick's potato industry. (Then as now, potatoes were an important provincial export. The McCain company, which sells half the world's frozen French fries, is still based in New Brunswick.) "Food," my father reasoned, "is something people *always* need."

At the time, F.W. Pirie Company was selling its regular potatoes and its premium spuds in similar, indistinguishable bags. My father, ever the innovator, suggested to it that an individual box with a transparent window to display the top-quality potato inside would make more appealing packaging for the company's best produce. Impressed, Pirie invited my father to join its sales force. He became the company's agent in Quebec, marketing potatoes mainly to the groceries and to a company that owned a chain of Murray's restaurants as well as to a separate company, Crowley McCracken, that supplied vegetables to the region's soup kitchens.

We moved into a house in a commercial block of Sherbrooke Street West in Westmount, about four kilometres west of downtown Montreal. Our home had two floors and we did what generations of immigrants and entrepreneurs have done before and since: Mother opened her business on the street-level floor. We lived upstairs.

(Today's commuter lifestyle is a relatively recent phenomenon. It has really only existed since the invention of trains, which carried city workers from suburbs to offices downtown and home again before cars and throughways became the norm. For most of history most people have lived near their workplace, often sharing it with their living quarters. Too many aspiring entrepreneurs today burden their businesses with excessive costs by adopting elaborate management "systems," fancy quarters and expensive lifestyles before they've made the first dollar.)

There was no one bankrolling Sam and Ida Campbell's gamble on a new life in Montreal except their own gumption and hard work. They wisely took every possible measure to improve their new venture's chances.

There is no better way to know your business intimately than by living with it. People who do so normally find they give their businesses more of their time—for a Type E, the hardest thing to find!

IV THE AUTUMN OF 1932 and the winter of 1933 were to prove the very bottom of the Great Depression. Things slowly began to improve after that. Of course, we didn't know that at the time. In fact, many things seemed only to get worse. The government began setting up "relief camps" where single unemployed men could get a cot, meals and twenty cents a day for labouring on public construction projects.

I'm certain my parents went through many sleepless nights over that first winter in Montreal and in the years that followed it. My father's income remained unsteady and my mother's enterprise continued to keep the family afloat.

"Afloat" was hardly affluence. "New" clothes or anything else usually meant new to us. Nothing was ever thrown out that could be repaired or used again. The smallest luxuries were the subject of agonizing family debate.

The day we brought a radio home and set it up in the living room of our small apartment was a huge family occasion. It was followed by many months of anxiety about whether my father would be able to keep up the instalment payments on the indulgence.

As I tried to find my own footing in this new setting, to win acceptance from other teenagers and make an impression on the world, I inevitably noticed those possessions others had that I did not. The must-have personal accessory of my years in high school—the equivalent of today's cellphone—was the wristwatch. A watch was much more expensive when it contained tiny springs and gears rather than microchips.

After weeks of wheedling, pleading and tears, I persuaded my father that my entire future rested on getting a wristwatch. He didn't have the money for one, but he agreed to go into debt at People's Credit Jewellers to satisfy my longing.

I recall my excitement as we set out to walk to the store to pick out a watch and make the arrangements. And then the desolation when the manager turned down my father's request for credit. We had "moved around too much," he said. I remember my hurt and shame as we walked home together. I can only imagine my father's emotions.

There were other new realities for my sister and me to deal with as well. Our mixed neighbourhood had French and English, Jewish and Christian families, and they all had children. I found myself making friends with many of them, from all groups. If there were rivalries and tensions, they were not on language lines. The French and Jewish families got along pretty well with each other; the English, as a rule, treated us both with an element of disdain, what the French might call *hauteur*.

An immigrant who had done well for himself heard that New York City's famous Bloomingdale's department store was for sale. He contacted the seller. A few days later he went to meet the vendor at the property, bringing his wife with him.

"Take a look around," he told her, as he headed into his meeting.

She returned an hour and a half later after touring the famed establishment.

"Don't buy it, Morris!" she whispered to her husband. "I've seen the place from top to bottom, and there's *nowhere to live upstairs!*"

THAT FALL I ENTERED my last year of elementary school. Inevitably, we had to buy some supplies: pencils, scribblers. I had observed that most of my classmates bought their small school supplies from the corner variety store. It charged exorbitant prices, but there was nowhere else nearby that sold paper supplies. The owner was basically using his local monopoly to gouge the neighbourhood's kids.

One day soon after school started I was sitting with friends at the store's soda fountain. A truck pulled up. The driver got out and brought in a load of school supplies. I saw that the name of the company was on the side of the truck and committed it to memory. Later, I contacted the company and asked if anyone could buy scribblers and pencils from them. The answer was yes.

I asked their prices, and the distributor's charge for pencils and notebooks was so much less than the storekeeper's that I knew I could easily resell them to my classmates for huge savings to them and still make a profit. The store's owner, I'm sure now, had his own bottom line to meet. But his gouging had left room for a competitor to move in with a better price and take away some of his customers. I had learned a lesson that would stand me in good stead for a lifetime: *never* gouge! When you overcharge, you leave the door open for a competitor.

Even so, the first few times I did this I was careful to order from the company only when a friend wanted to buy a particular item. That ensured I had a sale before I put my own money at risk. Rudimentary inventory management! Later, I began to keep some items "in stock" under my bed in our flat.

We had been in Montreal a year when I entered high school and confronted another new reality. In that era there was no charge to attend public elementary school, but once you reached high school you were expected to pay a dollar a week towards the cost of your education, plus another dollar a week for textbooks. As little as this sounds, it was going to be a significant strain on the family economy. There was no option but to go out and find a way to earn the money myself.

There was nothing original about how I did it. Like tens of thousands of boys (and girls) before and after me, I got a paper route. The paper was the morning *Gazette* and my route was two long parallel blocks of Victoria and Grosvenor Avenues—uphill both ways. I started with fifty-eight customers. The paper paid five cents a week for delivering each one six days a week and promised a bonus of ten cents for every new customer I could sign up.

The papers were delivered to a local depot each morning. My parents set up a cot in our small apartment hallway at the top of the stairs, so I could slip out at 4:30 AM without disturbing the rest of the family. Let me tell you: five dozen newspapers can make for quite a weight, especially if you're humping them over snowdrifts in January before the plows have been out!

I kept that paper route for as long as I was in high school and increased it from fifty-eight to, eventually, 105 accounts. I would ask the newspaper company for a few extra copies and leave them at the door of households that weren't customers yet. The next day I'd leave a note, expressing the hope that they'd enjoyed the paper—and pointing out some stories they were missing in that day's *Gazette.*

I also polled my customers about how they liked their paper delivered. "Do you *want* it at the front door?" Not everyone did. Some preferred delivery to a side door. One man asked me to put his paper in the window beside his front door. This turned out to be his bathroom window; by me putting the paper there, he could reach for it first thing in the morning without having to present himself in pyjamas at the front door!

This sort of extra service was reflected in the tips at Christmas. But even without these, or the dime bonuses I got for signing on each new customer, the weekly income of $2.90, rising eventually to $5.25, allowed me to pay my school and book fees each week throughout high school, with something left over.

Dollar figures from another period can be difficult to put into contemporary perspective, but it's interesting to reflect that my $2.90 a week starting income from that paper route was more than twice what men in the relief camps were paid for heavy labour (of course, they also were fed and were "housed" under canvas). By the time I got the route up to 105 subscribers, that paid me twenty-one dollars a month (worth about $270 in today's inflated currency).

That income was important to an eager teenager. Our neighbourhood was mixed, but Westmount was also home to many wealthy families. There wasn't a lot of obvious social division along wealth lines. At Westmount High School, playing hockey in the streets or cards in someone's house after school, we were pals. But I did notice that some of my friends never had to worry, as we constantly did, about where the money would come from to do anything. When I wanted to see a movie or buy a model airplane kit, when I wanted to build a "ham" crystal radio set, I had to find some way—*any* way (that wouldn't get me into trouble)—to earn the money to do it.

Through hunger and reward, those classic forces of conditioning, I was acquiring the foundations of the Type E personality's eye for opportunity. I was forever looking around for a chance to do something for somebody for which they might pay. By osmosis, I was learning to put the customer first, to look for a need and a way to meet it at a profit.

IV ANOTHER VENTURE FOUND me partnered with Charles Darwin. This was a school chum, not the evolutionary thinker. One day we walked into our family's kitchen and found my mother cautiously pouring a thick, acrid liquid from one bottle into another.

The liquid was something called "Javel"—concentrated bleach. For some reason (possibly to keep shipping costs down) manufacturers in the

1930s sold liquid bleach only in a highly concentrated form. Housewives needed to dilute the concentrate with water before using it or risk painful chemical burns. Indeed, there was a risk just in diluting the stuff.

Charlie and I took one look at this and thought, "This is stupid! Women shouldn't have to do this. We should be doing it for them!"

We rounded up some empty bottles and bought some Javel. It took a while to learn to pour carefully enough to avoid getting chemical burns ourselves, and you had to keep the windows open or the fumes would knock you over, but soon we were selling diluted Javel to quite a number of housewives. It saved them an unpleasant chore and earned a few pennies a bottle for Charlie and me.

It wasn't apparent at the time, of course, but these youthful enterprises, as amateurish as they were, reinforced the traits that would later be vital to my entrepreneurial success: an eye for opportunity, the initiative to act on it, respect for the customer. The paper route—six days a week, rain or shine; and then I took on a second, afternoon paper—developed my discipline.

In the last summer before my senior high school year, I got a summer job as well: guiding tours on a sightseeing bus. I haven't often worked as an employee (I've always much preferred to be the boss!), but what this job failed to teach me about business it more than made up for as a window into human motivation and Type E opportunism.

The bus drivers worked year-round. We guides, all young college or high school kids, worked seasonally. Our job was to provide colour commentary at each local landmark, from Montreal's historic old town to the Kahnawake Mohawk reserve across the St. Lawrence River. Our pay was a minimum wage—about twenty cents an hour as I recall—and tips that we split with the drivers.

These veterans knew every angle. Early in the season, one told me to make sure the passengers knew I was a student working to pay for college. Believing that they were helping some ambitious young fellow better himself always helped passengers to loosen the purse strings.

For some passengers, the drivers made "special" stops. When business conventioneers (in those days, overwhelmingly male) were in the city, we would often take a busload of men down Ontario Street and turn in at 312. We'd park in the rear yard and I would help the passengers down so they could file in the back door of a large house. Ten or fifteen minutes later the driver and I would follow.

We'd only make it as far as the kitchen, however. There, the "madam" of the establishment would greet the driver like an old friend and offer us both coffee and cookies. Half an hour later, she'd hand the driver an envelope and we'd return to the bus. Within minutes our passengers would begin to reappear; when all were back in their seats, we'd resume our sightseeing. Later, the envelope would be opened and the "commission" added to the tips to be divided.

Brothels weren't the only establishments to pay commissions: The wax museum and midgets' palace had similar standing arrangements to encourage us to bring sightseers to their doors. The same did not apply to the city's most visible and possibly most famous landmark, the Catholic shrine to Saint Joseph high on Mount Royal.

The shrine had been the lifelong project of poor but pious Brother André. He was reputed to have performed miraculous cures while raising money for its construction and when he died, in that January of 1937, more than a million people visited his body, delaying his funeral by days. For many visitors to Montreal that year, his still-incomplete oratory to Saint Joseph was the highlight of our sightseeing tour. But if the priests didn't pay commissions for the visitors we brought, that did not mean this attraction was immune to exploitation by my canny mentors in prompting larger tips.

"Go in with them," my driver told me the first time we visited the shrine.

"I can't," I said. "I'm not Catholic."

"Never mind. Just follow them in and do whatever they do. Kneel the same as they do."

"But I'm Jewish. We don't kneel."

"They don't know whether you're Jewish or Catholic or Muslim. But if you want tips, just kneel. They'll assume you're one of them and that's enough." I did as he suggested and the passengers did as he predicted.

On one especially hot day, I left my gunmetal-blue uniform jacket behind on the fender of the bus when I escorted the passengers up to the shrine. When we returned, I helped the passengers back onto the coach and followed the last one aboard the bus. It wasn't until we were well on our way that I remembered my jacket. I was horrified that I could have been so careless as to forget it. And worse, we were responsible for the cost of our uniforms: if I lost it, it would come out of my wages.

The driver told me he couldn't turn the bus around, but he would stop and give me time to run back up the street to the shrine to see if the jacket was on the ground somewhere or if someone had found it. I raced back up the hill and up all 300 steps to the oratory. No jacket.

Flushed, sweating and downcast, I returned to the bus. The grinning driver met me at the door with my uniform cap in hand—and it was brimming with dollar bills. In my absence he had explained the situation to the passengers, including my liability for the loss of the jacket. Touched, they had been especially generous in their tipping.

Still, I was glum at the end of the day as we divided this bounty. "You don't look very happy," my driver remarked.

"I still have to pay for a new jacket," I reminded him.

The driver stood from his seat, turned and lifted the cushion. From under it he produced the jacket, neatly folded. He handed it to me with a sly grin.

FOR A SEVENTEEN-YEAR-OLD entering his last year of high school, it was not such a bad time to be alive. I had stopped putting on height at five feet nine inches, but I was solid, weighing in at over 190 pounds. Bulk and staying power, more than athletic grace, won me a spot on the football team for a second year.

Campbell, the joke went, got his football uniform from the Montreal Tent and Tarpaulin Company! I played on the line—both ways; there were no "offensive" or "defensive" units in those days. That autumn Westmount High won the city football championship, doubtless due to its heavyweight line.

When winter set in, a favourite weekend activity was to take the train up into the Laurentians, get off at one stop and ski cross-country. We would stay the night at one of the region's many small hotels, then meet the train going back to Montreal late the next day at another station.

On one of these jaunts I got to know a vivacious brunette my own age named Vivian Rothbart. I enjoyed her company well enough but was deterred at first from pursuing a closer relationship. Vivian's mother, I quickly discovered, felt strongly that her little girl could do better than this eager but socially undistinguished youth!

Meanwhile, beyond my own agreeable circle of friends, family, paper routes and school, ominous events were gathering pace. Canadians had gone off to fight and die in Spain's civil war, which pitted left-wing Republicans against right-wing Royalists. Germany's chancellor, Adolf Hitler, had sent bombers to help the Royalist side.

That spring of 1938, my last year of high school, German armies marched into Austria in the unopposed annexation that came to be called the *Anschluss.* By summer, Hitler's propaganda machine and guns were turned on Czechoslovakia.

The quickening drumbeat of war was picked up in the economy. Factories, especially those in the defence industries, were hiring again as Canada began to rebuild its neglected armed forces.

CHAPTER 3

LIFE IS A **RISKY** BUSINESS

Yesterday is history.
Tomorrow is a mystery.
Today is a gift.
That's why we call it the 'present.'

ANON.

THE CRISP INDIAN summer morning seemed to vibrate. With a shattering roar from its one big radial engine, an airplane gathered speed down a runway and then lifted off on low-set wings. Its fresh coat of bright-yellow paint glowed against the clear blue sky. Beneath the glass canopy two leather-helmeted heads were visible: a pilot in front and an observer sitting behind.

The thunder of the engine faded as the aircraft climbed, spearing nearly straight up into the sky. High over the St. Lawrence River the plane performed a few lazy rolls, banks and circles. Then the pilot pushed forward on the stick and pointed the nose towards the ground. From five kilometres up, the 400-horsepower motor screamed at maximum revolutions. The propeller clawed the air under full torque. The crew hurtled towards Earth at 400 kilometres an hour. Just as it seemed the craft must plunge to disaster, the nose was pulled back. The plane shook and the riveted airframe creaked and vibrated at the limits of its designed tolerance. In the cramped cockpit, the men in the leather helmets felt the skin on their faces sag and the strange sensation of their internal organs being sucked down into their pelvises by a force three times that of gravity.

But then the plane was climbing again. Once more morning light glinted on fresh paint the colour of sunflowers and the blue-around-white roundel, with its red bull's eye, on its flank.

A few minutes later the plane touched down again on the same runway and taxied to the apron. The clear canopy slid back and the helmeted men climbed down to the ground. One of them, the figure who had occupied the passenger's seat behind the pilot, signed a printed form. With that casual signature, another Harvard trainer airplane was officially accepted into the growing squadrons of the British Commonwealth Air Training Plan.

The year was 1940. Canada had been at war for over a year and so far the battle was not going well for the Allied side. The casualty rate among British aircrews had been especially heart-rending—and alarming. Canada was the centrepiece of the Allied effort to replace those losses. By the time the war ended some 11,000 Canadian and 8,000 Australian, New Zealand and British airmen would learn to fly and train for dogfights using the rugged Harvards.

Today's flight, including the heart-stopping dive and last-minute climb from otherwise certain death, had been a test, putting this particular Harvard through its paces before it was put into service. Acceptance rested with the 20-year-old acting flight lieutenant who had flown in the observer's seat behind the pilot: Acting Flight Lieutenant David Campbell. I never told my wife.

I HAD GRADUATED from high school in 1938 hoping to find a career in advertising. I loved the idea of being called on to be creative every day. In my senior high school year I had won a city-wide contest, sponsored by a big agency, to design advertising for a hospital fundraising campaign. But war had changed everything—first the expectation of it, then the reality.

This wasn't by any means all bad. There was a gathering sense that the Depression might finally be behind us, for one thing. And even though the news from overseas was often dark, for a young man just entering adulthood in what was then Canada's biggest city, with no firm idea of his own talents or destiny, the air held the thrill of opportunity as well as of danger.

The circumstances of my childhood had forged in me a personality that was fundamentally optimistic and, more than that, opportunistic. Adolescence had been, for me, one long search for opportunities to do something different that no one else had thought of yet, and to make a few cents at it. Now the first years of my adulthood would introduce me to a far wider world of opportunity. They would also begin to make me aware that not everyone responds to opportunity as I do, by seizing it.

One opportunity did not present itself: university. Montreal's McGill was then world-renowned, but it was simply not an option for me. I didn't have the money, for one thing. In those days there were no student-loan programs and few scholarships. I also didn't have the marks: earning money had always come before hitting the books in high school.

The second barrier was a particular handicap because of the family faith. Jews needed academic averages of 75 per cent or better to be considered for acceptance into McGill. I certainly did not have that. (As a consequence of this policy, of course, Jews were significantly over-represented in the top tier of McGill graduates; not, perhaps, what the policy's framers had in mind.)

Instead of McGill, I found a seat at an institution that was then pioneering a new approach to education. Sir George Williams College was named after the British founder of the YMCA. North America's first YMCA had opened in Montreal in the 1850s; it began offering night courses a few years later. Since being formalized under its new name in 1926, the college had expanded. It had graduated its first full university day class only two years earlier.* More than half its students still attended in the evenings; this would be a good thing for me, as it turned out.

_____

* Sir George Williams College merged with the French-language Loyola College in 1974 to create Concordia University.

I enrolled in the general sciences program. How things worked had always intrigued me. I was the kind of kid who would take something apart to figure out how it went together. If I could understand how it worked, maybe I could figure out a *better* way for it to work.

NEVER ASSUME!

Four Sir George Williams students were from families all said to be "in oil."
I had visions of derricks and overflowing bank accounts and I could not imagine why they were attending such a working-class college.
Until I learned the businesses their families were really in:
The fish-oil business
The tanning-oil business
The olive-oil business
And yes, one was in the petroleum business.

SOUTH ACROSS THE St. Lawrence River from the Sherbrooke-Claremont neighbourhood where I had attended high school was the community of Longueuil. Now largely suburban, it was then still mainly farmland. Its flat terrain was also home to several minor airstrips belonging to aircraft builders and air-services companies. None of these were yet the giants of the "aerospace" industry. Most of them were overgrown workshops run by their thoroughly Type E founders, a mix of engineers and self-taught amateurs. Buoyed by the reviving economy and a rearming military, many of these were hiring.

I soon found a night job at Fairchild Aircraft Corporation. I was a "doper." That word has another meaning today; back then it meant responsibility for one step in building an airplane. These were first-generation production aircraft. Their fuselages were framed from wood or steel or aluminum tubes, then covered with fabric. We dopers painted a chemical "dope" on the fabric that, as it dried, contracted and pulled the fabric tight, almost like the skin of a drum, creating a light-weight covering for the plane.

The fumes were intoxicating, but the wages paid my college tuition and more. I was able to buy my first car (used). With it, naturally, my social life improved. I was invited into a fraternity, which I joined. I had known Vivian Rothbart since high school, and now our dating became more serious.

Abroad, the crises were piling up. Japan's imperial armies were methodically working their way across China and into Southeast Asia. Italy's "Duce," Benito Mussolini, invaded and annexed Albania. Then, on September 1, 1939, Hitler unleashed his Wehrmacht in blitzkrieg against Poland. Two days later, Britain declared war. On September 10, Canada did the same.

Beyond noting the headlines and Canadian Broadcasting Corporation (the CBC) news on the radio, I was generally too busy and always too tired to follow each unfolding crisis. Taking classes by day and working ten-hour shifts each night, I grabbed sleep when I could—and never enough of it. After I drifted off behind the wheel once too often, nearly killing a carload of friends, I rearranged my schedule. I started studying nights and working days. This way I slept in class, instead of on the way there.

The Allied retreat from Europe left Germany poised to invade Britain. The Luftwaffe began bombing British ports and air bases, turning the airspace over England into the war's front line. Training fresh pilots and resupplying their squadrons with aircraft became a matter of life or death for Britain and its allies.

Canada, under the Commonwealth training agreement signed at the beginning of that year, stepped up to both roles. Tens of thousands of Allied pilots and associated aircrews received their basic flight and battle training in Canada. Aircraft production gathered speed and scale at an almost explosive pace.

As important, anything new that could give our side even a momentary advantage against the Axis forces was instantly seized upon and tried. If it worked, it was put into production.

"The champion of today is obsolete tomorrow unless one takes constant advantage of new developments and discoveries," one reporter remarked after touring several aircraft plants. The principle matched my temperament perfectly. It became the central conviction by which I would live the rest of my life.

Even today, it's difficult to get one's head around the numbers from that time. In no full year between 1935 and 1939 did Canadian aircraft builders produce even as many as forty airplanes. By 1942 they were turning out 400 *a month,* from fighters to heavy bombers. In employment terms, the industry grew forty-fold, adding 2,000 employees a month.

There was a constant race to innovate in design and production processes. Not long after I started at Fairchild, fabric doping became obsolete. I moved to a company called Noordyne, where a new genera-tion of planes was being built with aluminum skins instead of fabric. These were stitched together with hundreds and thousands of aluminum rivets. Each one of these had to be snugly seated or it would eventually vibrate loose in service. If that happened, whole sections of aluminum skin might peel off in midflight. At first I was assigned to individually inspect each rivet to ensure it was tight and correctly seated.

The hectic race to expand and speed production was meanwhile creating millions of additional square metres of factory space and demanding thousands of new workers to fill them. In that environ-ment, "young men of 21 are veteran craftsmen," as a *Globe and Mail* reporter put it in the spring of 1941. I was soon inspecting not only rivets but other parts of the aircraft under construction as well.

For no particular reason that I ever understood, I was declared "expert" on the airframe of the new Harvard trainer and entrusted by the Royal Canadian Air Force with the job of "accepting" individual planes as airworthy. This determination was not reached by any sophisticated protocols; we simply took the plane up in the air and tried to tear the wings and sunflower-yellow skin off it. If they stayed on, we accepted it.

As the output of aircraft picked up I rode through the test routine of aerobatics, followed by that screaming nose-dive and gut-sucking recovery, as many as half a dozen times a day. You'll have figured by now that the wings never did come off. The skin sometimes did.

I WAS STILL LIVING at home and helping my parents meet the family expenses, but I wasn't spending much time in the flat on Sherbrooke Street.

Sir George Williams was still a very young institution then, with the energies and irreverence of youth. The year I began, a group of its students had started a satiric sketch-performance troupe under the name "Georgiantics." The group staged irregular variety shows with music and comic scenes built around personalities and events of the day. Its members wrote the scripts, built the scenery and acted the parts.

Somehow, between work and school (and probably at the considerable expense of the second), I found the hours to become a charter member of the troupe. Physique was again casting destiny for me, as it had been on the high school football squad. Then I had provided ballast to the scrimmage line; now, girth won me the role of Mussolini, to my friend Don Quinn's Hitler, in Georgiantics' patriotic send-ups of the Axis leaders.

The experience bears noting here for two reasons. First, no quality (and it *is* a quality as much as a skill) is more essential to the Type E personality than salesmanship. Whether you are introducing a new product to a customer or pitching a new business to a banker, the challenge is to communicate your enthusiasm about that product or business. Any top salesperson will tell you that his or her job is as much performance art as it is anything else.

The Georgiantics shows greatly bolstered my confidence in the spotlight and honed my performance skills both on the page and on my feet. It was an investment in myself that I maintained later on: reading books and articles on public presentation; enjoying—and committing to memory—books of jokes.

A second benefit from the Georgiantics experience I would come to appreciate only later: the unpredictably rich dividends returned when you pursue sociable occasions for their own sake.

Some of these are purely personal. Although I am sociable, at a deeper emotional level I have always been somewhat of a loner, admitting very few other people to any degree of personal intimacy. The exceptions have been those few deep friendships forged in the camaraderie of that long-ago student troupe; they endure to this day.

Other benefits of these kinds of contacts are pragmatic. Social networking exposes a person to new people and, with them, to new ideas, new facts, novel points of view and different experiences. Some of these challenge your own views. That serves a purpose, too: it obliges one to examine and redress the weaknesses in one's own views. And inevitably, by osmosis, you broaden your knowledge, you expose yourself to possibilities you might not have considered before.

You don't go in consciously thinking, "I'm going to meet a lot of powerful or useful people." But now and again some contact or some fact, some fragment of a conversation, some off-hand product of complete serendipity will prove to be of inestimable value.

The experience on stage was probably the most lasting and valuable benefit of my stab at higher learning. With all the competing demands for my time, I abandoned night school and, with it, my attempt to earn a degree. Either out of charity or in hopes of soliciting alumni contributions, Sir George Williams eventually listed me as a "graduate." But it is not the case.

III AS GREAT BRITAIN's fate hung in the balance and the need for replacement aircraft became more urgent, work and the war effort transcended all other priorities. Friends, including some recent classmates, went into uniform and overseas.

One of these was Don Quinn, my co-star from Georgiantics. His letters home, written from "somewhere in blackout Britain" and often chiefly concerned with his romantic intrigues with Wrens and other servicewomen, were especially likely to provoke bouts of resentful envy that I was not overseas.

I itched to join them. After receiving one of Don's missives I walked into a recruiting office and enlisted. The following day I informed my supervisor at the Noordyne plant.

"You can't go," he told me. "You're in an essential industry and you're an expert. You can't go."

"It's too late," I said. "I've done it."

"Don't worry," he replied. "You'll be out tomorrow."

I don't know to whom he spoke, but the next day my enlistment was cancelled. Instead I was given the rank, pay and benefits (although never, for some reason, the uniform) of an acting air force flight lieutenant—and instructed to report to my "essential" employment!

This exemption from combat enlistment was far from unique. Competition for manpower between the suppliers of war materiel and the uniformed services was intense. The same reporter who noted the elevation of 21-year-olds into "veteran craftsmen" also observed that "conscription of these workers for four months' military training is a threat to essential expansion of production. Each one of these [aircraft] plants has lost trained men...to military service."

I was not to be one of them. Neither, as it transpired, was I very long to be an acting flight lieutenant. Day after day of screaming dives towards the earth followed by that last-minute pullback on the stick and that gut-wrenching—again, literally—moment of multiple gravities eventually had an unfortunate and somewhat embarrassing side effect on my body. After having my guts sucked into my pelvis several times a day by "three-G" forces for many months, I developed a severe case of hemorrhoids.

The air force declared me unfit for further test flights.

> Bedside Manor
> Near Little-Puddle-in-the-Mire
> Drizzleshire
> England
>
> Dear Dave:
> No wonder the English have conquered half the world—the fact is they couldn't stand the climate of this benighted little island. I'll take Greenland!
> English coinage is another eccentricity. If you take the square root of a quid and add a florin, dropping tuppence every other stitch, by throwing in an A.T.S. girl and a dozen assorted omnibuses you'd probably end up with a slap on the face (these women are just like the climate...cold and getting colder)...
>
> LETTER FROM DON S. QUINN, SOMEWHERE IN ENGLAND, JULY 22, 1941

FROM EUROPE CAME word that Don Quinn had died in action. Early in 1943 I enlisted once again. It sounds like idiocy, perhaps, from today's perspective, but I simply felt I had to be in uniform. This time I was accepted—into the army. And this time I was allowed to stay long enough to be issued a private's uniform, even if I got no closer to the action. I was assigned to a motor pool and turned into a "grease monkey," changing oil and tires and doing mechanical repairs on military transport vehicles.

My relationship with Vivian continued to deepen, and I had a jeweller turn my old Alpha Delta Phi frat pin, retired from collegiate duty, into an engagement ring. On April 4, 1943, we married. I wore my uniform.

On my private's pay of $1.30 a day, allowance of another $1.10 for living off-base and Vivian's secretarial salary of $11 a week, we moved out of our respective family homes and into a studio apartment on Shuter Street. It was one of those where the kitchen is also the hall to the john and the sofa unfolds into the bed. We got rid of guests at the end of the night by telling them we needed the sofa to go to bed!

By the end of that year it was clear that the war, while far from over, was on the way to being won. Canadian, American, British and other Allied troops were on European soil, working their way up the "boot" of Italy. In Asia, the Chrysanthemum Emperor's troops were in retreat.

In Montreal, the military service of Private David M. Campbell came to an honourable if unremarked end. The uniform I had at last received had included a pair of painfully ill-fitting boots. In these, the route marches of basic training became a form of patriotic torture that eventually resulted in one of my toenails becoming severely ingrown to the point that my entire foot became inflamed with infection.

Once again I was mustered out of His Majesty's service.

IV WITH HITLER'S AIR FORCE mostly in ruins, Allied aircraft production was tapering off. Production of other forms of war materiel was still in full swing, because the enormous demands of the Normandy invasion and drive to Berlin lay ahead. I soon found work at Northern Electric Company.

Physically, this was a vast old factory of stone foundations, red brick walls and multipaned windows. It occupied most of a city block across the abandoned Lachine Canal from downtown Montreal. Bell Telephone

Company of Canada owned a little more than half the company; American AT&T, through its manufacturing subsidiary Western Electric, owned the rest. Until the war, Northern had manufactured mainly telephones and switching equipment, under licence from Western, for Bell Canada. Much later it would win its independence, develop its own technology and be celebrated as one of Canada's most successful corporations under a new name, Nortel. (Sadly, it would also enter the next century brought low by mismanagement and scandal.)

With wartime mobilization, the company had diversified into military equipment. I had maintained my fascination with electronics, devouring every piece of knowlege I could get my hands on about the subject. So I was excited when Northern Electric decided that my smattering of science courses at Sir George and my aviation background qualified me for management in its electronics department. I became assistant to the "production reports manager."

The first encounter with this function was disillusioning.

My boss's job, essentially, was to convene a weekly meeting of the heads of the various production subdepartments, canvass them on their output and compile a report from this information. At the first meeting I attended, he directed me to take notes. I did this, faithfully recording the amounts—122 units; 75 units; 500 units—until we heard from department number 916, which was making radio transmitters for the tank corps.

"No production this week," the department head reported. "No parts."

I looked over at my boss. "Just write down what you heard," he instructed. I found this mildly surprising but did as he said.

When the same thing happened the following week—"No production, no parts"—I pushed back. I had a number of good friends in the tank corps, and it angered me that they might be left without some vital piece of kit because we hadn't produced it. Besides, I was just plain astonished. I blurted out: "But then what do you do all week?"

This from a newly hired youngster was brazen impertinence to the older manager of department number 916, especially in that more formal era. "You're not here to question me," he snapped. "You're here to take the notes." He added: "I could have you fired for that kind of cheek."

I can only say I was young and full of piss and vinegar. I looked at the man and said, "I'd rather be fired than take my salary under false pretences, doing nothing and getting paid for it like you."

"You can count on it!" he lashed back.

The meeting broke up minutes later. I went back to my desk and began cleaning out the few personal belongings I had accumulated in my ten days' employment. The call came to present myself before Work Manager Cy Peachy.

"Do you know why you're here?" he asked when I stood before him.

"Yes. You're going to fire me," I answered.

But Cy Peachy wasn't an impetuous executive. "First, why don't you tell me your version of what happened?"

I did, repeating what I'd said to the head of department number 916.

"Well, if you're so smart," he said, "what would you have done if you'd been managing department number 916?"

"Call the supplier!" I replied. "Find out why there aren't any parts."

"Why don't you do that," Cy Peachy said, and he filled out the requisition form the company required before you could make a long-distance telephone call.

The supplier in question was in Brockville, Ontario, just 200 kilometres from Montreal. He had 4,000 of the missing parts waiting at the door.

"Why haven't you shipped them?" I asked.

"I can't," he explained. "The order says 'ship in entirety' and we haven't filled it yet."

"Ship them!" I ordered.

"Who the hell are you?" he wanted to know. "And what's your authority for changing the order?"

I reported this stalemate to Works Manager Peachy, who promptly got the order moving and gave me authority to order partial shipments in future to keep the production lines going. ("Just in time" inventory keeping would be another few decades coming.)

IN ONE RESPECT, not even Northern Electric was immune to the fast-moving changes in a society under the pressure of war. With the extremely high demand for good employees and high turnover in human resources, one of the rules at Northern that made better sense than some others was that the moment you took on a new position one of your first tasks was to train your successor.

Not long after my encounter with department number 916, my boss was moved into another position and Peachy named me production reports manager. I'd had a taste of both the bad and the good of corporate behaviour. Now I was about to get a taste of the somewhat surreal.

I called my first production report meeting. At the established time I appeared, took a seat and waited for the department heads to arrive. No one came, not a single department manager or even a junior stand-in. At the end of thirty minutes I was dejected. I thought they had won, punishing me for my insubordination. Then I had a better idea.

I went down the list of production departments and filled in the report. "Department #901—not working this week." "Department #902—not working this week"…"Department #906—not working this week," and so on. They hadn't come to the meeting. There was only one conclusion to be drawn: their departments must not have been working! An office runner distributed my report, the era's equivalent of hitting "send" on an E-mail today.

Twenty minutes later I had a lineup of irate department managers at my office door. "You know damn well we're working!" they all huffed. "Not as far as I'm concerned," I replied. "Not if you're not present at the production meeting."

The next production meeting was fully attended, but it was clear to me that the can-do attitude I had shared so fully with the aircraft industry in its pell-mell rush to meet the demands of war was foreign to the complacent corridors of corporate Northern Electric.

A few weeks later Cy Peachy summoned me to his office again. It was a curious conversation. Cy opened by informing me that I was a "disruptive" presence at North Electric—but that was fine with him. He assured me that my future with the company was secure, "but I'm sure we won't be able to keep you."

He explained that he could continue to offer me advancement in small increments, but Northern Electric's policy was to promote based largely on seniority and there were too many men ahead of me on the seniority list. "You'll want to move faster," he said. "And I'll have to accommodate them. But please, stay as long as you can."

I left his office with divided emotions.

V MY INTERESTS IN RADIO and performing had continued. Somehow, mostly because nobody else wanted the job, I landed the Sunday overnight announcer's slot on Montreal radio station CFCF (Canada's oldest radio station and, by a matter of a few weeks, the second-oldest in the world). Other alumni from the old Georgiantics troupe were writing plays for the CBC, and I was happy to be roped into acting in a few.

Vivian and I also threw ourselves into the activities of the Montreal Repertory Theatre. The amateur group had been very active before the war, but many of its headliners and mainstays had enlisted in the professional service shows being mounted to entertain troops overseas. There was ample opportunity for both of us. Vivian was active in the wardrobe department; I secured the role of "Top Banana"—lead comic and MC—in the company's *Tin Hat Review* of variety skits.

It was fun. But it was also evident to me that show business was no place to look for a steady income. I had no patience for the constraints and inefficiencies at Northern Electric, but neither did I have any clearly formed alternative ambition.

With Allied armies mopping up the remnants of the Third Reich's divisions on the road to a broken Berlin and American bombers within range of Tokyo, people began to think for the first time about what a postwar economy might look like. Governments braced for the return and reintegration into civilian life of millions of servicemen and women, and some experts even worried that the economic strain might trigger a return to depression. Ordinary Canadians began looking forward to a day when everything from coffee and eggs to rubber tires and gasoline was no longer rationed.

At Northern Electric, I began thinking ahead. Under wartime restrictions there had been very few radios made in the last five years for household use. We made radios; indeed, we had all the parts we needed to start making radios for home instead of military use at the drop of a hat. I suggested to my supervisor we begin setting aside some units of each of the parts we would need, against the coming day when we could officially use them.

"You can't do that," he told me. Northern Electric, like other companies under contract for war production, was forbidden to waste its time and effort making consumer goods.

"I know we can't *make* the radios," I protested. "But look..." On lines where we had, say, 1,000 units of some tube or wire harness ready for assembly, why couldn't we segregate a couple of hundred to one side? If those units were ever needed for war production, they were there and available. But if we did the same with all the parts for a consumer radio, then we would be ready to jump off the mark the moment peace was declared.

That's how a Type E personality thinks. We have trouble understanding the word "can't." We see most rules as obstacles to be worked around, sidestepped and overcome on the way to accomplishing our chosen objective.

Reluctantly, Northern Electric agreed that setting aside parts was not the same thing as actually making unapproved radios. As a result, when the time came to shift from military to consumer designs, Northern Electric was back into the market a step ahead of its competitors.

Still, my conversation with Cy Peachy remained on my mind. If I wanted to make a mark, it seemed clear that it would have to be outside Northern Electric and without the assured, slow-but-steady promise of advancement through its corporate ranks.

Ex-servicemen were being strongly encouraged to go into business for themselves. Over cups of wartime "coffee" heavily extended with chicory, Vivian and I frequently batted around ideas about what we might do.

I can't say that the idea we eventually settled on was reached in any very strategic or thought-out way. We certainly did not reason that a wave of returning soldiers, rushing to make up for six years of lost time, would be in a hurry to form new families and equip households. Nor did we foresee that this eruption of pent up demand would coincide with the introduction of entirely new categories of products, as technologies until now reserved for the military were released for use in consumer goods.

We just thought it would be fun to open a record store. Both of us loved music. Popular music was just coming into its own as a mainstream entertainment, and through my part-time job at CFCF I was aware of all the latest titles. "I'll Be Seeing You" was the big tune in the last year of the war; like the rest of the hit parade, it was from a musical film. There were stores in Montreal that sold records, of course, but most of these were big department stores. There were only one or two small places specializing in records.

Our minds made up, I contacted the RCA Victor Company with a request to order records from them. They turned me down flat. This, remember, was 1944. Recordings came in only one format: discs that spun at 78 revolutions per minute and were made from a composition of carbon black and shellac. Shellac is a natural product that came exclusively from Southeast Asia, and war in the Pacific had disrupted supplies. RCA Victor informed me that they had enough shellac to supply only their existing customers and they weren't interested in any new accounts, even for an ex-serviceman.

I called another of the big record labels, Columbia, and got the same answer. I tried Decca and heard the same reply: no shellac, no new accounts.

"Spend as much time and attention on learning how to communicate well as you spend learning technical matters."

RICHARD A. MORAN, PROFESSOR OF SOCIOLOGY

CANADA AND ITS ALLIES were winning the war, but victory was not without cost. The casualties of battles in Africa, Asia and Europe filled

Montreal's service hospitals and convalescent wards. Looking for ways to contribute, our amateur Montreal Repertory Theatre performed its *Tin Hat Review* in armouries for the care of convalescing troops and often took its show into the hospitals.

To acknowledge one of these performances at a convalescent ward, someone in the Montreal business community invited the cast to an after-show reception at their elegant private home. As I stood with a drink in my hand and enjoyed the post-performance release of tension, a man stepped up to me. He identified himself as our host and thanked me for donating time to entertain troops. Then he asked me what I did for a living.

I told him I worked for Northern Electric, adding, "And what do you do?"

"I run a company you've probably never heard of called the Compo Company," he said.

"Yes, I *do* know that company," I replied. "You make Decca records."

The businessman looked startled. "How do you know that?" he asked.

"Because I want to go into the record business," I told him. "I applied to your company for records, and the company turned me down."

"Why did they do that?" he wanted to know.

"They said there was a shortage of shellac."

"That's right; there is no shellac," he said. "Did you ask RCA?"

"Yes. And they turned me down."

"Why?"

"A shortage of shellac."

He nodded, then asked: "And Columbia?"

"Them too. And they turned me down as well."

"Why?"

"The shortage of shellac." I was beginning to get exasperated. "I don't think this conversation is getting us anywhere," I said.

"Yes, I think it is," he said. "Call me tomorrow at my office." He gave me his card and walked away. On the small oblong I read his name: H.S. Berliner.

The next day I made a few inquiries. Herbert Samuel Berliner, it turned out, was the son of Emile Berliner, who had patented the first flat record in 1897 before selling the rights to his technology in the

United States to RCA Victor. "H.S." had retained those rights in Canada, pressing discs for the family's Berliner Gram-O-Phone label and other companies until the patent protection expired in 1917. The following year, he installed record-pressing equipment in a leased building on Lachine's Eighteenth Avenue and created Compo Company.

By 1945, Compo was the biggest company pressing records in Canada. In addition to manufacturing for most major American as well as Canadian labels,* Compo recorded and released its own catalogue under the Sun, Apex, Ajax and Radia-Tone names. It also had Canadian rights to the Decca library.

Canada's national sound archive much later recognized H.S. Berliner as the "Father of the Canadian Recording Industry" for his numerous innovations. His company was the first in Canada to use electronic microphones and amplifiers to boost sound being recorded; until then, "acoustic" recordings depended on a singer's own lung power to mechanically inscribe record grooves—with predictably uneven results! He also began experimenting with 33 $\frac{1}{3}$-rpm records nearly twenty years before they appeared on shelves. And while other music labels such as Columbia stuck with classical repertoire, Berliner's Decca carried musical film soundtracks and many of the day's hot young acts, including Bing Crosby and Frank Sinatra.

I would discover only much later that H.S. also harboured a lingering resentment against RCA Victor. He blamed the company for making off with his family's patent rights for...well...a song, and he would seize any opportunity to compete with RCA.

A few days later I visited his office. Once again, Berliner had me go through my litany of rejections at the hands of every record company in the city.

He looked at me for a long time. Then said: "Go to RCA. Tell them we're giving you fifty records a month and come back and tell me what they say."

---

* This remains a little-known national specialty: Canadian companies are dominant players in the international business of duplicating music CDs and making release copies from movie master prints.

"Are you giving me fifty records a month?" I asked.

"I didn't say that," he corrected me. "I said, just go to RCA and tell them what I told you to say. Then come back and tell me exactly what they say. I want to know every word."

Somewhat uncertain but willing to play along, I called on RCA. Once again they told me they were not opening any new accounts—"No shellac."

"Well, Compo-Decca's giving me fifty records a month," I told the RCA representative.

"That bastard!" the RCA man swore. "We'll give you a hundred a month."

The next day I took this conversation back to H.S. Berliner. I quoted the man from RCA: "That bastard!"

Berliner smiled and said, "I expected them to say something like that."

"Now what?" I asked.

"Now you go to Columbia. Tell them you're getting a hundred records a month from RCA. Then come back and tell me what they say."

The conversation with Columbia went much as the one with RCA. "Those bastards," the rep swore. "We'll give you 200 a month."

I was beginning to get the gist of this game. I returned a second time to Berliner's office. He laughed at Columbia's answer and said, "I expected that."

"Well, now I have a hundred records a month from RCA and 200 from Columbia," I said. "What are you going to give me?"

"You learn fast," H.S. Berliner said with a smile. "We'll match both of them."

VI THANKS TO A CHANCE conversation after a volunteer variety show, if Vivian and I chose to go ahead with our venture into the music business we now had an assured supply of records.

Peace came to Europe in May 1945 and to the Pacific in August. In Montreal, I was determined to seize the day. I did not yet consciously think of myself as an "entrepreneur," but Type E attributes clearly marked me apart from many of my contemporaries.

I knew the value of curiosity and self-improvement. My mother's investment in her skills as a beautician and the new technology that created permanent waves in hair had seen our family through the Dirty Thirties. My father had introduced me to the fundamentals of critical thinking and the possibility of taking an inventive approach to things.

I understood who came first in business. When I put the customers first and tried to see things their way—relieving housewives of a distasteful chore, delivering the daily news to a bathroom window instead of the front door, catering to the varied tastes of bus tourists—I made money. It was probably also important that I "got" the potential of the hot new technology of the day. Today, it is the Internet. Then, it was radio.

I had not proved to be an academic whiz. I had always been so focussed on finding ways to make a few extra dollars that formal learning had suffered badly. There was only one discipline in which I had ever earned reliably good grades and, fortunately, it was the one subject that would be vital to my future in business and technology: I was good at math.

As a child and adolescent, I had seen my father regularly become taken by this or that promising idea, only to lose interest or energy before he had half completed it. I had also seen first-hand, in the aircraft industry on the eve of war, what could be accomplished with a very few resources, a can-do attitude and a tireless pursuit of innovation. Northern Electric had shown me how corporate inertia and rule-bound behaviour could stand in the way of achievement.

The importance of maintaining an active social circle also was clear to me. Striding the stage with the Georgiantics crowd and later with the Montreal Repertory Theatre had reinforced my self-confidence. In H.S. Berliner, I had met the first of several astute men who would become invaluable business mentors.

I heartily disliked working for someone else. *I* wanted to be the one making the decisions, right or wrong, taking the risk and reaping any rewards that came along.

The war years had taught me that all of life is a gamble. Some of my best college pals were dead before any of us reached twenty-five.

Playing it safe was the worst thing to do. Life isn't about *avoiding* mistakes. It's about making them, coming to terms with them, learning from them and then taking a new direction that may lead to a far more interesting result.

With the end of the Pacific war in sight, it was possible to look forward with optimism to the future. There seemed no better time to set out on the uncertain sea of a new enterprise.

CHAPTER 4

FOOLS **RUSH** IN

"If you are afraid of making mistakes, you will never have any ideas."

ANON.

IT WAS AUTUMN IN Montreal once again but now it was evening, the Indian summer day turning sharply towards frost once the sun set. On busy west Sherbrooke Street, drivers had their vehicles' headlights on. Pedestrians either hurried or drifted, depending on the urgency of their lives, from lit-up storefront to glowing shop door.

At the corner of the commercial block there was activity behind one window, but no customers. The sound of good-natured ribbing and friendly laughter drifted out to the street. Inside the open door, a small party of twenty-something men and women, dressed to get grubby, were wielding brooms and dustpans, buckets, mops and soapy rags.

The tiny space, barely 3.6 by 7.5 metres, had last been occupied by a shoe-repair shop. The smell of leather and boot polish lingered, especially where decades' worth of dust, snippets of old cowhide and twists of waxy thread had formed small drifts in the darker corners. Filth crusted every surface.

Huffing with effort, a stocky young man with curly hair and a neat moustache emerged from a stairway near the back of the shop. In his arms he hefted a metal trash can brimming with ancient rubbish. The shop's former tenant seemed to have used the basement as a disposal site for old boxes, cast-off tools and more leather scraps.

The young man humped his load out to the sidewalk. There he dropped the can at the curb and turned back. Flushed and sweating, he stood for a moment, taking a breather from his labours. He scanned the narrow storefront, then raised his eyes to the area over the window. One or two passersby followed his gaze, but all they saw was a blank space where ghostly letters showed through a crude cover-up of thin paint. The young man on the sidewalk broke into a cocky grin.

Anyone who noticed it as they drove or walked past that evening late in 1945 probably gleaned no more than a vague impression of activity in a hole-in-the-wall store even less significant than its mom-and-pop neighbours. But this young man saw something they didn't: When he looked at the modest facade and the cramped sales floor behind it, he saw the future home of Dave Campbell's Melody House.

I had been going to call it simply "Melody House." It was Vivian's mother's idea, oddly enough, to call it *"Dave Campbell's* Melody House." It was the second-best thing she ever gave me, after letting me marry her daughter.

ONE QUALITY THE Type E character possesses perhaps more than any other is the readiness to *try*. To "just do it." To run the idea up the flagpole and see whether anyone salutes. To build it and see if they will come.

There's always the chance they might not! That's the *risk* in chasing the *reward.* The Type E mind has a blind spot for failure: it always discounts the risk of disaster.

An entrepreneur is the essential optimist. Maybe he, or she, is just too stupid to realize the potential trouble ahead. I don't remember most of the things I tried over the years that didn't work; you blank them out. There were lots, I know, but I couldn't tell you what they were. You only remember the successes. And to me, at the beginning, anything that wasn't a failure was a success.

Many people spot what they think might be a business opportunity. They may even mention it to a friend or to their spouse. But that's the end of it. The Type E not only *sees* that opportunity, he *seizes* it. And like the dog with the bone, he does not let go. Sometimes the gamble works, sometimes it doesn't. If it doesn't, he picks himself up off the floor and he tries again.

It's not just a case of being bright and lucky—although never underestimate the role of luck. Successful Type Es are bright *and* lucky. They inquire and probe to determine whether the opportunity is real, what it might require to produce profits. And if it still looks good, they act. They do whatever it takes to get things done, to "make it so."

Type Es see "luck" as an acted-on opportunity. They rush in where others fear to tread.

> "The purpose of business is to create and keep customers."
> **THEODORE LEVITT, EDITOR, *HARVARD BUSINESS REVIEW***

RAISING START-UP CAPITAL is one of the most frightening tasks any would-be entrepreneur faces. Certainly it is one of the most often complained about or raised as a reason *not* to pursue some promising business idea. A zillion brilliant ideas have been summed up with the regret that "if only I had the money, I could make a million dollars."

The problem is amplified in today's climate of "spend it to make it" management thinking. I've lost track of the number of business plans I've received over the years from people who seem to think they can't start a hot-dog stand on anything less than $3 million in seed money. But even at a time when more businesses than today opened on sweat and shoestrings, *some* cash was almost always needed.

Reams of good advice for today's entrepreneurs exist on Web sites like the one maintained by the U.S. government's Small Business Administration. Many other government agencies as well as community colleges offer counsel and courses on the subject. But even those note that most brand new businesses still rely for their first infusions of capital on two humble, even old-fashioned, sources: personal savings and family.

After all, if you can't sell your own family on your business proposition, how do you expect to sell it to skeptical customers—let alone even more skeptical, not to say cynical, bankers?

THANKS TO H.S. BERLINER and his canny mentorship, the country's three leading record labels had all approved me as an account. I could order records. But if I wanted to actually receive any, these companies expected to be paid. And, of course, having a supply of records to sell was of no value without somewhere to sell them.

The answer to both requirements—stock, and a shop to put it in—was money.

Although Vivian and I had some savings, we knew they would not be enough. But whenever we visited my parents or hers, we were bubbling over with enthusiasm about the prospects for our proposed record shop. After six years of wartime rationing, to say nothing of the decade of depression that preceded the conflict, people felt overdue for better times. Music, we felt certain, was an affordable indulgence that would be eagerly snapped up as soon as it was more available.

We had only instinct to back up this assertion, but for my mother, who had carried her own entrepreneurial initiative through to fruition, that was enough. She stepped forward with a generous offer to close our financing gap.

My mother owned a life insurance policy that carried a loan value of $2,000. That is, it could be used as security to borrow up to that amount. Now she put that collateral at our disposal. It was a more significant offer than may be apparent today. Corrected for inflation, the amount we were able to borrow on Mother's policy provided us with the equivalent of more than $20,000 in 2004 terms. It would, of course, need to be repaid, but the debt was a risk I was happy to take on.

My side of our family had solved our capital problem. Vivian's side would, after a fashion, help solve our space problem.

We were living then not far from my parents' apartment in lower Westmount. One day, walking along Sherbrooke, I spotted a corner storefront whose tenant, a cobbler, seemed no longer to be in business. It was tiny, with barely enough room to swing the proverbial cat. But it was on a busy shopping street and, given its size, the rent could not possibly be excessive.

I made some inquiries and determined who owned the building. The landlord, a Mr. Feldman, was a wealthy property investor who also owned one of the city's bigger discount department stores. As it happened, I recognized his name as a friend of Vivian's family, so I placed a call to his office and asked for an appointment. An assistant informed me that Mr. Feldman had no time for me. I placed another call, this time to an uncle of Vivian's who knew Feldman. He made a call on my behalf and with his help I finally secured a meeting.

I will always remember it. Feldman was one of those people who pursue every psychological advantage, carrying on their gamesmanship to an almost childish extent. In Feldman's case, he had actually placed his desk on a riser and then provided only low chairs for visitors. The effect was to ensure that when you sat in his office you were obliged to look up at the man.

This ruse became apparent the moment I entered his office, which was decorated in aggressively masculine style. I approached the massive desk.

"Sit down," he said. It wasn't an invitation.

I wasn't going to sit looking up at this guy. "I can't," I said. "I can't see you."

"Sit *down.*"

I remained standing.

"Well, I can't talk to you unless you sit down," he finally said.

"Well, I guess you won't talk to me." I turned to walk out.

"All right," he said. "What is it you want?"

I told him I wanted to rent the store on Sherbrooke Street. He looked at me with disapproval. Grudgingly, he said, "I know your uncle." Technically, it was my wife's uncle, but I wasn't about to correct him. "If I didn't, I wouldn't even be talking to you."

"This has nothing to do with him," I said. "*I'm* the one renting the store. And by the way, it's empty now, if you remember. You're not getting *any* rent from it."

"Okay, okay. Don't be smart-assed." Feldman paused for a minute. "Your uncle says you're all right, so I'll rent you the store."

"Fine," I said. "But let's get one thing straight. My uncle has nothing to do with this. I am responsible for this."

"Yes, but I'll be looking to him to guarantee the lease."

"Then I won't sign." For the second time I turned to go.

"Okay," Feldman said, relenting. "I'll give it to you without your uncle's signature."

That first encounter set the tone for every other I had with the man. I was glad, some years later, when I no longer had to deal with him.

But we had our shop!

WAR TENSIONS HAD BEEN winding down all through that summer and fall of 1945. Even as the full horror of what had gone on under Nazi rule in Europe began to emerge, and scenes of devastated Japanese cities made clear the power of the new atomic age, nothing could counter the mood of rising optimism. On September 2, Japan's rulers submitted their unconditional surrender to U.S. forces aboard the battleship *Missouri*. For the first time in six years, the world was at peace.

Four weeks later, Vivian and I celebrated an event of much bigger significance in our own small lives. After enlisting friends to help us clean, paint and build a sales counter and shelving in the small corner shop on Sherbrooke Street, we had stocked it with a modest inventory of popular, jazz and classical records. On Monday, October 1 (at the time, one of two days in the year that most commercial leases in Montreal were renewed or expired; the other was April 1), we opened the doors of Dave Campbell's Melody House, with Vivian behind the counter.

I was at my desk at Northern Electric. While we were optimistic about our new business, we did not want to be foolhardy. Our domestic expenses—rent and so on—remained, and there was the matter of repaying the loan we'd taken out on my mother's insurance policy. Our plan was that I would keep my "day job" until the store was generating enough profit to pay me a weekly salary of fifty dollars, the amount of my salary from Northern. That required selling about 150 one-dollar records a week. If—*when*—we reached that benchmark, I would devote my full time to the store.

Too much happened later to leave me with any clear memory of that first day in business. I do know that by opening day we had run through almost all our $2,000 start-up kitty. The money had gone to Feldman in rent on our tiny premises, to paint and lumber for shelving, to record companies for inventory and to a handful of other things we could neither do ourselves nor cajole from friends; we had, for instance, reluctantly hired a professional to make our outdoor signage. There was about fifteen dollars left in the cash drawer to make change.

But no new record store had opened in Montreal in years—nor would they, at least until the shellac "shortage" eased. For a while, Melody House was a novelty just by having records for sale. And our instinct had not been wrong: Canadians were eager to begin enjoying some of the fruits of a peacetime economy. We had sales from the first day of business and our first month was profitable.

Of course, ours was not the only new enterprise being launched on the rising tide of postwar optimism. From the start I knew that Melody House would need to stand out and my strategy to achieve that rested on two principles.

First: be different. Second: make sure that people know about our difference.

Innovate. Promote. The two ideas became the guiding poles not just for Melody House but for every business in which I subsequently became involved. I still believe they are fundamental principles for entrepreneurial success.

On the day we opened there was little room for innovation in our product line. There was only one format for recorded music at the time, and everyone used it. The 78-rpm flat shellac record had been standard for several decades, despite being so fragile that to drop one was to shatter it like glass.

Instead, we innovated in customer service and what today's M.B.A.s might describe as "point-of-sale marketing." In our naïveté we simply thought of it as giving the customer a reason to walk in the door, then stay long enough to make a purchase.

In addition to counters and shelves, we had built a couple of extra features into the store during our evenings-and-weekends renovation. Behind the counter we installed a record turntable and amplifier, wired to a speaker mounted outside over the front door. The strains of music broadcasting to the street all day not only distinguished our store from its neighbours (and competitors), they promoted our product in a way that no static window display could have.

And even though our space was cramped, we also built along the wall beside the sales counter three listening booths equipped with record players. If you were interested in a recording, you could ask to hear it in one of the booths. Today virtually every music store does exactly the same thing, using headphones. Back then, however, the idea was novel; most retailers avoided such "previews" for fear of damaging the fragile shellac discs.

Instead of thinking like a vendor, I tried to think like a customer. How was anyone going to buy any record, I reasoned, if they had no idea what it sounded like?

In no time, this novelty made Melody House into something of a mecca for local teenagers. They would come from school straight to the store, pick some records and crowd into a booth, two or three at a time, to listen to them. Sometimes they would buy something, sometimes not.

Several friends scolded me for letting the shop become a teen "hang-out" like this. But I wasn't seeing what they were seeing, cliques of self-absorbed and boisterous adolescents. I was seeing future customers.

Some businesses seem to regard their customers almost as the enemy. I always saw them as allies—not just the people who kept me in business, but a resource that could help my business grow. Later, when I could afford it, I became a strong believer in advertising. In those early weeks and months I was a strong believer in another principle: that word of mouth is more effective than any promotion you can buy. It's also cheaper.

Positive word of mouth comes only from satisfied customers, and at Melody House we went out of our way to make sure our customers were satisfied. The listening booths were a start, but only a start. Whenever I was behind the counter, I made a point of engaging customers in conversation. People like to talk; too many people fail to listen. I used these occasions to get to know patrons and their tastes. If they mentioned a particular recording, I ordered it.

Melody House quickly became the "it" spot for Montreal audiophiles. Pianist Oscar Peterson, his worldwide fame still ahead of him, was then still living in St. Henri, a neighbourhood he memorialized with a movement in his masterpiece *Canadiana Suite*. He often performed with Johnny Holmes and his orchestra at Victoria Hall, not far from the store, and dropped in shortly after we opened. He became a regular customer whose requests pushed me to expand our selection of jazz recordings.

Another frequent customer was H.S. Berliner. I took this as a sign that we must be doing *something* right. No one—but *no one*—knew more than he did about sound recording.

(His patronage did have one unexpected downside. One day Berliner gestured me into one of the listening booths. "Hear that?" he asked, drawing my attention to an almost inaudible clicking in the background of a recording by his long-standing rival, RCA Victor. "That shouldn't be there." It was a lesson in critical listening that made me more aware of the flaws in recordings. But I found thereafter that it was harder to listen to records for pleasure: I kept hearing the flaws!)

My weekend night-shift radio job also paid dividends. I had come to know many of the city's popular daytime radio hosts. In those days, immediately following the war and with shortages still widespread, record labels were not yet distributing "promo" copies of records; that came later. So I provided a number of hosts with records that they could give away to listeners as prizes. In return for the price (at *my* cost, not full retail) of a few discs, Melody House got regular on-air "plugs."

When new radio station CJAD entered the Montreal market we became one of its first advertisers, taking advantage of the low rates its management offered to attract business.

Later, we introduced annual customer appreciation days. We'd bring in some wine and cheese, invite a couple of these radio "personalities" to attend as masters of ceremony and hold an open house. This tactic, too, has become a commonplace in retailing and in radio promotion, but in 1945 it was novel.

> "Profit in business comes from repeat customers, customers that boast about your product or service, and that bring friends with them."
>
> **W. EDWARDS DEMING, CONSULTANT**

WITHIN SEVEN MONTHS, Melody House had achieved our initial income target. I quit my job at Northern Electric and became, for the first time, a full-fledged self-employed business operator—an *entrepreneur*—paying myself the princely salary of fifty dollars a week. It felt great, as much as I had time to feel anything at all.

The Canadian Federation of Independent Business Web site points out some interesting statistics on which anyone contemplating an entrepreneurial path would do well to reflect. Self-employed small business owners, they show, work more than people who work for others and earn less for their efforts. Indeed, the CFIB says, "eighty per cent of small business owners reported working at least 50 hours a week.... [and] about half devote over 60 hours a week to their business." At the same time, those entrepreneurs took home salaries that in 1998 averaged 20 per cent less than the income of employed workers.

A recipe for resentment and unhappiness? Not at all. The same study found that people who were self-employed were very much likelier to be "somewhat" or "very" satisfied with their work life than ordinary employees. Sixty-three per cent of entrepreneurs surveyed said they were "very satisfied" with their work experience. Only 40 per cent of employees could claim the same thing.

Those figures certainly reflect my own experience. Sixty hours a week was far from unusual. I was at the store before 9 AM to sweep the sidewalk and prepare for the day. I was there late into the evening every Friday, all day Saturday and into Saturday evening. Often, we were so busy that there was not even a break for lunch. When I finally got the chance to eat I would wolf down a sandwich, barely noticing what it was — then order a second without thinking. And always I felt the pressure and uncertainty of keeping everything rolling.

In retrospect, I medicated much of that stress by eating even more unwisely. Dave Campbell the once relatively trim ex-serviceman began to look more like the "Fatty" he had been as a youngster in Fredericton.

But Dave Campbell's Melody House prospered, putting on a different and altogether more desirable kind of weight. We began selling radios along with records, then added players for records.

As traffic picked up and with each extension of our product line we needed more display space. Within eighteen months Melody House had outgrown the former cobbler's shop. We moved, first two doors down (to another of Mr. Feldman's properties, unhappily), then again and again—five times in all over the years, always to bigger sales floors that could accommodate our expansion.

Throughout that period I was learning from trial and error. There were no rules—at least none of which I was aware. It was entirely seat-of-the-pants navigation. I did take a few night courses in business basics, bookkeeping and so forth, but mostly I was making it up as I went along, trying things out and seeing what worked. Anything that didn't fail, I chalked up as a success and kept doing.

I couldn't tell you today what our retained earnings or cash flow or EBIDTA were. I only knew we were making money. And for that I had a very simple formula, one I'm sure the whiz-kid M.B.A.s at Enron or WorldCom would have mocked: if revenue exceeded costs, that difference was my profit. And I worked just as hard to keep one down as I did to push the other up.

For a child of the Depression, frugality was second nature. Just as we had roped in friends to keep down the cost of opening our first Melody House location, when the time came to prepare a new, larger space to move into, again I did as much work myself as I could.

When you are struggling to make and hold on to that first dollar, you're more concerned with the nickels and dimes. Recalling my childhood lesson from Stephan, I bought a jar of rubber cement and turned the backs of old letters and envelopes into serviceable scratch pads. When I could finally afford to buy advertising, I put Melody House's precious cash into the cost of the air time or newspaper space. Given my own interest in the field, I designed the layouts and wrote the ad copy myself.

I had sold my old used car during the war; to keep our family expenses to a minimum, it would be years before I replaced it. If a room light could be turned off in the apartment or at the store, I turned it off (I still do that).

Looking back, we might have done better to purchase some of the properties we occupied. But I felt—correctly, I still think—that if I put $15,000 or $20,000 into a property (yes, you could buy a building in those days for that kind of money) my capital would be frozen until I sold the building. I preferred to use any earnings we retained to make more money, not park it in real estate when that was not my business. I also wanted to avoid a conflict of interest in which I might be offered a good price for a building we occupied but then be forced to move the store to a less desirable location.

Today I might look at things differently. It's all a matter of return on capital. It might be better to put down a small payment on a property and take out a mortgage, paying it off over time and eventually owning the building. But at the time I had not yet grasped the powerful potential of leverage.

Besides, debt made me nervous. I had enough worries about meeting my existing obligations to the bank, first for the money we had borrowed on Mother's insurance policy and later to finance inventory, without entertaining any additional debt-carrying costs.

▐▐▐ I WAS ALWAYS ON the lookout for new products to give people a reason to come into the store. I was a voracious reader of the consumer electronics industry trade press, sifting every story for any new item I might possibly carry. As soon as we could afford it, we added cameras and film to our shelves.

My motto was Make Melody House First—and I meant the motto for my own attention as much as my customers'. I wanted shoppers to think of Melody House first among the city's record stores, but I also wanted to be sure that ours was always the first store in Montreal to carry each new product being released by the emerging "consumer electronics" industry.

The war had been over for three years when the trade press began to buzz with anticipation over what today we'd call a new format of sound recording. It was one that my mentor, H.S. Berliner, had experimented with years earlier. Now Columbia was introducing it to consumers. The new generation of "long play" records turned at 33 ⅓ revolutions per minute. They could hold twenty minutes or more of music a side, three to four times what you could get on a 78-rpm side.

Columbia introduced the new format first in the United States. I had made friends in the industry there and arranged for one of them to send me a few samples of the new releases.

What I needed next was a player. Naturally, these new discs wouldn't play on our 78-rpm equipment. As it happened, a Northern Electric–brand radio we were carrying boasted a spare input jack. I called around and tracked down a 33 ⅓-rpm electric motor. Then I took a regular 78-rpm turntable and "tone arm" (that piece of an old record player that pivots out over the disc and holds the needle in contact with its surface) off the shelf. With it and the new motor I retreated to the basement.

In my cramped workshop I removed the 78-rpm motor from beneath the turntable and replaced it with the 33 ⅓-rpm one. The new motor turned the table perfectly; the tone arm tracked the groove on the record nicely. The electronic signal that came from the needle through the tone arm, however, was very, very low, certainly far too weak to drive loudspeakers. It needed to be amplified before the sound it made would be audible. I plugged the output wire into the spare audio input jack on the radio. *Et voila!* A 33 ⅓-rpm record player!

We announced "Another Melody House first."

We were the first store in Montreal—and in Canada, as far as I know—not only to have the new generation of long-playing records for sale but also to offer something to play them on. Audiophiles and gadget freaks then were no different from today. We soon had eager customers for the new format and I was kept busy for hours each night making "radio-players" in the basement.

Columbia Records promptly fired off a scorching cease-and-desist letter to Melody House. The music company had not yet introduced 33 ⅓ records into Canada; indeed, they were having a hard time producing enough to supply demand for them in the United States. I suppose they didn't want me jumping the gun on whatever their marketing strategy was. They threatened to sue me to the ground, put me out of business, heaven knows what else, if I didn't stop selling "LPS."

These guys, remember, were one of the three biggest suppliers of my core inventory: records. If they really wanted to take me out behind the woodshed, it could be very painful indeed. I'd never faced this kind of business threat before. I called my lawyer. He asked whether I had purchased the LPS legally in the United States, imported them properly into Canada and paid duty on them. Happily, I could answer yes to all of this. "Forget it," he assured me. I had done nothing wrong.

I kept selling LPS and my lawyer duly fired back a "stick-it-up-your-nose" letter in legalese to Columbia. Within sixty days, the company introduced 33 ⅓ LPS in Canada—and discontinued my trade account.

I went back to my lawyer. Of course, Columbia had no grounds to cut me off as a customer. But even after he pointed this out to them, the company found other ways to make life miserable for what they doubtless regarded as an upstart wise-ass. Orders took forever to be filled, or came back short, or were filled incorrectly.

One of those misfilled orders must have come in one day when other things had already stretched my temper. I blew my top and wrote out a scorching letter to the company, tearing a strip off them and threatening all sorts of legal action.

Before putting it in the mail, I called my lawyer and told him the situation. I read him the letter and asked, "What do you think, is there anything I should add?"

He paused and took a deep breath. "Is that it?"

"Yes, that's it. Should I add anything?"

"Do you feel better now you've written the letter?"

"As a matter of fact, I do."

"Okay. Now tear it up. Don't send it," he said. "You got it off your chest. You feel better. Sending it will just aggravate things. Letters like that are not conducive to business relationships. Tear it up."

He was right, of course. I cooled down. Lesson learned.

A little later, RCA Victor introduced 45-rpm records that played one song a side. Columbia evidently came to the realization that its tactics were merely hurting sales of its own format and decided to make peace. Things went back to normal with the company.

> "Try not to burn bridges. You never know when you may need to cross one again."   ANON.

MEANWHILE, I KEPT making record players in the basement. Eventually I was spending too many weekends and evenings down there and found someone else to make them for me. (That chap went on to expand his business, a company called Fleetwood, into a substantial manufacturer of record players, radios and other appliances.)

To this day, electronics manufacturers still introduce some products—such as Apple's immensely successful iPod music player—in the United States first, releasing them in the rest of the world only later. To stay ahead of my Canadian competitors I travelled regularly to the States to see what was coming down the pipeline.

Eventually Melody House added major appliances to the lines it carried: Moffat ranges, Kelvinator refrigerators and Fedder air conditioners. In addition to selling individual appliances we sold entire kitchens, including the cabinets and whatever interior design might be needed, at an "all-in" installed price.

When the first television signals reached Canada from broadcasters in upstate New York, we brought some of the first television sets into Canada to receive them. Then Melody House began to sell and install the tall outdoor antennas that most Montreal homes required to receive the signals clearly.

This "be first" strategy was not without hazards. Even the decision to be one of the first stores to bring televisions into Canada was more of a risk at the time than you might think. Quite a number of prominent commentators had doubts about the new medium. One "expert," noting that North Americans were listening to five hours of radio a day, opined that television would never take radio's place.

"After the first few months of novelty wears off, five hours of television broadcasting a day would be next to impossible for the average listener," warned Warren Dygert, in a book on advertising. "Television viewers will have to give full attention to the broadcast. No playing bridge, washing dishes, reading the newspaper while a television program is on. By its very definition, it demands both eye and ear and more concentration, a thing which John Q. Public is extremely short of today."

Then there was the expense. Televisions cost around $400, or over $3,000 in today's terms. At first, this expense bought viewers at best only one single, ghostly channel snatched from the fringes of an American station's coverage. Not for the first time, some of our friends thought I was crazy to expect the expensive novelties to sell, let alone to sell briskly.

I was right about TV, of course. But even when I correctly pegged my customers' appetite for new products, I discovered that innovation exacted a price I should have anticipated. It instantly devalued any older stock. When new automatic washing machines began to appear, we had to drop the price on older wringer machines in order to move them off the floor, sacrificing margin on older stock in exchange for our regular markup on the new.

The Type E person's infectious enthusiasm conceals another un-expected hazard: Type E individuals are often instinctive salespeople. They automatically orient whatever they're selling to what the customer desires. That skill helped me grow my paper route as a teenager; now it helped me move music and appliances off the floor at Melody House.

Looking at your service or product through the customer's eyes encourages you to focus on their benefits. But that invites a terrible weakness: you can wind up loving the product too much. When that happens, the unwary Type E, instinctive salesman that he is, buys too much. Suppliers don't help, of course. Manufacturers are not inter-ested in how much you sell, only in how much you buy.

One day the telephone rang. It was my bank.

"Mr. Campbell," the fellow on the other end said, "don't sign any more cheques."

"Why not?"

"Because you're at your limit."

I swallowed hard. We had run down our cash account at the bank and I had just run up against the limits of my credit line. The bank was giving me a heads-up, for which I suppose I should have been grateful. The next cheque I wrote would bounce unless more money went into our account.

I thanked the caller and gathered my thoughts. Then I took a large piece of cardboard and a black marker and printed the words SAY 'NO' TO BUYING ANYTHING ALL DAY! on it. I put it where I could see it. And I said no all that day and for many days thereafter. I concentrated on selling the inventory we already had, and in time we worked our way out of that crisis.

But it was a terrifying moment that drove home a lesson I would strive to remember: know your business's position at every moment. Entrepreneurs, virtually by definition, operate in climates of fast-changing opportunity. It is essential that they be attuned, moment to moment, to the environment around them. New developments in their industry's products; the actions of competitors; shifting priorities and preferences among customers: a moment's inattention to any of these may invite disaster.

That is why successful Type Es are those who *live* their businesses on a twenty-four-hour-a-day basis, the ones who dream about it at night and wake up in the dark with ideas they can't wait to try out. They know instinctively how healthy their bottom line is at any given moment. They don't wait for the monthly statements. They know that *figures come late.*

Bringing a fledgling enterprise from infancy to robust, healthy growth requires constant vigilance. The Type E in action is as alert to what is going on in the life of his business as he is to the feelings of his own body. Maybe more.

IV AT MELODY HOUSE, if a customer asked for something unusual we did our best to accommodate them. And often I would learn something valuable or new from the request.

A man who had become a regular customer came into the store one day. A.L. Lawes (I never learned what the "A.L." stood for) was a Montreal shipping magnate married to a woman who was a concert pianist. He wanted to equip a recording studio for her. He asked me to help him acquire and install all the components, since I had some exposure to audio technology.

He had also heard about a company in Chicago with the latest in sound-reproduction technology—what would later become known as "hi-fi," for its higher fidelity than any previous audio systems. A.L. asked me if I would fly, at his expense, to Chicago to look it over. If I thought it measured up to the company's claims, I should buy him a set.

"I expect to pay anywhere between $2,500 and $3,500," he said.

I nearly fainted. That was the equivalent of spending $30,000 on a stereo today. But I was certainly prepared to accept the assignment.

In due course I made the trip, found the equipment as advertised, purchased a unit on Lawes' behalf—and made an enduring contact at a company that went on to become a power in the electronics industry. On my return to Montreal I presented a list of my expenses, thoroughly documented with receipts for airfare, taxi, hotel and meals.

He looked at the itemized account. "This isn't complete."

I was mortified. I thought I had been meticulous. I certainly did not want Mr. Lawes thinking I had tried to pad the account.

"Where is the item covering your time?"

Hello? "I felt the contact and exposure in Chicago were my compensation," I answered, truthfully.

"That's very commendable," he said, a little dryly. "But within reason, always try to make a profit, small or large, on everything you do." He added a sum for my time and wrote a cheque for the full amount. "Oh, and by the way, I hope you asked them for the Canadian rights to their equipment."

It's embarrassing to admit that I had not. As soon as we parted I got back to the Chicago firm, which was happy to give me rights to its products in Canada without charge. No one had ever asked for them before!

Thanks to Lawes I had not only earned a profit on my jaunt to Chicago, I had learned another important lesson. It would not be the last from this rather formal but always forthcoming businessman. He would become a deeply influential mentor.

ALONG WITH UNUSUAL products, I was also always on the lookout for new customers.

The first two Melody House locations faced across Sherbrooke Street to the Westmount movie theatre. The building remains; the movie house has long gone. One day the theatre manager came into the store, looking for a recording of film music to play in his lobby while patrons bought their tickets and popcorn (before the days of Muzak). I happily sold him some records. Then I started thinking. I went to the phone book, flipped to the back and found "cinemas" in the Yellow Pages. Hmm!

Within a short time I was supplying new LPS every couple of weeks to a dozen Montreal theatres. I would select new releases, deliver them to the various cinemas around the city belonging to United Amusements Limited and then drop off one single invoice at the company's offices.

I had considered offering the chain the records in exchange for exposure of Melody House's name, but the company was willing to pay. And by that stage in the store's development the predictable recurring revenue of a cash sale looked a lot more attractive then additional exposure. Even so, I could not predict what this association would lead to later on.

The services I gave United Amusements or A.L. Lawes seemed obvious to me. They were the simple practice of an oft-quoted and too-oft-ignored principle: always, *always,* put the customer first. What does the user of my product want? How can we get them to say yes to our service, rather than a competitor's? How can we make him or her feel comfortable? How can we get them to say "Hey, these guys think I'm important. I want to give them business"?

The professional manager puts great faith in the metrics of internal financial reporting: debt-equity ratios, return on capital, inventory cycle time, labour cost per unit. All of these can convey useful information about a company's health, of course, but without a customer *there is no company.*

Never take Joe or Jane Customer for granted. That is a fundamental truth too many large corporations today forget. No entrepreneur can afford to do so for a single hour.

IN THE WIDER WORLD beyond Montreal's island, not all the promises of the bright autumn of 1945 were being fulfilled.

The war in Europe had been over for less than a year when Winston Churchill warned that a new "Iron Curtain" of Communist occupation was falling across the continent. When the United Nations created the state of Israel in 1948, its neighbours promptly invaded; the Soviet Union seized the moment to isolate the western-occupied part of the former German capital, Berlin. And just six years after VE Day, Canadian troops were again under fire, in Korea.

But in Montreal life was good and the Campbell family was growing. After I began working full-time at the store, Vivian's presence there became less essential. In September 1947 our first child arrived.

We named him Henry after Vivian's father. The studio apartment was now emphatically too "cozy." On the strength of the business we secured a mortgage and bought a modest duplex, moving into the ground floor and renting out the upper apartment.

Any spare cash was still something for the business to use, not for personal pleasures. I had only one day off a week, and on many Sundays the height of our recreation was to sit out on the front porch and watch the neighbourhood go by. Now and again a friend with a car dropped by and took us out for a drive; this simple pleasure was always appreciated. But I often found myself envying the leisure time and disposable funds that allowed other people I knew to spend their afternoons driving or on the golf course.

Ours was, from the perspective of the twenty-first century, a very traditional domestic arrangement, the often-critiqued "working Dad/stay-at-home Mom." But let me say a word in its defence. In many respects, it worked.

In innumerable ways, Vivian has always been my greatest asset. It is impossible to overestimate her contribution to the success I have enjoyed in business. She managed our home life superbly, taking responsibility for expanding our domestic establishment into its new and larger quarters. She was an unstinting provider of affection, patience and care for infant Henry.

Astonishingly, she still had time and energy on most evenings to listen to my complaints about the stresses of my day at the store. Vivian's unsparing spirit and efficiency at home allowed me to give Melody House the constant energy it demanded.

At the same time, the responsibility of meeting the bills for an expanding family added to the stress I felt at work. I was seldom home, too consumed by the need to sell, sell, sell. And when I was home I was often preoccupied and ill-tempered with worry. Were there sometimes tensions? Of course there were. Anyone who stays married through six decades of stress and challenge and tells you otherwise is lying. But last year Vivian and I celebrated our sixty-first wedding anniversary.

It's beginning to look like a permanent thing.

Outlets for work tensions are important. Vivian and I joined a curling club and we kept up the sport and the hearty camaraderie that goes with it. Later I joined the Rotary Club, as well, and found time to get involved with community work. These sociable encounters continued to provide good company, spiritual renewal and the occasional serendipitous contact that starts something brand new and potentially profitable.

Meanwhile, without it being a conscious process I was learning, by living it, how to be an entrepreneur. Only later would I look back over the bruises and strains and conclude that I was earning my education from the U. of H.K.: the University of Hard Knocks!

I had manifested the prime characteristic of the Type E personality by just *doing it:* bringing an abandoned cobbler's shop to new life as Dave Campbell's Melody House.

We had made our store *different,* distinguishing Melody House from its competition from day 1 with music on the street and listening booths inside.

We had *made the first dollar*... and then I had *watched every penny.*

I had worked with determination always to *see things the customer's way,* to the point that at least one customer had trusted me to spend $3,000 of his money.

And I had learned always to keep my eye out for the *next new thing.*

CHAPTER 5

THE **NEXT NEW** THING

"Imagination is more important than intelligence."

ALBERT EINSTEIN

THE CONTEMPORARY WORLD is so full of astonishing technology—wireless phones with built-in cameras, robot airplanes, laptop windows on the World Wide Web—that it may be difficult to conceive of how many "everyday" items were unknown to most Canadians as recently as 1945. Modern staples like ballpoint pens and frozen food had been invented but not yet commercialized. The same was true for television. There was hard black Bakelite but no household plastic, either literally or figuratively; garbage bags and MasterCard were yet to come. Contact lenses, the pill, the pocket calculator: none of those were even on the horizon. Virtual reality was truly the stuff of science fiction.

The end of a hot war against one kind of totalitarianism and the beginning of a cold one against a different kind, however, marked the start of the most inventive half century in human history. As soon as North American manufacturers stopped turning out tanks and airplanes and Liberty ships, they began adapting engineering breakthroughs achieved in wartime to products targeted at civilian buyers.

I had started Melody House with only records to sell, but my motto Make Melody House First applied to offering every new technology for the home. To radios and record players and kitchen appliances we added home-movie cameras. I keenly followed the trade publications' coverage of what manufacturers were developing. When I could, I travelled to U.S. cities to see what was on the market there.

On one such trip in 1948, a white enamelled steel cube on a display floor caught my eye. A company that would later become Whirlpool Corporation had unveiled the first automatic washing machine.

That load-and-forget appliance in your laundry room is the end product of a century and a half of tinkering and refinement. Electric-powered washing machines had appeared in the 1920s, using a wringer to squeeze water from cleaned clothes in a laborious and potentially crippling operation. The wringers were also called "mangles," which is exactly what they did to an incautious hand caught between their rollers.

At the end of the war, wringer washers were still the state of the art. The new machine, with its automatic rinse and spin-dry cycles, would make laundry chores far less dangerous and unpleasant. The next year Westinghouse brought out a similar model that I brought to Canada. I unpacked it the moment it arrived. Tucked inside the tub was a small cardboard box of ALL, a detergent. Believe it or not, this too was a brand new technology. Soap has been with us since the Babylonians, but detergent only since 1946. The Westinghouse manual recommended using the new cleaning product in its new washing machine because detergent created far fewer suds than traditional soap.

I put the box back in the tub and thought about this for a while. ALL was not for sale in Canada. A customer who couldn't use her new washing machine for lack of detergent was going to be an unhappy customer—or no customer at all. This was a problem.

Or... I looked again at the box. Then I picked up the phone and called a company named Detergent Incorporated, in Columbus, Ohio. I got someone on the line. I identified myself and explained that I'd just opened a washing machine, found a box of the company's product and wanted to buy some more.

"That's what we do here," the voice on the phone said cheerily. "We sell ALL."

"But I also want the rights to Canada."

I didn't say anything about *buying* the rights to Canada, only that I wanted to have them. But as it turned out, Detergent Incorporated was running as fast as it could to keep up with demand for its product in the United States. It had no time to think about developing the market anywhere else.

"We're so goddamn busy down here, we don't care," the company's man told me after a little more conversation. "Come on down."

I paid a visit to Ohio and signed a five-year contract to distribute ALL to Canada.

> "Always keep the ball in their court."
>
> **RICHARD A. MORAN**

IT'S OFTEN REMARKED that the Chinese character for "crisis" integrates the ideas of both danger and opportunity. The decades after 1945—like the decades ahead of us now—offered an abundance of danger but also unlimited opportunity.

The essence of the Type E personality is not only to *see* an opportunity, but to *seize* it. An opportunity is only a potential. To be reached, it must be *acted on.*

When I opened that first machine and discovered the box of recommended soap substitute, unavailable in Canada, I could have seen an impediment to selling washing machines—a danger. Instead, I saw an opportunity to sell both products.

And then: I picked up the phone. Many people say to themselves from time to time: "You know, there's a business in that!" Their opportunity sensor is functioning. It astounds me how very few take the next step to action or even the first step. A clock-watcher who insists on walking out of the office on the dot of 5 PM every day will never be a self-made millionaire. The kid who meekly turns over his peanut-butter-and-jelly sandwich to the class bully in grade 6 can't expect to win a lot of showdowns later in life.

As a teenager, I had always had my eye out for any new idea that might earn some money. The only certainties an entrepreneur can count on are relentless, unpredictable change and fast-moving opportunity. Survival under those conditions requires nothing less than total attention at all times to what is new around us.

"Always," A.L. Lawes reminded me frequently when we spoke about business, "*always* be open to new ideas."

What the Type E thinker understands is that you don't have to be Microsoft owner Bill Gates to have a monopoly on what everyone else wants—at least for a little while. The same dynamics apply at a smaller scale.

Begin where everything starts: with the customer. Whatever it is you are selling—movies to meatballs, it doesn't matter—it has to give the customers what they want. It must solve their problem, satisfy their desires and aspirations, *meet their need.*

Usually, there are lots of ways a customer can meet any particular need and many vendors competing to supply it. Consider buying a litre of milk on your way home from the office: there are probably a few dozen places you could stop to get it.

Every now and again though, someone devises an entirely new way to meet some need. They slice the bread at the bakery and save you the trouble later. They find a way to put a digital camera in a cellphone and save you buying and carrying around both. They get a machine to wash, rinse *and* drain your jeans and underwear all in one operation, when no one else has done that before.

For a little while, whoever has that unique product for sale can charge a premium. They have, after all, a monopoly. This, of course, is the basis for things like patent protection and copyright.

But this is also the sweet spot of the Type E's game, the grail and the motherlode. As long as your door is the only place a customer can find the latest hot new thing, your business can reap profits at the top end of what is fair.

That benefit vanishes like a pumpkin coach at midnight as soon as the first competitor appears on the scene with a similar product. The competitor's product may improve on yours or it may not, but even if it is only just as good as yours it will certainly compete on price. To meet that competition, you will have to give back some of that "monopoly premium" profit: you'll have to drop your price.

Or innovate yourself. Or both. (This is also why it is wise to remember a lesson from chapter 2: Do not gouge. Gouging just makes it all the easier for a competitor to enter the market and underprice you.)

The only way to continue to enjoy premium profits, then, is to stay always one innovation ahead of the next guy. Always be the only place in town with that must-have next new thing.

This isn't rocket science; it's just market common sense. But many people overlook the implications.

1. You don't need to be Microsoft to enjoy the benefits: monopolies come in all sizes and categories. Anyone can play.
2. The moment you *do* enjoy a monopoly, the clock is ticking towards the moment you don't any more, because some competitor got to the next innovation ahead of you.

Figure 5.1: The Innovation Cycle

North America is still coping with the consequences of the "baby boom"—the result of the most intense and concentrated period of what statisticians call "household formation" in western history. Nearly a million Canadian men, out of a population of only 12.5 million people, were in uniform at the end of the war, most of them at sea or in Europe. In 1945 they started to come home, get married and begin making babies. Canadians produced more children the following year (and each year for many more after that) than the adults among 32 million Canadians did in 1999. (All this without Viagra!)

Among the other household products yet to be introduced was Pampers. Diapers still had to be washed. It was a good time to be the only guy in Montreal selling automatic washing machines, and now I could also provide the detergent the easy-to-use machines were made to work with. Soon, detergent sales to people who had bought machines from me were turning a separate and satisfying profit.

It didn't last, of course. Soon other manufacturers introduced competing automatic washers and within months every appliance store in Montreal was selling them. Profits shrank to more competitive levels. But within a year the new models were outselling the old-fashioned kind ten-to-one. And all of them were supposed to be used with low-sudsing detergent, not soap.

And I was still the only guy in Canada with the right to sell ALL detergent.

I had started out importing ALL in small shipments of one-pound boxes and got a few boxes onto the shelves of local grocery stores. Soon we were selling it in five- and then twenty-pound boxes. Eventually we were bringing the stuff in from Ohio in carloads.

I called Detergent Incorporated. "Look," I said, "this is nonsense. Why don't you just give me the formula. I'll pay you a royalty and we'll mix it here."

They agreed. In fact, they had a box-filling machine they were replacing. I bought it, moved it to Montreal and installed it in rented factory space.

We had labels printed in French and English. This wasn't a matter of respecting the law, it was just good business sense. "Make it easy for the customer" starts with speaking his or her language. We were selling into a bilingual market; I wanted my customers to be comfortable with my product in either language.

Soon I had boxes of ALL on the shelves of most of the big Montreal supermarkets and was getting it into chain stores across Canada.

"Nothing focuses the mind better than the constant sight of a competitor who wants to wipe you off the map."   WAYNE CALLOWAY, FORMER CEO, PEPSI COMPANY

MELODY HOUSE CONTINUED to sell washers. That made for a bit of tension when I called on other appliance stores. Their customers were also looking for the new detergent but the stores bridled at buying it from a competitor. To deal with this, I registered a new company to handle the detergent business: Dave Campbell Enterprises. Other stores could now order all the ALL they liked, without feeling as though they were lining the cash drawer at Melody House.

Not every washing machine buyer was convinced that detergent would produce a better result than the flaked soap that they'd been using for years. To persuade doubters, we organized demonstrations— we called them "clinics"—to show off the effectiveness of the new generation of cleaning. I'd show up at an apartment building laundry room, armed with ALL, and invite the housewives there to bring me their stained tablecloths and their husband's underwear. I'd show them how our product got the stains out then send them home with a free sample and a list of all the local retailers that carried it.

At the same time, we continued adding to Melody House's lines: refrigerators, ranges, dryers, air conditioners and other major household appliances. In the music section, 45s were now on sale alongside 33 $\frac{1}{3}$ LPs and the disappearing 78s. Hi-fis eclipsed record players.

Within a year or so of opening the store I had hired counter sales help. Now, overseeing the expansion of both Melody House and ALL was putting crushing demand on my available time. Vivian had no interest in re-entering the business. Her hands were full at home with one active three-year-old and a second child was on the way. If I wanted to seize the potential evident in this detergent business, it became clear that I had no choice but to hire someone else, as well, to manage Melody House on a day-to-day basis.

Hiring effectively is one of the most difficult skills a business owner must master. Like so much else, the function has changed dramatically over the decades and become a profession on its own, commanding entire "HR" bureaucracies in large corporations. There wasn't much sophistication in the way I chose my first manager for Melody House: I simply promoted a fellow I had hired to help me on the counter, who had proved reliable and shown good judgement. No batteries of personality tests or aptitude profiles!

It took me longer to absorb something else I would need to learn as my business and its staff grew. No matter how well I hired, or how good the person I hired, they would never do a job the way I would. *Nobody* was going to do it the way I would, for the very good reason that there could never be two of me. I had to keep reminding myself to let people do things their way—and judge their performance on *results*, not on *process*. That way I got along much better. And so, I imagine, did they.

Hiring is one challenge. The other end of the relationship can be just as hard. Happily, I have had less practice getting rid of people than I have hiring them. I have always preferred to innovate continuously, staying in expansion mode with lots for everybody to do, rather than find myself on the defensive and cutting positions to preserve a bottom line.

"You're fired!" The American millionaire Donald Trump's signature line on his television "reality" show goes with the rest of his arrogant, "I-know-best" attitude to management. It seems to be popular on television, but in my view it is bad business in practice. In fact, I don't believe I have ever actually used the F-word. When someone is not working out, I have generally found it is enough to go along and ask how they feel they're doing.

"Are you happy? Do you think you're making progress?" Most people have a fine sense of when they are *not* working out in a situation; they are seldom happy about it. "Can I help?" I usually ask. "Or would you like to take some time to look around for something else?"

In my experience, people always got the message and "de-hired" themselves with little further prompting. In any case, my inquiry had been entirely sincere: I *did* want them to be happy.

An essayist in the *New York Times* had this to say about "The Donald's" style: "The Trump approach is all about Mr. Trump. On his show, he's the answer to every question, the source of all wisdom. In his companies, he revels in micromanagement. The Trump model of leadership boils down to this: nobody is as smart as me."

This is not my approach. That kind of superior attitude turns people away. It puts customers off and breeds resentment in employees. It may also make you blind to something you *don't* know yet, but need to. More is going on out there than you can possibly keep up with on your own, no matter who you are. In a world of relentless, unpredictable change, arrogance is not only not required, it can be a handicap.

I know lots of people smarter than I. I tried to hire as many of them as I could in areas where I knew I was out of my depth.

> "I see life almost like one long university education that I never had. Every day I'm learning something new." **RICHARD BRANSON, FOUNDER, VIRGIN GROUP**

THE CENTURY'S MIDPOINT was the year of my thirtieth birthday. It went by in a blur. In 1950 we added Barry to the family, making the duplex an even busier place for Vivian. She shouldered the load of two preschoolers heroically.

I was little help to her. Melody House still demanded my presence six days a week; most of the time I spent serving customers directly on the sales floor. I was also dedicating many additional hours every week to the expanding detergent business. And on at least some evenings I was back at Sir George Williams; now, rather than general sciences, I studied practical economics.

However, I learned far more from the people I met on the store floor and in other encounters, both business and social. Some people hear but don't listen. I was always a good listener, and I was never afraid to ask a question or to keep asking questions until I understood the answers.

A young American singer appeared recently on the TV news magazine show *Sixty Minutes*. Mary J. Blige is described as being to her generation "what Billie Holiday, Aretha Franklin and Tina Turner were to theirs"—a singer whose talent overcame a hard childhood. She explained to interviewer Ed Bradley that her inner-city school graduated her with an eighth-grade reading ability. Now she finds herself in meetings where her money and career are the subject of complicated contracts.

"It hurts a lot when you cannot comprehend what a person is saying in a meeting or what you're reading in a contract," Ms. Blige told Bradley. Rather than be embarrassed into silence, she said, "I just drop my pride and say, 'You know what? I don't understand what you just said. Could you explain it to me again?'"

That's the attitude!

In men like Lawes and H.S. Berliner, and others whom I got to know over a Rotary lunch or drinks at a curling bonspiel, I found freely given sources of tremendous experience and insight, as well as fresh ideas. Looking back, I see that I was very fortunate in the quality of many of those individuals. I was a sponge, always absorbing; I could easily have been directed the wrong way.

And I continued to read voraciously anything to do with electronics. In the pages of the industry journals, one subject dominated all others: Television.

TV, as a technology, is older than some people realize. The first primitive pictures were broadcast and received on experimental equipment in the 1920s. My family arrived in Montreal in 1932 just a few months too late to join the thousands of others who lined up outside a department store that year for a glimpse of a primitive, experimental red-on-black television system that was being demonstrated there. By the late 1930s, some programs were being broadcast in Britain, Germany and the United States to tiny audiences of hobbyists and engineers.

All those broadcasts ended with the war. But in 1945, broadcasting resumed from the Empire State Building in New York City and elsewhere. By 1950, television broadcasting was spreading fast across the United States but had not yet arrived in Canada.

Television *watching* was another matter. Canadians didn't wait for local stations to come on-air to begin enjoying this exciting new medium. Melody House and other stores like ours across the country sold 10,000 sets in 1949, 25,000 the following year. With not a single broadcaster in the country, TV sets were already the equivalent of a $100-million-a-year industry in today's currency.

This despite import controls that had been in place since the war. The government's goal was to preserve Canada's limited foreign exchange, mainly U.S. currency, for what it considered more strategic purchases of capital equipment for industry. The result was that major appliances and home "white goods" were in perennial undersupply.

Frustrated customer demand and transferable quotas created a secondary market in the quotas themselves. When Melody House used up its own quotas in a category, I would often be on the phone to other importers who might have unused quotas they wanted to sell.

How and when Canadians would get their own television *broadcasters* was a hot topic. A Royal Commission on culture was debating, among other things, whether the CBC should be given a monopoly in television, like the one the BBC enjoyed in Britain. Private investors were also clamouring for a shot at the new medium.

In 1952, Canadian authorities decided. Private companies would be allowed to build and own television stations in Montreal, Toronto, Halifax, Vancouver and other major cities. But the CBC would provide most of the programming.

THEN ONE DAY I got a call from Ohio. It was my contact at Detergent Incorporated. "How would you like to sell your company?" he asked.

"I don't want to sell my company," I told him. "I like this business. It's the only business I've ever been in where I can sleep in Monday morning and people everywhere are using my product."

"Well, think about it," the caller from Columbus said. "Because we're selling down here, and I can tell you that the people buying us already have an operation in Canada. They won't renew your distribution contract in four years. Be smart, sell your business with us."

I hemmed and hawed a little. I did like the business and I didn't want to sell—but he was right about the contract. Timing is everything to the entrepreneurial cycle. When to get into an opportunity, when to get out.

"Look," the guy from Detergent said. "Would you like us to put a price on your end of it for you? We know how much product you're selling and how much you've invested in equipment."

I had no idea what kind of a price to ask for, so I said, "Sure. Just do me a favour: Before you tell them the price, tell me?"

"Of course," he said, and rang off.

Within forty-eight hours he called back and gave me the figure. Monsanto Corporation was willing to pay me $25,000 for the Canadian side of the ALL operation (equivalent to more than $175,000 today). I would never have dared suggest such a price. I thought he was nuts and told him so.

"Not nuts," he said, laughing. "That's just what they'll pay because they want your end as well."

The next day he called again to confirm the deal was done. Thirty days later I received a cheque and handed over my remaining stock and the keys to the mixing and packaging facility to Monsanto Corporation.

I was no longer in the detergent business.

THERE'S A CAUTIONARY aside to Detergent Incorporated's experience. As that generic-sounding name implies, the company was a pioneer in its field. It was such a leader in the chemical engineering that created detergent that it was able to claim a name that embraced an entire class of products. It was as though a Silicon Valley firm had been able to register itself as Microchip Incorporated. (Or, for that matter, as though in the infancy of television a company had trademarked Cable TV Limited—as we were to do.)

But Detergent Incorporated mixed its product from ingredients bought almost exclusively from Monsanto. As the company grew, its management elected to reinvest most of its cash flow in selling and promotion, while neglecting to pay off their mounting account with

Monsanto. By the time the chemical giant moved in, it picked up Detergent Incorporated for not much more than its founders' overdue tab for ingredients.

For me, it had been a shorter than hoped for but certainly profitable ride. In less than thirty-six months my venture in ALL had gone through the entire entrepreneurial cycle, from ignition to exit.

With Type E thinking, I had seen opportunity—rather than threat— in that first sample box of detergent. I had seized the moment and called the company. I had expended shoe leather and time to make the first sales outside Melody House, then risked an investment in mixing and filling equipment to bump the business up to another level. It was well on its way to successful maturity in the marketplace when Monsanto presented me with both a carrot and stick to time my exit.

And yes, we'd enjoyed a gratifying stretch of those high profits that can only be sustained by the latest unique product.

One day, soon after the deal to sell ALL closed, I received another phone call. It was from the Canadian president of Monsanto.

"We've just bought your company, as you probably know," he began.

I knew.

"And I'd like you to have lunch with me."

I said that would be nice.

"Fine, then. Meet me at the Mount Stephen Club."

I knew the club. I also knew I couldn't meet him there.

MATTERS OF CHARACTER

"He who hesitates is not only lost but miles from the next exit."

ANON.

"MEET ME AT THE Mount Stephen Club," the president of Monsanto said.

I knew the place well, from the outside. I had walked past it hundreds of times on my way to and from classes at Sir George Williams. It sat directly across the street from the college.

The ornate nineteenth-century mansion was the former home of George Stephen—later Lord Mount Stephen—president of the Bank of Montreal and later the Canadian Pacific Railway, in which he was a major investor. Since 1926, it had been a private club. In short, if there was a spiritual home to Montreal's moneyed upper crust, which in 1951 still meant Canada's financial elite, it was the Mount Stephen Club.

I had never set foot inside it. Now, I hesitated at the invitation. After an awkward silence the voice on the phone asked: "Why are you hesitating? Is there something we still need to do before we meet?"

"No," I said. "No, everything's been discussed. We've agreed on the price. But I can't go to the Mount Stephen Club. I'm Jewish. And the Mount Stephen Club does not allow people of the Jewish faith as members or guests."

Now it was his turn to hesitate. Finally he said, "I wasn't aware of that."

"Why would you be? You're not Jewish. But look at your roster; there are no members of the Jewish faith there. I can't step inside the place."

This time he thought for only a moment. Then: "I'll call you back," he said.

I did have lunch with the president of Monsanto, who invited most of the Mount Stephen Club board to join us. A couple of months later the club dropped its exclusionary policy.

AS SHOULD BE CLEAR by now, success for the entrepreneur is seldom a question of job skills. It is a matter of possessing a Type E personality—a unique combination of ambition, outgoing interest in the world and what used to be called "gumption." In brief, success is a matter of character.

Our character proves itself in how we handle ourselves under stress. The entrepreneur's stress filled life is full of opportunities for such proof. Every business has its own particular kinds of worries and all entrepreneurs share (or should) a few fears in common: Will the customer want my product tomorrow? Can I stay in front of the guy who is coming up behind me with something new?

Stress brought me physical anguish often: stomach pains, headaches, burning sensations in my chest, sleepless nights and more. That sort of stress comes with the game, but the serious person expects to put his or her shoulder to the wheel and get on with it.

Choices don't come only in adversity, however. Once a business begins to succeed, there is often ample opportunity to direct rewards back to the founder, either in salary or in "perquisites." The long, friendly, expense-account dinner with business associates is a tradition. The same tradition can be made to cover much more spectacular indulgences— as we've seen in the criminal trials of some U.S. executives recently.

It's far from unusual for weaknesses of character to emerge once an individual has begun to "make it" and discovers, too late, that they can't handle their own success. The same restless energies and wilfulness that make the successful Type E formidable in business can make him equally excessive in his leisure pursuits. Self-made successes who party away their success are not limited to Hollywood.

But there is another kind of adversity you may run into. It's the hurdle that presents itself when you encounter another person who holds a prejudiced view of you for reasons that are entirely gratuitous, arbitrary and unjust—in a word, biased.

Despite my family name (which I did not control), I have never sought to conceal my Jewish faith. Neither has it been an especially defining part of my life. I have certainly striven to act ethically in business and in life, but I am one of the least formally "religious" people you will ever meet. Indeed, I find much about organized religions of every stripe to deplore. They have killed more people over the centuries than any other man-made force. My own ambivalence towards organized religion has perhaps only underscored the shock and, yes, the hurt when I have encountered bias at work.

In this, I know, my experience is far from unique. As recently as the end of the war to defend our "freedoms" against Nazi aggression, many Asian Canadians did not have the right to vote or to work as lawyers, pharmacists or accountants. That legal discrimination ended less than four years before my telephone call from the Monsanto president.

Much has changed in half a century since then, but not human nature. Even as we each value our cultural, ethnic, racial or religious identity as a source of personal strength and social support, it may sometimes also attract unhelpful attention. Bias persists.

For that matter, you needn't be one of any so-called visible minority to face unjust barriers. The ignorant and unthinking are just as ready to prejudge others on the basis of their manner, looks or sexual orientation (or merely of what the bigoted observer imagines that to be).

And yes, it *can* sting—deeply. This is an admission I might not have made back when I needed to appear as tough as nails in negotiations. In fact, I have sometimes considered such vulnerability to be my greatest defect as an entrepreneur. But it is true, I am extremely sensitive. I am easily hurt; about some things I cry very easily.

How, then, to respond to the hurt of bias, whether individual or institutional? In anger? With retaliation? Resentment? Denial? Retreat? A chip on the shoulder?

Or with a polite, but clearly drawn, line?

"Never be embarrassed about where you grew up, where you went to school, how you look, your name, or anything else that it's too late to fix. Be proud of who you are."   RICHARD A. MORAN

AS A CHILD GROWING UP in Fredericton, religion never seemed very important, either positively or negatively. Our family made some effort to educate my sister and me in our faith. My father and the only one of my grandfathers whom I knew (my mother's father) were both very religious men, but with only a couple of dozen Jewish families in Fredericton at the time, the community had neither a synagogue nor a full-time rabbi. The usual extent of our practice of the faith at home was on Friday night, when my mother would light the candles and my father would lead us in prayer.

There was a part-time rabbi who taught us the letters of the Hebrew alphabet and to sound out the Torah verses. He never did bother to explain to us what the words meant, however, so I mouthed the syllables without understanding any of them. The books of the Torah meant nothing to me; not surprisingly, I found it pretty boring. Only much later, when I encountered English translations, did I find there was more to appreciate.

Among playmates on the streets of Fredericton or at school, my family's faith was never an issue; it just never came up. Far more hurtful were the taunts and teasing I endured for being fat (unless I blame that on the *taglah!*).

It was much the same after we moved to Montreal. The deeper social divide was along language lines, between the French and English. But then I was twelve and Montreal offered not just a synagogue but a choice of them. I was approaching the age, thirteen, when I would be bar mitzvah. My father thought that I should introduce myself to a rabbi, tell him my age and ask him how I should prepare for this initiation ceremony, an important milestone.

The following Saturday I dutifully got ready for synagogue. I didn't give much thought to what to wear; in any case, my choices were severely limited. I grabbed whatever shirt was clean and a pair of what we called "knickers" then: three-quarter-length trousers that tucked into knee socks. I knew enough about the protocol of the service to know I should cover my head. I threw on a peaked cap and set off.

On my father's instruction, I introduced myself after service to the rabbi. I told him where I was from, who I was and that I was approaching the age of bar mitzvah. "How should I prepare myself?" I finished.

The rabbi scowled and said: "When you come to synagogue, be properly dressed and wear a fedora. You cannot come to synagogue in shorts and a cap. If you can't wear long pants and a fedora, don't come to synagogue."

I was devastated. "I guess I won't come, then," I blurted. "I don't own a fedora." Tears came as I turned away from him and walked towards the door. On the way I passed an older member of the congregation.

"Here," he said. I looked up and saw a man with a fedora in his hand. He held it out for me to take. "This is yours for your bar mitzvah." He leaned towards me and added, "Don't let the rabbi tell you what to wear. In the eyes of God, clothing has no meaning. The rabbi is trying to be officious. He should know that one of the reasons for the *tallit* [prayer scarf] is that it covers up any finery and that in the eyes of God, we are all equal."

The elder's wisdom mitigated my hurt feelings somewhat. And I did eventually have my bar mitzvah, an event celebrated by nothing fancier than a small glass of wine and a little piece of cake in the rabbi's office afterwards. But I could never again feel entirely comfortable in that synagogue or any other. Friday evening prayers and Passover seder dinners continued to be part of my adolescence. If I made it to service once a year, that was it.

And yet at other moments I could not escape my Jewish identity. As a teenager in high school I dreamed of going into the ad business. It was not altogether new, but neither was it the ever-present goliath it has become in today's media-saturated age, when marketing messages plaster anything that moves or stands still. As a Depression kid in Montreal I certainly was not foreseeing the industry's explosive growth, but I am an instinctive salesman and you can be creative in advertising.

That ad contest I won during my senior year offered as the prize a framed certificate, twenty dollars (not such an insignificant sum back then, the equivalent of about $250 today) and an internship at the sponsoring advertising agency.

I roughed out a dozen newspaper ads: what I hoped would be eye-catching pictures and captions. "Is this man's life in your hands?" one ad asked the reader, under a picture of someone on the operating table. There followed, of course, a pitch to save his life by donating generously to the new wing at St. Mary's public hospital. Another depicted the wing with several windows dark and invited readers to "light up a window" with a generous contribution.

I submitted my entry and eagerly awaited the outcome. One day I got a call from the agency and was invited to go to their offices, where an executive congratulated me on winning first place in their contest and produced my prize: a certificate and a twenty-dollar cheque.

"Normally," he said, "we like to offer first-place winners an internship in our company. Unfortunately we have a policy that people of the Hebrew faith are not permitted. We'll be pleased to give you a recommendation, but we cannot offer you an internship."

But why did they have such a policy at all, I asked him. He lowered his head a little and spoke in a more personal voice. "In *my* opinion," he said, "it's because people of that faith are extremely entrepreneurial and pretty soon we'd find them competing with us."

The caption of one of my winning ads noted that St. Mary's, a Catholic institution, served anyone in need of care, "Regardless of Race,

Colour or Creed." I doubt whether the agency sensed the irony, in light of its anti-Semitic policies.

> "Don't hire only people who look and act like you. It will make for a less interesting and less effective group."   **RICHARD A. MORAN**

AT SIR GEORGE WILLIAMS COLLEGE, I found myself invited to join a "Jewish" fraternity. Most other members were from families wealthier than mine and why they deigned to have anything to do with me I'll never know. But, aware of my circumstances, Alpha Delta Phi's membership committee waived its usual membership fees to allow me to join.

When I took up curling, I and a number of other Jewish enthusiasts founded the Greystone Curling Club and participated in its bonspiels for years. For a while I held the lead position on a team skipped by Charles Bronfman. (Although as the only Campbell on the roster I really should have been made president of the club, given the game's Scottish origins. . . .)

Both of these were fundamentally social associations. They were rewarding in the same way that my involvement in Georgiantics, the Montreal Rep Theatre, or later the Toronto Symphony Orchestra or Art Gallery of Ontario would be: enjoyable on their own, with the additional benefit of expanding my knowledge and personal network.

When the United Nations ordered that territory under British mandate in the postwar Middle East be partitioned to make room for a new Jewish state, I was elated. When its neighbours promptly attacked the new state the day after it assumed independence in May 1948, I shared every other Jew's concern for its fate. And when Jewish organizations in Canada solicited us to buy Israel bonds, we did. Vivian and I would eventually visit Israel in 1973 and later contribute significantly to the Weisman Institute there—but would also feel both free and compelled to comment on some of the directions Israeli governments have taken and continue to take.

Still, as unobservant and non-"religious" as I was, I was still too Jewish for some people. This became apparent when I was courting the Toronto Stock Exchange for the rights to disseminate its trading data. It was the only major exchange that did not yet allow our company to provide its trading prices to the financial community.

Each month or so, I flew to Toronto for the day and took the general manager of the stock exchange out for lunch. We talked business. I asked him for the rights to the TSE trading data. He said no. I picked up the bill. This went on for months and the months became years. At last my patience ran out. At one of our lunches I said, "Look, this has been going on for three years. I need to know *why* you are not considering giving us the rights everyone else has given us."

Perhaps the man had begun to consider me a friend, perhaps it was the (customary, for him) third martini: I'll never know. But he finally blurted it out.

"You have three strikes against you."

"And what are those?"

"One: you come from the wrong city [Montreal]. Two: you went to the wrong school [Sir George Williams, not the University of Toronto]. And three: you go to the wrong church."

There it was.

Now, I'm not generally a bellicose guy. I won't pick a fight just for the fun of it. I don't make a display of my Type E, alpha-dog personality in the manner of Donald Trump or some other "celebrity" CEOs. I well recall my father's advice to pick my quarrels carefully. But neither did my mother raise a doormat. She had me stand up for myself against Fredericton's schoolyard bullies. It is no less important to stand up for myself later in life.

There were no human rights commissions back in 1937. Much later, however, the big agency that had declined to have me as an intern began making earnest attempts to get some of Melody House's advertising business. I routinely declined their solicitations. Eventually an account executive called me, baffled. He wanted to know why I wouldn't do business with Montreal's largest ad agency.

"I don't do business with people who are biased in their hiring policy," I told him.

By the time I encountered the explicit bias of the Toronto Stock Exchange, times had changed. And, perhaps, so had I.

"Three: you go to the wrong church," the general manager of the TSE itemized.

"And number four: we go to court!" I responded.

He shook his head to clear away the martini fog and blustered, "You can't prove what I just said."

"Maybe not," I answered. "But you're not going to like the publicity. Because I am going to tell the press *and* see you in court."

I stood up. "By the way, this lunch is on you. I've picked up my last lunch check for you." I walked out.

By the time I got back to my Toronto office, there was a phone call from the stock exchange. I did not return it. About an hour later a letter arrived by courier. The general manager of the TSE suggested we get together "to discuss" our service. I didn't dignify this with a typed response. In thick black wax pencil I scrawled across the letter, "Discussion time is over. See you in court." Then I sent it back.

Half an hour later another letter arrived. This one said in essence that it was "the intention of the TSE to consider allowing your company to disseminate" exchange data. This at least was progress. This time I used the wax pencil to write: "Intentions are fine—when and under what conditions?"

Within thirty days, we had signed a contract and had the rights we needed.

THERE IS SUCH A THING as oversensitivity. Don't try to hide what you are; that's the worst thing you can do, and in the end it will probably come out anyway. In the meantime it fills you with shame and fear. And most certainly do not stand for abuse. But don't go around with a chip on your shoulder, either. Keep your eye on the things that really matter and learn to let the rest roll off you. Get on with life.

Your own expectation of bias can hold you back as much as its reality.

WHEN CMQ WAS EXPANDING across Canada very rapidly in the 1970s, we needed a larger technical and sales base in Vancouver. Positions were offered to several proven Montreal employees, francophone Quebecers. The jobs came with big raises and the chance to work on leading-edge technology. As well, the company would pay for all the costs of relocating, including helping them find acceptable residences.

To my great surprise, all the Québécois employees turned down the advancement. "Why?" I asked. They explained that their wives, none of whom had ever been to Vancouver, were afraid of being ostracized by "English" British Columbians! The positions went to others.

"If everyone is thinking alike, then somebody isn't thinking."

GENERAL GEORGE S. PATTON

THE WORLD'S PERCEPTION of us may be unjust and undeserved, or it may be pointing out something about ourselves we would do well to examine. In the 1950s, I decided the second was true about my weight.

With the pressures of running Melody House, a lethal combination of snacking to relieve stress, little exercise and irregular eating habits sent my weight soaring. I was on my feet from 8:30 in the morning until after 6 PM, focussed so intensely on selling that frequently I would not stop to eat. By evening, my head would be so busy with one business problem or another that I would shovel my meal into my mouth compulsively, wolfing it down without noticing what it was for the first few minutes.

I became increasingly aware of, and embarrassed by, my size. Then, one day at my doctor's, I was appalled to discover that I had reached 229.5 pounds. Believe me, that's more than even a well-cut suit can hide on a five-foot-nine frame!

"How healthy am I, doctor?" I asked as I stepped off the scale.

"You're fine," he said, "except that you're overweight."

"I know that. So give me a diet."

"Before I do that, I want you to do something," he said. He pointed to two large black briefcases in the corner. "Those are full of medical books. I want you to pick one up in each hand and walk around the room for fifteen minutes."

I walked over to the cases and hoisted one in each hand. My doctor stepped to the door. "Start walking. Don't stop," he said. "I'll be back." And he walked out.

Needless to say, by the time he returned I was puffing and sweating as I circled the room, bags in hand.

"Each one of those cases weighs between twenty-five and thirty pounds [11.3 and 13.6 kilograms]," my doctor said, fixing his eye on me. "Together that is fifty or sixty pounds. That's what you're doing all day—carrying around fifty or sixty pounds of extra weight. You're healthy now, but that will eventually cause you a problem you won't be able to correct."

"So give me a diet," I asked again.

"No, I won't give you a diet," he said. "But I will give you some advice."

"Okay, what advice?"

"Eat anything you want—deny yourself nothing. But I want you to *chew* more *slowly*. Take your time. Chew, then chew some more. Then some more. I guarantee you'll never finish whatever is put in front of you."

Coincidentally, I had happened to win one of those contests manufacturers hold to reward top-selling outlets; Melody House had moved more Fedder air conditioners than any other store in Canada. The prize was a ten-day trip to Italy, and our bags were already packed. I made a vow to begin the chew-many-times routine when we got home.

Rome in autumn is delightful. We both enjoyed the wine, the art and architecture—and the food. In our sightseeing, I also noticed a number of places offering to tailor a custom-fitted suit within three days. Reasoning that I wouldn't get another opportunity like this for some time, if ever, I went into one of these and ordered a suit in a lovely spring-weight silk.

In due course I returned to the shop and picked it up. It fitted flawlessly. Well satisfied, I went back to the hotel. By the time we got home to Montreal a couple of days later winter had descended on Montreal; it was far too cold for a light silk suit, no matter how nicely tailored. The Italian suit went into the closet to await the spring.

I also put my doctor's "chew slowly" rule into action. As simple as it sounds, especially in contrast to today's celebrity diets, the program worked for me. By the following spring I had shed fifty pounds. Most of them have stayed off ever since.

The loss of that extra weight boosted my energy as well as my confidence level. I can easily understand why so many of today's young (and older) entrepreneurs schedule weekly hours in the gym into their personal business plans. A fit person is bound to generate more assurance than a fat one. Appearances count.

My lovely Italian suit, however, now fitted me as though it really did come from a tent and tarpaulin company. I consulted a tailor in Montreal, who said he could cut the trousers down all right—so long as I didn't mind reaching around to my buttocks to put my hands in my pockets.

Someone shopping at Goodwill not long after that got a heck of a bargain on a brand new Italian silk suit.

THERE ARE WORSE shortcomings than compulsive overeating. Many people with the intensity and focus it takes to be a self-made success release their stresses in ways less healthy than by devouring a jumbo smoked meat on dark rye. The phrase "work hard, party harder" could have been coined for some of those flamboyant Type Es.

You needn't look far to see examples of promising businesses run into the ground by proprietors who lost control over their fondness for alcohol or drugs, casino tables, illicit romance or simply their own excessively lavish household tastes.

Perhaps I was just lucky. I worked hard. But I also enjoyed people. I preferred to blow off steam by throwing myself into social activities outside the office: curling, volunteering with Rotary, or later in community work with organizations like the symphony and the art gallery. For whatever reason, I never developed the kind of out-of-control appetites that have destroyed too many entrepreneurial ambitions.

I did pick up a few artful devices to conceal the fact that I was not keeping up with harder-boozing associates drink for drink. Especially in the days when business lunches were more often lubricated by multiple cocktails, I didn't want to lose control. Ordering water and ice to guzzle while I nursed a drink; spilling some of a cocktail into the potted palms or table centrepiece; outright watering my drinks: I became adept at them all. I kept my wits about me.

Patience was something else: that, I often lost. I am demanding of employees and don't easily "understand" when a commitment goes unmet, a deadline is missed or an instruction is mishandled. I have no time for excuses and know that some employees have dreaded encountering me when I was displeased. I know I yelled sometimes, but they stayed and we built great companies.

The Type E personality is typically impatient with anything less than 110-per-cent effort by anyone. He or she demands commitments of ambition, energy and focus so bottomless that many other people may regard them, perhaps not entirely unjustly, as obsessive. We carry forward in single-minded pursuit of our objectives, often heedless of the hurt feelings and bruised egos we may leave in our wake. Am I easy to work for? No. I can be a son of a bitch. And often I handled people poorly. I am forever asking "Why not? When? So what? What if…?" I do not tolerate slipshod attitudes. I insist on target dates being met, reports coming in on time, consistent follow-up; I am impatient with excuses, want promises kept and figures checked twice. I sometimes react too quickly, am short, sharp-tongued, impatient, overbearing and dominating.

A fellow named Finkelstein changes his name to Kelly.

But he finds that people keep asking him what his name was before he changed it.

"Finkelstein," he has to say each time.

He goes back to court for permission to change his name a second time. This time he wants to be known as Johnston.

"But you already changed your name," the judge says. "Why do you need to change it again?"

"Well," the fellow says, "if I change my name to Johnston, when people ask me what it was before, I can say, 'Kelly'!"

I AM AS COMFORTABLE being Jewish among "Scots" as I am wearing my Scottish name in a synagogue. No one has a right to ask me to change my faith, or to treat me differently because of it.

Bias may be less common today than it was, or it may be directed at different distinctions than in the past, but it has not disappeared from human relations.

Keep provocations in perspective. Many people carry burdensome and unfair disadvantages—some visible, others not. Think carefully about your fights before you pick them. Then stand up for yourself.

OTHER **PEOPLE'S** MONEY: PART I

"Give me where to stand, and I will move the earth."

ARCHIMEDES

THREE TIMES IN the past 100 years, "disruptive" new communications technologies have set off economy-wide booms. The latest, the "killer-app" combination of the Internet with affordable personal computing, has followed a trajectory blazed by those who went before. A creative burst of enthusiasm soon attracts a rush of new participants. Illusory expectations and speculation eventually lead to a painful shake-out and consolidation of the industry. Yet these new technologies have a lasting and profound effect on the conduct of human affairs.

The first of those disruptive technologies, radio, helped bring Hitler to power. Winston Churchill and Franklin D. Roosevelt each mastered the same medium to muster his nation's will to resist.

We are still assimilating the immense impacts of E-mail and the World Wide Web, but just three reference points give some hint of their scale. The Internet has altered everything from how North Americans date (good-bye Mr. Goodbar; hello singles.com) to how they buy cars (the biggest used-car dealer on earth doesn't have a car lot, it has a Web site: eBay), and it has transformed life for terrorists and criminals (no more cloak-and-dagger; now it's click-and-send).

But of these three great revolutions in communications, neither radio nor the Internet has yet changed the world as thoroughly as the one that came in the middle—almost exactly at the midpoint of the twentieth century. During the stock-market bubble that closed the century, tech-heads were fond of saying, "The Internet changes everything."

What is for sure is that television already *has* "changed everything." The adoption of television, in fact, foreshadowed that of the Internet. At the beginning, a handful of early adopters—engineers, hobbyists and the curious wealthy—paid steep prices for a very limited experi-ence. But the experience was so novel that more and more people demanded it, driving sales volumes up and hardware prices down in a cycle that lit a rocket under the economy. And like radio before it and the Web later, television was a technology everybody could use. Indeed, once they saw it in action almost everyone wanted it.

You didn't need to be visionary to see that television was going to be huge. And Melody House, which had quickly outgrown its infancy of nothing but records to sell, was poised to profit handsomely from supplying this latest new entertainment appliance to Montrealers.

At the same time, my customers and I faced a common problem. Once you owned a television, the entertainment it offered was avail able at no extra charge. But acquiring the television in the first place involved a very substantial outlay.

LEVERAGE IS PERHAPS the most powerful ally an entrepreneur has. It makes your every asset work harder than it normally does. The astute Type E is always on the lookout for it—and finding it in unusual places.

With Melody House, I had leveraged our initial success at selling 78-rpm records into expanded profits selling new 33 $\frac{1}{3}$- and 45-rpm discs, as well as the turntables and tone arms that allowed our customers to play them. We encouraged our customers to associate Melody House with both a high level of personal service and the latest innovations. Profits from operations paid the overhead costs of the store and staff.

All those assets of reputation, infrastructure (overhead) and cash flow provided the fixed point from which to lever our existing customer traffic into an expanding range of home and entertainment goods: radios, cameras, kitchen and laundry-room appliances. And, by 1950, televisions.

By then I had become more familiar with "leverage" in its purely financial sense. The notion was a shift in perspective from the one I had been raised with. My father had a deeply ingrained, and not entirely misplaced, fear of debt. He would read a company's report and point to the lines indicating its huge debt. "See that?" he would say. "This company has always to remember that that money is not theirs and that its repayment can be demanded at any inopportune time."

Debt can indeed be a burden—if it's undertaken for the wrong reasons and without making sufficient provision for repayment. The critical question for an entrepreneur is: what are you going to do with the money? Use it for a *productive* purpose that will more than repay the amount and cost of the loan? If the answer to that question is yes, then you are simply using someone else's money instead of your own to extend your reach. You are leveraging your financial credit.

If the answer is anything else, there may still be good reasons to buy some item over time, so long as you don't forget to add the cost of that privilege to your purchase decision.

By 1950 Melody House had a line of bank credit to maintain its expanding inventory. Since then I have also encountered, and sometimes struggled to understand, increasingly sophisticated forms of finance. Some of these are useful to the entrepreneur (taking in outside equity investors, for one, as we shall see).

Others, in my view, are not. Financial specialists have nothing to do with their time but study, devise and sell financial products. The natural outlet for their creativity is to devise new products in ever more baroque layers of complexity. They can get so convoluted that you lose yourself and wind up paying more attention to the bankers and the financial people than to your own business.

Unless you're a financial genius, in which case you should be *in* their business, my advice is: Don't get involved in complex financial structures. Keep it simple, Sam. Any financial "instrument" so complicated that only the "experts" understand it is likely to prove just a new way to make money for the financial institutions by extracting it from you—and in the process make the institution look as if it is doing your business good.

But even plain-vanilla bank debt was a rarer experience in the mid-twentieth century than it is today. Or, to look at it another way, today's young people often find that by the age of twenty they have something older generations needed to take the initiative to establish: They have a credit history.

From Times Square to Ste. Catherine Street, New Year's revellers ringing in the half century paid for their champagne in cash. The option to put the party on "plastic" simply did not exist: There were no credit cards. Diners Club introduced its first card, for well-heeled U.S. corporate executives, in 1950. *No one* left home with an American Express card until 1958, when the company began promoting it to corporate travellers. BankAmericard (later Visa) came out that same year, but it wasn't for another decade that banks began marketing credit cards aggressively to ordinary consumers.

Now, of course, all the card companies begin courting young people while they are still in high school. Banks and trust companies market credit in association with "loyalty" partners like sports clubs, charity causes and universities. Their promotional efforts dwell cheerfully on everything one can *buy* with plastic; at bottom, of course, all credit cards are really devices for *borrowing.*

Those who use credit cards responsibly—taking advantage of the bank's money for a month but paying off every charge in full as it comes due—quickly establish a positive credit history. It will give them good standing when they look for other kinds of leverage later: loans for college, a home mortgage, or cash to build a business.

Too often the young and naïve mistake the banks' expensively shot commercials and their inducements to indebtedness for "free" money. They can easily wind up deep in a financial hole and with a reputation as a bad credit risk.

Before the introduction of consumer credit cards, it took more care and consideration to establish a reputation as a good borrower. Luckily for me, I had the benefit once again of a willing and wise mentor.

One of our first customers at Melody House was H.S. Berliner. On one visit, he asked: "How much do you owe the bank?"

"Nothing," I said, proudly.

"That's very commendable, but you're never going to get anywhere without a line of credit."

"I don't need any money right now," I protested. "Maybe later."

"Ah, but you don't want to leave it until you *need* the money," the more experienced man countered. "The time to establish a banking relationship is *before* you need it.

"Let me tell you what to do. Go to the bank on the corner. Introduce yourself to the manager. Tell him you have just opened a record shop down the street and you just want to say 'Hello.' He'll ask you, 'Are you dealing with any bank?' Tell him the truth: that you have been using your own money until now, but maybe later you'll need a small short-term loan. Then say good-bye.

"Then, a week later, go back and suggest you would like to borrow $100 or $200 for one week. [This suggestion wasn't quite as preposterous as it seems now: Those sums were the equivalent of $1,000 to $2,000 in 2004 dollars.] Tell him you need to put in some shelves or something. Don't bother asking what interest rate he's going to charge. He may offer you more than you've asked for, *but don't take it.*

"If he gives you the money, *do not use it.* Take it and put it in a separate account at another bank. Do not touch it for a week, or ten days, or however long you told the manager you needed the funds for.

"Then, *two days before the money is due,* walk back into the bank and give the manager the exact amount you borrowed plus any interest you owe. Don't argue about the rates or any charges; just pay them. Thank him for his accommodation and invite him to visit the shop to see what you're doing.

"Three weeks later, go back and do this exact same thing again, only this time ask for $300. Keep doing this, always for a little more money and *always* repaying a few days before the money is due. You'll establish a reputation for being a good credit risk and for always paying back when you said you would."

I followed H.S.'s advice to the letter and before too long had established a credit line of $10,000 (the equivalent of ten times that amount today). As Melody House expanded, of course, I also found a use for that new borrowing power: financing our growing inventory.

By 1950 Vivian and I had also bought our duplex, putting some money down and acquiring a mortgage for the balance. The extra income from the upper suite helped pay the mortgage.

Bank credit, in short, is certainly important. But two other things are worth remembering:

· financial debt isn't the only kind of leverage you have
· believe it or not, bank officers are human too.

In effect, Vivian and I were leveraging not only our financial credit but also our *ownership* of the duplex. Our willingness to take on the additional responsibilities of being landlords extended the advantage of ownership: we now enjoyed both accommodation and recurring rental income.

In expanding our product range from shellac records to automatic washing machines and televisions, Melody House leveraged more that just its cash flow and stockroom space. I leveraged my *knowledge* of consumer electronics (an asset assiduously cultivated through reading and intelligence-gathering trips) to discover new, high-margin products sooner than some competitors.

Our *reputation* with both consumers and suppliers became another "fixed point." Consumers extended me the value of their confidence in our selection of new—and, hence, unproven—technologies. Suppliers of those products extended me the value of net-thirty-day shipments for the same (often in-demand and hard-to-get) technologies.

An even mistier asset had already supplied the "fixed" point for other important instances of leverage: *social connections,* which though they ought not be pursued with material gain as their object often prove immensely valuable in unexpected ways. An instance was my unscripted meeting with H.S. Berliner.

Another example of another kind of unconventional leverage lay in the "white lie," a.k.a. *"the bluff."* By presenting an at-best ambiguous commitment from Decca as more solid than it was, I had induced RCA Victor and then Columbia to advance me the value of scarce inventory. In a turnabout that H.S. had of course anticipated, I then used the "asset" of those companies' commitments to wring a less ambiguous one out of Berliner's own Decca.

Yet another encounter introduced me to another concept: the leverage of *time*. Vivian and I were walking in Montreal one day when we passed a store called Art Lenders. We both liked art, but until then we had not acquired any; we could not afford it. But there's no harm in dreaming, so we went in.

There was a seascape on the wall, a powerful work in a vigorous Impressionist style. The artist was a Newfoundlander named Robert Pilot. We both fell in love with the piece, but the price was $350, the equivalent of about $3,500 today. That was far beyond our budget. Still, we lingered, unable to tear ourselves away.

"You know," a voice said, "the name of the shop is 'Art Lenders.' We rent this art if you can't buy it."

"What do you mean?" I asked.

"You rent it by the month, at one dollar a day—thirty dollars at the end of the month. You pay in advance and you can do this for up to three months. At that time you can either return the piece and lose the ninety dollars, or buy the piece and put the ninety dollars toward the purchase price."

I could afford a dollar a day, so I said, "Sure." It was the beginning of my education in instalment selling, the principle that people pay for *use*. Their continued use generates the result: recurring revenue.

(That painting, by the way, is still in the family. It hangs in one of our sons' houses. At the end of ninety days I told the gallery that I wanted to buy it—on the same terms on which I had been paying: thirty dollars a month. I subsequently bought many other pieces of art on the same basis, insisting on "trying" works before I committed to buying them.)

Consumer demand for televisions was skyrocketing. In twelve months over 1952 and 1953, sales of sets tripled. For stores like ours, there was a tide of high-margin profits to be had as Canadians spent

$150 million on TVs in 1953, a bonanza equivalent to sales of more than $1 billion in today's currency.

There was no doubt that everyone *wanted* the new medium in their living room. But like Vivian and me with the Robert Pilot, not everyone could *afford* it. Sets cost between $400 and $500 each, which today would be $2,800 to $3,500. That was well beyond what many young, single-salary families could afford.

But why not use the same principle that had worked with art to sell television? People pay gladly for usage. There were plenty of people who couldn't scrape together $400 all at once but would happily part with a dollar a day, payable a month in advance.

We began selling television sets on the same basis on which Vivian and I had bought the Pilot painting. After three months the customer had either to agree to buy the set over time, with ninety dollars credited towards the purchase, or we took it back. We sold a lot of televisions that way: once people had a chance to watch one, they usually didn't want to give it up.

- Don't let price be a barrier to entry. Make the product affordable.
- People value and pay for use, not the thing itself.
- Once people "touch it, feel it, taste it and live with it," a good product sells itself.

ANON.

AS SUCCESS BUILDS on success, the value of all your assets increases. In general, the more substantial the asset forming your "fixed point" in any deal, the longer the lever you can rest on it. But never forget that one asset underlies all the rest: *you.* Your personal qualities, your skills and knowledge of your market and product: those are the foundation stones of all your other assets, whether those are as hard and quantifiable as cash or as "soft" as social connections.

This is especially true for the self-made entrepreneur who doesn't have a corporation at his back. Your reputation is only as solid as your own behaviour. Knowledge you haven't acquired through the investment of time and attention won't support any lever at all. Social assets similarly are as strong as whatever *you* have brought to your relationships with others.

It's for the same reason that it is so important to *sell yourself first* on any new business proposition. When you take any new idea forward, whether to your first potential customer or to an investor, what you are doing is, in fact, just another very sophisticated kind of leverage. You are resting the lever of your personal credibility on the "fixed point" of your own confidence. And with that leverage you hope to move your audience (customer/investor) off their initial skepticism until they share enough of your confidence in the product (or business plan) to buy into it. If you just mouth the words of a "pitch," you are not going to be credible to your listener. Once you have sold yourself on your idea, it's easy to sell others. But beware: you can oversell yourself sometimes and fall too much in love with your own ideas. When you have no money, there is a natural discipline. But when bucks abound, watch it.

As with so much else, good habits established early tend to stay with you for life. I still keep on top of electronic and digital developments; wireless connectivity with technologies like Bluetooth is especially exciting in the new century. And I remain an inveterate pack rat of newspaper and magazine clippings: Insightful expressions, curious facts and inspirational thoughts all attract me.

You get the point: Assets lurk where you least expect them. Leverage can be exerted in many dimensions. The Type E not only knows where to look, but what to look *for.*

SOONER OR LATER, even an entrepreneur is going to need to deal with a bank, for the same reason that Willie Sutton, the famous bandit, did: "Because that's where the money is."

Bankers understand leverage intimately. Their industry is built on it. The heart of a banker's business is to hold money from "depositors" (who are, in fact, *lenders,* lending their money to the bank in return for interest) and in turn lend a portion of it to borrowers at interest rates that must, in aggregate, exceed what depositors are paid for the use of their money. In practice, so long as banks keep a certain percentage of the money entrusted to them in cash or its equivalents they are allowed to lend out many times the amount they have "borrowed" from depositors. Thus, banks leverage our collective confidence in them as both borrowers and lenders to "create" money, in effect from thin air.

It's a neat trick, verging on the magical. Maybe it is the reason banks have rattled millions of other Canadians since the humorist Stephen Leacock wrote about the experience.* With their deliberately imposing architecture and power of financial judgement, banks can be intimidating.

They also have a long history of being as much use to small business as ice in winter. War stories about unsympathetic bankers and their disdainful rejection of credit requests are legion. As the old saw puts it, "If you have trouble repaying a million dollars *you're* in trouble; if you can't repay a hundred million, *the bank's* in trouble." Since the introduction of automated teller machines (which one chartered giant introduced under the name "Personal Touch"), it is nearly possible to believe that some Canadian banks would prefer never to see a customer personally enter their doors.

Yet, despite all this, bankers are human too. Yes, they have their formulas and procedures and policies. But at the end of the day, *people* make decisions. *Fallible* people.

I remember a manager at a bank where I was looking for a line of credit years after my initial effort to establish a good credit rating. The banker had all the manners of the typical stereotype. He seemed to enjoy letting me know what a favour the bank was doing me by agreeing to lend me money, despite all the collateral they'd demanded.

Finally, he said: "And you know, we make very little money when we lend to you. We have to pay depositors three per cent and can only charge you six per cent—so you see, we only make three per cent."

---

* "When I go into a bank I get rattled. The clerks rattle me; the wickets rattle me; the sight of the money rattles me; everything rattles me. The moment I cross the threshold of a bank and attempt to transact business there, I become an irresponsible idiot." The opening passage of Leacock's "My Financial Career."

I actually felt sorry for him for half a minute. Then: "Hold on!" I said. "Back up! That sounds like 100 per cent to me: you pay three, and get six. And it's not even your money; it's the depositors' money."

He gave me a dark look. But he signed the loan.

Credit cards are a wonderful invention. As well as being valuable for establishing a good credit history, more directly they let you use the issuer's money for as long as twenty-eight days at zero interest. Bearing in mind that you always have to have the money available to pay off that debt when it becomes due (or a couple of days before!), you have the chance to make that money work for you during that period, rather than for the credit card company. If you miss the due date you could attract extremely high interest rates.

Never be afraid, either, to challenge a bank's error or bad arithmetic. From the six-dollar service charge that appears by mistake on a credit card bill to the three zeros dropped in error from a deposit record (to take just two examples from the many I have encountered over the years), *bankers are human too.* They make mistakes.

But because bankers are human—for better and for worse—it does still help, even in the age of ATM machines, actually to *know* yours. Most banks still won't advance business loans through a machine. H.S. Berliner's advice is still sound.

So is Robert Baden-Powell's: "Be prepared!" Have your homework done and your story straight *before* you meet your banker. Know the facts of your business, your customers, your product and your competitors. *Sell yourself first.* Show them you're so confident in the business that you have invested not only your time and your research but also your own money. Here is where the meticulous, intimate knowledge of your business we talked about in chapter 4 (*"figures come late"*) repays itself in spades. Know where your own money is coming from and going to, and you will go far to alleviate the banker's fear for his.

Don't let your finances get too complicated. Deals that are not crystal clear arouse a banker's natural suspicion and should, by the way, arouse *yours.* And never lose sight of the fact that for all their mystery and cultivated importance, banks are in business for the same reason as the rest of us: to make money. They can only do that if they sell you their services. Without you, they wouldn't be in business either.

As Mother said: "Stand up for yourself." Don't be intimidated. Bankers are (only) human too.

> "Big corporations play a vital role, but so do small, emerging ones. When you lose small businesses, you lose big ideas. People who own their own businesses are their own bosses. They are independent thinkers. They know they can't compete by imitating the big guys—they have to innovate, so they're less obsessed with earnings than they are with ideas. They are quicker to seize on new technologies and new product ideas. They steal market share from the big companies, spurring them to adopt new approaches. This process promotes competition, which leads to higher product and service quality, more jobs, and greater wealth. It's called capitalism."   **TED TURNER, ENTREPRENEUR**

LOCAL TELEVISION FINALLY came to Montreal in the fall of 1952. The first station offered just two hours of programming a day at first, although that schedule quickly expanded. The station belonged to the Canadian Broadcasting Corporation and, because there was only one, it broadcast in both English and French, depending on the time of day, to accommodate both of the city's language groups.

In retrospect, the shape of many of the debates that echoed through the decades to follow was already clear. Within a year of that first Canadian television station going on air in Montreal (the CBC's Toronto station followed two days later), pundits were fretting about the amount of American programming on the tube. Brewers had already bonded to live hockey broadcasts.

Melody House was sending a steady stream of television sets out the door. In keeping with my determination to focus on our customers' convenience, we were also installing rooftop antennas for many. The necessity for these had to do with a combination of physics, geography and the state of TV technology in the middle of the last century.

Television signals, unlike amplitude modulation (AM) radio (but like frequency modulation, or FM), travel in straight lines. And when they hit an object sufficiently solid, a mountain, say, they do not pass through it.

Until late 1951, the only television signals coming into Montreal came from distant U.S. stations. These transmission signals, of course, travelled in a straight line that was increasingly higher above the receding surface of the curved Earth. By the time the signals reached Montreal, most homes needed to raise an antenna in the air to pick up signals. The higher the antenna, generally the better the signal.

Reflecting the principles that what customers want is the *use* of something and that a satisfied customer was our best advertisement, we also promised that if a Melody House antenna did not produce a clear picture we would remove it and there would be no charge.

Montreal has a small mountain in the middle of the city. For the fortunate few who lived on the south-facing slope of 620-foot (189-metre) Mount Royal, this accident of geography actually enhanced their reception of distant U.S. television signals. But the much larger number of people who lived north of the mountain paid the price: its bulk blocked all the incoming broadcast signals before they could reach that part of the city. People living north of Mount Royal might as well have tried to sunbathe in the shadow of an office tower as pick up a TV signal from Plattsburgh, New York, or Burlington, Vermont.

This only became clear over time, however. And not every address was in the signal shadow of the mountain. You often couldn't tell until you had already spent the money to erect an antenna. A lot of people who at first couldn't get a good picture tried adding sections to their mast, investing more money in hope of getting the antenna element high enough to grab a signal out of the air.

Then unforeseen hazards began to emerge. Wind and ice storms blew down some antennas. Others were installed improperly (by homeowners themselves, usually) and damaged the structures on which they had been erected. Insurers began to charge extra for coverage of houses that had rooftop television antennas. At Melody House, we were suddenly taking down more antennas than we were putting up—and eating the cost!

People were as eager as ever for a good night of television, but my customers' difficulties in receiving a secure, high-quality signal alerted me to a yawning need that was about as unmistakable as a schoolhouse fire bell.

I understood the nature of the problem. My background as a ham-radio hobbyist and at Northern Electric had acquainted me with the basic physics of the waveband used for television signals. But I had also been reading the trade literature closely.

As early as 1948, a handful of experimenters in Arkansas, Oregon and Pennsylvania had jury-rigged ways to get television signals from distant antennas to one or two remote hamlets in those hilly states. The idea was called "community television."

The theory of community TV—what became cable—is simple: Stick up one antenna (today, more often, satellite dish or dishes) and share its signal around many television sets.

As it happened, Melody House had recently landed a contract to install television sets in an eight-unit apartment building on Côte St.-Luc Road. That street is on the western slope of the mountain; picking up a clear TV signal from beyond the city with an indoor "rabbit-ear" antenna would be problematic. It seemed a perfect place to put the idea of a "community" antenna into practice.

We erected an antenna on the roof of the low-rise building and began running connections to televisions on the floors below. The antenna cable delivered a strong, sharp picture to the first television set we hooked up. At the second set, the picture was not as good but still acceptable. But with a third one connected, the image was badly degraded. Shivering grey "ghosts" wavered across the screen in a blizzard of static "snow." We had a problem.

I consulted the journals. The U.S. experimenter with the most promising technology was a fellow named Milton Shapp, an electrical engineer and radio parts dealer in Pennsylvania. He was trying to solve exactly this bug in the technology.

The theory is simple: one antenna, many users. The reality is more complicated. Every television set needs to receive a signal of a certain minimum strength—call it 100 units—in order to produce a clear, stable picture. But the signal flowing through the air and received by a television antenna is a little like water in a pipe: Every time you open a tap in the pipe and let out some water (signal), the pressure (signal strength) of the water left behind in the pipe drops. Less pressure (signal) is available for the next user along the pipe's flow.

In television terms, it meant that sets "downstream" were receiving too low a signal (too little "pressure") to produce a clear picture. Instead of 100 units, they may have been getting eighty, fifty or less, as the number of sets connected rose.

Shapp was reported to have developed an economical amplifier that could be installed between the "taps" on the television cable, boosting the signal strength so that everyone got enough. I tracked him down near Philadelphia.

Milton J. Shapp turned out to be another of those extraordinarily high-quality business people it has been my occasional good fortune to meet. He had been an army signalman in North Africa and Italy during the war. The year after war ended he had started Jerrold Electronics Corporation with two employees and $500. He would much later be lauded as the "father" of cable television in the United States.

With Jerrold's "little black boxes" installed between every few sets, we managed to get a clear picture to all eight television screens in the apartment building on Côte St.-Luc. If we could manage that, there was no reason we couldn't do the entire city of Montreal!

That's how a Type E thinks: "Today, my garage; tomorrow, the world!" He's either so dumb—or so optimistic—he doesn't think he can fail. If he knew the risks, would he try? If I had known the dangers ahead, I probably would not have.

But I didn't. That wasn't how I thought. This was *new!* And as the stories of fallen antennas, damaged houses and poor-to-nonexistent

TV reception mounted, it was clear there was a crying need for something else.

Still, developing this new technology and installing it in the marketplace was going to cost a fortune. Sure, we'd done it for eight apartments; there were bound to be a few road bumps on the way to 80,000. And building out the connections was going to cost money every inch of the way. In addition to cable and Jerrold's black boxes, I'd need to hire lawyers to secure rights-of-way, access points and whatever licences the government might throw in our way.

We'd need to move fast, too. I wasn't the only one who read the electronics trades or heard the complaints about bad signals and hazardous home antennas. Indeed, over the next six years something like thirty companies would come and go, trying to take a bite of potential pie.

Melody House was doing well. But it wasn't doing well enough to spin off that kind of money. Its cash flow, moreover, was already leveraged to the hilt to finance the store's inventory. I found myself in a situation not that different from my customers who stood outside the window, looking in at the television sets on display and fingering their pocket change. I could see opportunity plainly in front of me. But how was I going to finance it?

> Milton Shapp sold his electronics business to run for governor of the state of Pennsylvania. I asked him why.
>
> "I'm going to show them how to run the government," Shapp replied.
>
> Some years passed before we met again. By then he had served two terms as Pennsylvania's governor. "So how did you make out?" I asked.
>
> "I moved the system an infinitesimal amount," he said, "but it was an experience."

I WAS CAPTIVATED by the potential of this new approach to delivering television signals. People were desperate for television and demonstrably willing to pay a monthly charge to watch it. Cable service would give them more stations than off-air reception, far clearer pictures, and it wouldn't wreck the roof of the house. Customers would, of course, be paying me a few dollars a month for the use of this signal. Once we built out our network to the limits of the market, however, that *recurring revenue* would, I hoped, become a cash cow.

I was also tormented sick by the risk and the unanswered question of where I was going to get the money.

As I twisted on the horns of this dilemma, A.L. Lawes happened to come into the store one day.

"You look worried," he said. "What's the matter?"

"Nothing," I said, getting my "game face" on. "Why?"

"Don't say that. I can tell by your face you're worried. Let me tell you, your business and mine are the same."

I looked at him incredulously. This was a man whose company ran a worldwide fleet of merchant ships, each one worth many times the value of my modest Montreal appliance and music store.

"No, really," he said, reading my expression. "I deal in $100,000 or more chips. You deal in chips of $100 or $1,000, but the principle is the same. On any business question, you have to ask yourself three questions:

"One, can you afford to lose? If you can afford to lose and feel the risk is worth it, then you have made the decision.

"Two, you cannot afford to lose but you still like the deal, so you have to ask yourself: 'If it does not succeed, can I afford the salvage of the assets if it fails?' If you can afford the salvage, then you have made the decision.

"Three, you cannot afford to lose, you cannot afford the salvage, but do you still like the deal enough that you will go for broke and bet the whole ranch?

"I don't recommend number 3 unless you want to go out of business."

He tipped the brim of his hat and left the store. I thought about all he had said and decided to go for it.

WE HAD ACCOMPLISHED a great deal at Melody House, but I could already see some signs that concerned me. As the baby boom continued to roll, the retail appliance business was attracting increasing competition and it was becoming harder to be "the only place in town" to get the hot new home gadget.

Cable TV offered an entirely new model of business that, I hoped, would put me back in the entrepreneurial "sweet spot" as the only supplier of this new service. I wouldn't be selling a product just once, but ensuring recurring revenue from the sale of a service. I was going to rest the longest lever I could manage on the "fixed point" of everything I had accomplished to date in business and in my personal development.

A few days later I visited the registry office and registered the name of a new company: Suburban TeleService Incorporated.

CHAPTER 8

OTHER **PEOPLE'S** MONEY: PART II

"Things are seldom what they seem,
Skim milk masquerades as cream."
GILBERT AND SULLIVAN, *HMS* **PINAFORE**

THE YOUNG QUEEN smiled beneath her glittering tiara. Languidly, she waved a white-gloved hand in the regal style her subjects would come to know well over the decades of her reign. Today, on the day of her coronation, she still seemed new and fresh, the first queen after half a century of kings for Britain and for Canada. Bobbies in domed helmets lined the new monarch's parade route through London. Guards in bearskin hats escorted their commander-in-chief.

And for the first time ever, Canadians could watch everything—all the pomp and pageantry of a royal installation that was far more consti-tutionally charged in those days than it might be now. True, it was not exactly "live." But the CBC's new television service broadcast film of the royal investiture as fast as it could be flown back across the Atlantic and put on the air.

Canadians crowded around any small screen they could find to get a glimpse of the moment. The 1953 coronation broadcast was far and away the biggest hit of Canadian television's short history. It was also the best advertising imaginable for anyone still sitting on the sidelines, undecided about whether to buy a television set.

But what most Montrealers of either language really wanted to see were the programs they'd read and heard about from American networks, being broadcast from eighty miles away in Burlington, Vermont, and Plattsburgh, New York.

Imagine their frustration, after putting out the equivalent of $2,500 of today's dollars on a brand new television, when the picture on their screen was no better than watching ghosts in a whiteout blizzard.

Melody House customers felt better than most under these circumstances. We refunded their money and removed the unsightly sticks if they didn't pull in a picture. But stories about bad reception began to hurt new TV sales, and I was very far from pleased to be paying both to put these ineffective antennas up and then to take them down.

Clearly people were hungry for television. Just as clearly, there was that crying need for a new way to get signals to homes. My Type E antennae were on full alert.

When I incorporated Suburban TeleService in late 1953, for the third time I set out on the rising side of the entrepreneurial cycle. We began building cable service out from the rooftop of that same apartment on Côte St.-Luc. At first the enterprise was financed with the money banked selling ALL Canada to the Monsanto people and from the ongoing operations of Melody House. We also assigned some people working in the TV-repair and antenna-installation departments of the store to the new business.

But I wasn't the only Type E in Montreal who read the electronics trades. There was already a potential competitor in the field: Redifussion. It was an English company with a system that required customers to own special Redifussion television sets, equipped with circuits that understood the coded signal they were sending down the cable line. To me, this requirement was a deterrent to the customer. I reasoned that people wanted to own and watch the television set of their choice.

Still, Redifussion and others were out there, and once a customer signed up to a particular service they would be hard to win over to another. If I was going to get to the customers first, I would need to build out Suburban's system fast. And that was going to take a hell of a lot of money.

I was mulling all of this one day behind the counter at Melody House when A.L. Lawes dropped in again.

"How's your idea for television working out?" he asked.

I explained my notion of adapting the U.S. concept of community television for remote hamlets to big-city Montreal's appetite for distant American stations. "We don't know how far the signal will travel," I finished. "We don't really know what equipment we'll need. It's all brand new."

He absorbed my explanation. Then he said: "Do you want any partners?"

"'Want?' " I said. " 'Want' is not the operative word. *Need* is a better word!" I had to admit to A.L. though, that I had no idea how to proceed; I had no experience working with a partner.

"May I make a suggestion?" he said. "How much have you put into this?"

"Twenty-five thousand dollars."

"I'll match that," Lawes said, "for 25 per cent of the company. You'll keep 75, and I'll give you an option to buy my share back."

It was my first experience with an outside investor. Later, I would get to know the equation from both sides, as an investor myself in other companies. In retrospect, what I have learned since then has only deepened my appreciation for Lawes' integrity and fairness in business.

THERE ARE BASICALLY three ways an entrepreneur can bring new outside money into his business. The first and by far the best way is from profitable operations; hence, my preference for *making* a dollar before *spending* one. But later, when I had money, this natural discipline was lacking, and I sometimes spent too much money chasing crazy ideas.

For the Type E personality, who values autonomy and freedom of action above all, both of the other two ways have drawbacks. The offsets for exerting *leverage* to *borrow* money were discussed in the previous chapter. The third way—accepting someone else's money as an investment in exchange for a share of your enterprise—also has its upsides and downsides.

Lenders are really only interested in two things: They want you to keep making your regular payments, and they want you eventually to repay the principal amount of the debt. *Investors*—good ones, with what is called "patient money"—want to see the value of the business grow, and with it the value of their share. But they are willing (at least in principle) to see their money go down the drain if it doesn't.

In other words, while both investors and banks are concerned for their own profit, their strategies are different. The bank cares strictly for the preservation of its money, nothing for your business. The *backer* cares less about the original sum of money, per se, but a lot about the business—because it's his business as well. When I tried to become an angel investor, too many people wanted me just to be their banker.

These different interests drive different kinds of involvement in your business. Make your loan payments regularly and you may never see your banker at all. An investor reads the same business pages you do in the morning, sees a threat (or an opportunity) to "his" business and is on the phone to you before you've put your coffee down at your desk.

The hazards are evident: a back-seat-driver syndrome; the uncomfortable feeling of eyes looking over your shoulder at all times; pressure to manage for others rather than make decisions based on your own judgement; the loss of decisive control over the enterprise.

All of these risks are real, of course. But no great, or even substantial, enterprise is a one-man band (even Donald Trump has to rely on the decisions of others sometimes). Like The Donald, you're not as smart as you think: *you don't know everything.*

Good investment partners bring more than their money and their oversight to the table. Many are themselves Type E people who have already succeeded in carrying their own "crazy" ideas to fruitful maturity and now have the retained resources to invest in other ventures. They have expertise, wisdom and insight to contribute, as well as outside connections that may present unexpected new business opportunities.

I was glad to accept A.L. Lawes as a partner. It was bracing to realize that his offer valued the new company at $100,000; that meant that my $25,000 cash investment to that point was, on the same valuation, now worth $75,000. On paper, I had tripled my money! It didn't mean much;

we were still pouring every spare penny into building out the system. But it was gratifying all the same.

"If you do a lot of things to build business, you'll build a business. They don't have to be done perfectly to work, although the better you do them, the better they'll work. But the main point is that you have to do them—a lot."

JOE GIRARD, MOTIVATIONAL SPEAKER

THE NEW COMPANY's name, Suburban TeleService, sounded too limiting and technical. We applied for a new one that incorporated the simple, easy-to-remember name everyone was using to describe the new technology: Cable TV Limited.

That name gives you an indication of how quick off the mark we were. The term "cable TV" is so generic today that you couldn't register it as a name; the registrars would kick it back as being "too general."

We offered five channels and a clear picture for $3.75 a month. Hackneyed as the claim sounds, we were true pioneers of what has matured into one of the core networks of the "post-industrial information economy." Cable television today enters tens of millions of North American homes, delivering dozens of channels on basic services alone, hundreds more in tiers of specialty channels and pay-per-view movies; in some places cable delivers interactive shopping, Internet and phone connections as well. Cable is as familiar and important a part of postmodern life as the car, the airplane or the telephone.

Just by stringing a single cable across an alley to get our signal from the eight-plex on Côte St.-Luc to the apartment building next door, we had leaped into the unknown. Everything we tried was being tried for the first time. After a while, we had the engineering more or less down pat and a handful of buildings connected. Then we began to encounter hurdles of a kind we could not have imagined when our problems were no more serious than fading signals and ghostly screens.

It became clear very soon that to extend our system beyond a few neighbouring buildings we could not rely on "jumping" cable from one structure to another. The building owners didn't like it, for one thing; it put strain on their walls. And in any case, you couldn't cross all the distances involved that way. The solution was obvious: we needed to be able to hang our cable on the utility poles that carried telephone and electricity service. They went almost everywhere and had plenty of room.

I contacted Bell Telephone, who owned the poles along the alley behind Côte St.-Luc, and solicited permission to string our cable on them. The company turned me down flat.

"We don't allow outside companies to use our poles," was the message.

I left Bell's offices crestfallen and considerably annoyed. I didn't know I was about to get another of those unexpected payoffs from a non-business social connection that have so often turned things around for the better in my career.

I had continued my interest in curling as a member of the Greystone Club. As anyone who knows anything at all about curling is aware, an important part of any curling event is a drink or two with the other team after the last rock is thrown.

One day, after a game against a team from another club, its members and our rink settled into the bar for the after-game ritual. We exchanged toasts and tipped our glasses. The fellow sitting beside me and wearing the other team's cardigan asked, as one does, what I "did."

I told him I was in the television business, but that I was having a lot of problems, particularly in getting our cable across streets.

"Why is that?"

"Because Bell Telephone won't let me use their poles."

He looked at me and said, "Do you know who I am?"

"No, I'm afraid I don't," I admitted.

"I happen to be the chief executive officer of Hydro Quebec," he said. "And what you said about Bell Telephone is incorrect."

"What do you mean, 'incorrect'?"

"What they're telling you is against the law. They're obliged to give you space. Just as we are. We have a contract with them that says just that: they put up wire on our poles; we can put up wires on theirs."

Not for the first—or last—time, one of these unplanned social encounters ended with the invitation to "come to my office tomorrow, and let's talk about this." The upshot was that Hydro gave us access to its poles for a dollar a pole a year (cable companies nowadays pay closer to twenty). Bell had no choice but to follow.

That still left places where neither company's poles reached. In some of those, the only alternative was to put cable underground. Now, this was Montreal in the era of empire-building Mayor Jean Drapeau's first term and Quebec strongman Premier Maurice Duplessis' last. The space beneath the streets of the city was supposedly "public," which meant "political."

The army had given me one taste of government in action. It hadn't prepared me for the intrigue required to get anything done at Montreal City Hall. There were more committees to placate and permissions to get and requests for a "donation" than the American comedian Jack Benny had jokes. Some of what went on probably would not pass muster by today's standards for public officials.

Still, Cable TV got the rights-of-way we needed and eventually became a member of the volunteer city board that oversaw rights of access beneath the city streets—a contribution of my time that was to provide a critical source of unconventional *leverage* later on.

The politics would get more involved after 1958. That was when the federal government, responding to a Royal Commission into Canadian television, stripped the CBC of its role of regulating the country's broadcasters. Ottawa gave the job instead to a new panel called the Board of Broadcast Governors (BBG). It was replaced a decade later by the Canadian Radio and Television Commission (now "Radio-television and Telecommunications"), the familiar CRTC.

Even though distributing television by cable might not have been "broadcasting" in the technical sense (indeed, it is not treated as broadcasting under United States law), the BBG acted quickly to impose its jurisdiction on the new technology. That meant *more* licences and permits that we had to obtain.

"Nothing motivates a man more than to see his boss putting in an honest day's work."   ANON.

AS OUR NETWORK reached more neighbourhoods, we invested heavily in newspaper and radio advertising to persuade as many residents as possible to sign up for cable. Every door our cable went past was another sales opportunity; every family that didn't sign up was revenue lost.

We knew what our customers wanted. "American Programs!" we boasted in one ad: "Enjoy Jack Benny, Jerry Lewis, Steve Allen, $64,000 Question, Jackie Gleason, Sid Caesar.... Only 4¢ per channel per day!"

And we knew what worried them. In other ads, we reminded people that conventional antennas could fall and damage their homes, noting that Cable's subscribers paid lower home-insurance premiums. Once, when a particularly vicious wind and ice storm whipped across the city, we rushed an ad into print the next day, cheekily pointing out that: "If you had cable yesterday, you would have TV today."

We made it as easy as possible for homeowners to abandon their antennas, offering to remove the obsolete towers at no charge when they signed up for cable (selling the old metal for scrap, recovering at least some of our costs).

After a while, cash flow from subscribers began to make a significant contribution to the new business's expenses. But the cost of building out the system also rose. We needed more cable, more amplifiers, more installation and cable crews. For the first time in my business career I began to spend significant sums on lawyers to appear before panels of political and bureaucratic gatekeepers. The recurring revenue from subscriptions was good, but it also demanded additional staff to keep track of accounts and billing (all done by hand in those predigital days).

In short, while Cable TV was showing every sign of fulfilling its promise, there was still a lot of the city left to conquer.

LIKE MOST OTHER entrepreneurs, my social and business life have never been strictly compartmentalized. Business is play for the Type E; recreational contacts also generate business leads. I had kept up my membership and weekly attendance at the Rotary Club. Among the many interesting people I met through that involvement was Frank

Carlin, the general manager of the Victoria Hockey Club, a farm club for the Montreal Canadiens owned by the Molson family.

We happened to be seated at the same table one day. He asked me what I was up to besides the record store. Over lunch I told him a little about my venture into cable technology. He said, "That's interesting," and we moved on to other topics.

A few weeks later Carlin dropped into the store. "I've been telling the Molsons about you," he said.

If the Mount Stephen Club was the spiritual shrine of Montreal's old-moneyed class, the Molsons were its first family. The dynasty's founding beer business had been going strong since 1786. Along the way, Molsons had at various times been rich enough to issue their own banknotes, from a bank that later merged with Bank of Montreal. They also started the country's first steamship company, invested in its first railway and in 1957, just a year earlier, had bought the fabled Montreal Forum and its venerated National Hockey League franchise.

Carlin had come to know the two brothers directing the family fortune through their interests in the Canadiens organization. "They'd like to talk you."

"Sure," I answered. *The Molsons!* Now, *there* were people with an entrepreneurial background.

"Do you want partners?" he asked.

"Does bread need butter?"

He set up a meeting, and a few days later I went to the brewery and met Senator Hartland de Montarville Molson and his brother, Thomas Pentland Molson. I made a presentation, explaining the *need,* the *new product* we had to offer, its potential for *recurring revenue*—and the immediate requirement to put on steam to extend cable to as many neighbourhoods as possible before competitors got there first.

The brothers looked at each other. Then the senator spoke. "Well, we still don't quite know what it is, but we'd like to look at it."

He went on to explain what "looking at it" entailed. They would send in "an expert"—what today we'd probably call a management consult-ant—to review the entire Cable TV operation, at Molson expense. I was to make available any information he needed. When he was finished I would get a copy of whatever his verdict was, good or bad. They would call me when they received his report.

The "expert" turned out to be a man named Al Steiner, from one of the major consulting firms in the city. And he was certainly thorough. For three months Steiner shadowed our business, listened in at meetings, asked questions and pored through our books. It was an unsettling experience, the closest thing I could recall as an adult to the nervousness of undergoing final exams as a schoolboy.

Finally I received a call from the Molsons and presented myself again at the brewery. The senator and his brother both met me again; this time there was a thick document on the table in front of them.

"Here's the report," the senator began, sliding the document towards me. "This is your copy. And you should be very pleased with it."

"Thank you," I said.

"Because it is 100-per-cent positive. They're recommending that we make an investment in your company." Then he said something that made me swallow hard: "I think you should also know that they value your company at a million dollars...."

That was *ten times* what A.L. Lawes had thought it was worth just thirty-six months earlier. As I struggled to process this concept, I heard Senator Hartland Molson go on: "We would like to take a $250,000 position in that million dollars. We'll lend you another $250,000. We also have some first-rate management and accountants; you're welcome to call on them for advice any time it could be helpful."

"But...." The senator levelled a look at me. Then, very firmly, he added: "This is the end of our investment. We never send good money after bad. Make it or break it on this amount. But *do not come back to the well.*"

I told the Molsons I would need to discuss their proposal with A.L. Lawes, who already owned a quarter of the company. "Of course," the senator said, and the meeting ended.

The moment I got back to my desk I put in a call to Lawes. "Well, Dave," he said, "I think it's time to take some money off the table."

And so we did. We each sold one-quarter of our shares to Molson. That gave the brothers 25 per cent of Cable TV Limited. It also reduced my position to a little over 56 per cent—still more than half the shares and enough that I retained absolute control over management decisions. It was still entirely up to me, in Senator Hartland's resonant phrase, to "make it or break it." It was how I liked it.

It was also yet another valuable lesson from my mentor: Don't hesitate to take out profits. It's the same principle any smart player in Las Vegas ought to heed: When you're up, take something off the table and put it in your pocket. Lawes pocketed $62,500 in the sale to Molson, more than doubling his original cash investment on only one-quarter of his shares. My share of the payday was $187,500, equivalent in today's dollars to about $1.2 million.

To this day, when I see profits, I take some money off the table. You never know when reverses can happen.

The Molsons' involvement in Cable also turned out to be a tremendously positive experience. They had been admirably clear at the outset on the ground rules and I, of course, never tried to "go back to the well." I took advantage more than once of their professional management, in particular their accounting department, seeking advice that I much appreciated. Like Mary J. Blige, I just kept asking questions until I understood what they were telling me, learning by osmosis.

As our cable network evolved (and again much later when our pioneering data network was expanding), engineers often came to me with the request to "just try this." I was always willing to take a look at something new, but they first had to explain to me what they had in mind in terms that I understood. Then, if we approved the idea and gave them some money to work with, I also gave them a shot of the Molsons' advice.

I told them to get to where they planned on whatever amount of money we had approved, but not to "come back to the well" for fresh infusions of cash until they had a saleable product. There would be plenty of opportunity to tweak and adjust their idea later, after we were making *the first dollar.*

▌▌▌ WITH THE MOLSONS' investment, Cable TV had the resources to really take on the field. From that point on, my commitment to the new company became all-consuming.

We were building out to new neighbourhoods as fast as possible. We had begun in Côte St.-Luc, on the western slopes of Mount Royal, but we knew that other neighbourhoods in its "shadow" were desperate to pull in the U.S. stations it blocked. So we began our offensive there, cabling the neighbourhoods of Hampstead, Snowdon, Town of Mount Royal, Côte des Neiges and Westmount, in a clockwise advance around the summit, eventually reaching the more working-class Côte St. Paul, Verdun and LaSalle quarters on the southern flats of the city along the St. Lawrence River.

As the appeal of cable TV spread, other companies got into the game, racing to erect their own antennas and sign up households on streets we had not yet reached. Thanks to the Molsons' involvement, we were soon able to boast a major coup that our competitors could not. It had nothing to do, strictly speaking, with the family's investment. Instead, once again, it was a matter of *connection.*

The Molson company had recently bought the Canadiens hockey franchise. The purchase made possible some new departures—what might be called "synergies" in today's business jargon. Within months, Molson unveiled their new "Canadian" beer brand and began advertising it heavily during over-the-air game broadcasts. But those broadcasts were blacked out for home games.

Cable TV Limited had established its own community channel on our cable system. We called it Channel Nine. Our own small studios generated community programs and were always looking for something different to offer that would make our customers feel special.

This venue was a natural for the Habs' home games, since most of the team's appearances at the Forum were already sold out. The team and arena's management agreed that they had nothing to lose by letting a few thousand Cable viewers watch from home. Indeed, the experience only whetted their appetite for tickets to the live events.

We installed cameras at the Forum, hired a play-by-play crew and began to promote Cable on the strength of our unique programming: our Cable Channel Nine was the *only* station in Montreal carrying the Habs' local games.

The Molsons, meanwhile, stood to reap their share of Cable's growth as we signed up more customers. And we had many people who subscribed just for the hockey games. Later, we added home games of the Canadian Football League Montreal Allouettes, which were similarly "blacked out" for local off-air broadcast. When it was being used for neither purpose, we "broadcast" FM-quality music on Channel Nine.

I remained a very hands-on manager of the recapitalized company, signed every cheque, approved every capital expense and continued to write most of our advertising as well. "Antennas are for birds!" said one newspaper insertion, adding, "Cable TV is for people." Read another: "Old antennas never die. Their pictures just fade away." Accompanying a picture of a smiling mother and "cable subscriber" was the caption: "I get the best baby-sitters on the block...They know they can watch anything they wish on our TV set." We relentlessly pushed the advantages of a secure picture, all the American channels, no roof damage and exclusive programming.

AS THE CABLE business blossomed, my attention to and interest in Melody House dwindled. If our pioneering venture into cable TV had now achieved liftoff, the store Vivian and I had opened in the shadow of a world war was approaching the conclusion of its entrepreneurial cycle.

It was not that Melody House was no longer profitable: It was doing fine. But much of the zip had gone out of the business—and the industry for me.

From the day we had opened in 1945, and for fifteen years thereafter, Melody House had always enjoyed the competitive edge of being first to market with each new, "must-have" product. We had benefited, if not from true monopolies in the economist's sense, then from the serial advantage discussed in chapter 5, of being "the only place in town" to find those products. And we had been able to reap the profits to match.

But "must-have" home electronics products were becoming fewer. Those high-margin opportunities were becoming scarcer. The big post-war wave of pent up innovation in home appliances had largely run out of steam by 1959. A few things were still to come: colour TV sets in the sixties, cassette tapes in the seventies, VHS home video in the eighties. But until the computer chip unleashed a new springtime of invention in the nineties, there would be far less that was clearly novel coming onto the sales floor. Stores like mine would increasingly have to compete on cutthroat pricing and vanishing margins.

At the same time, the baby boom was fading. The big bump in "household creation" was behind us, along with its associated spike in appliance-buying. It wasn't a sandbox I wanted to stay in.

The decades since then have vindicated that judgement, I think. Price competition decisively shifted the advantage in retail towards those who cut costs. Improving distribution chains, "consolidating the industry," driving down wage costs and seeking out cheaper suppliers: these became the critical skills.

Those are all worthy enough pursuits. Sam Walton has certainly done very well out of them. But most independent electronics and appliance stores like Melody House have succumbed to (or recreated themselves as) one or the other of a very small number of big-box, very price-conscious chains like his Wal-Mart, or Future Shop.

In any case, I also firmly believed that Cable had the potential to be worth many times more than anything into which I could build Melody House. It was a business built on *recurring revenue,* one in which *new* programs could be introduced instantly for the marginal incremental cost of "lighting up" another channel. I could see no reason why we couldn't eventually have every household in Montreal as a subscriber and sending us a cheque every month. That was some-thing Melody House was unlikely ever to accomplish.

Or perhaps it just was a matter of my Type E personality. In retail, I would have been playing defence. I much prefer offence. Besides, pinching pennies in the warehouse didn't excite me the way radio and then television had done, and now cable did. Appliances were machines of steel and plastic. What we were building out, street by street across Montreal, was a live network of electricity and light!

I sold Melody House to the fellow who had been managing it for me. We negotiated a figure based on the store's operating profit, its assets and leases and accounts receivable and payable. Then we threw something in for "goodwill," a nebulous thing that is entirely a matter for negotiation. The final figure was in the neighbourhood of $50,000 (a little over $350,000 in 2004 dollars)—many times the long-since repaid $2,000 loan we had taken out on my mother's insurance policy.

There were also strictly selfish, personal reasons for "taking something off the table" at that point. Henry, our first-born, was a tall, active nine-year-old. His younger brother, Barry, was turning six and also expanding his horizons and demands on Vivian. With the birth of our third son, Jeffrey, in late 1956, the Campbell clan had finally and unavoidably outgrown its duplex. The following year we bought our first single-family detached house and moved in.

It was a lovely red-brick colonial, with a maturing tree on a corner lot in the Town of Mount Royal. It would be our home for almost two decades, the setting for our sons' adventures through childhood and adolescence, the springboard for their entry into the adult world. For Vivian and me, it would be a place to indulge our love of entertaining and socializing with our friends.

Another entrepreneurial cycle had come to its close, but there was no time to waste looking back. There was far too much to do in order to bring the young enterprise of Cable TV to its full potential. I had made a strategic decision: My future, and that of our growing family, would "make it or break it" on an idea as new and ambitious as the one that had earlier laid out electricity and telephone networks to every home.

IV I CONTINUED TO READ the electronics trade press voraciously. And when I read about a new technology for addressing radio signals selectively to individual receivers small enough for people to carry with them, I incorporated a company under the name Calling All Cars & Calling All People. It rented personal pagers and the service that activated them: another opportunity for *recurring revenue* from a (then) *new* capability.

Calling All Cars would never become the demand-driven monster Cable was, but it did grow into a gratifying side interest that generated steady profits for several decades. We later expanded the company's operations to Toronto under the name The Beeper People. Much, much later still, it would play a small role in a bid for a national cellphone licence.

Cable, however, consumed most of my time. It also presented constant challenges to innovate—in process, product and technology. Customers *not* in the signal shadow of Mount Royal needed some better reason to sign up for cable than just a clearer and more stable version of what they could already pick up off-air. It would be another decade yet before cable-only stations and "networks" made their appearance, but I already saw our subscribers as a potential audience apart from the mass free-to-air viewing market. We jumped on any chance to make our service unique.

ESPN was in the future; no network sports divisions yet existed to follow Canadian professional teams around their leagues. But the build-out of microwave networks among major North American cities in the 1950s made it economical to rent dedicated lines for real-time coverage of remote events. This opened up new horizons to our ambitions.

Emboldened by our success in broadcasting the Habs' home games to our "closed circuit" audience, we began sending our play-by-play team to the Canadiens' away games. Our advertising leaned heavily on this "exclusive" for Cable TV subscribers. We also broadcast prizefights and other sports events on the same basis.

Channel Nine broadcast community events like the McGill University drama students' annual satiric review (an event that had me wishing we had been able to do the same with Georgiantics' twenty years earlier). As soon as the U.S. networks' affiliates in northern Maine, Vermont and New York state began broadcasting in colour, our subscribers (those very few with colour sets, at any rate) enjoyed that innovation as well, years before the CBC finally introduced colour broadcasts in 1966.

At the same time, the scramble to lock up territory became more urgent. It was impossible to build out a network fast enough on our own; Montreal was simply too big and the demand too widely distributed. As the potential of the business dawned on more people, latecomers tried to shoulder their way into the party, signing up single streets and small neighbourhoods across the city. It became smarter—and cheaper—for Cable TV to buy some of these than to duplicate their small systems.

Indeed, some other Type E minds got into the "community antenna" business on precisely those grounds. When they saw our network getting close to a neighbourhood, they would enrol cable customers two or three streets ahead of us. They counted on "selling" us the customers at a profit over their own cost of signing up the accounts.

Buying up these companies was yet another face of investing: the acquisition. It quickly proved an illuminating window into the inventiveness of thieves and scoundrels.

On the face of it, it was not that difficult to figure out how much to pay for a small cable system. Our rule of thumb was the equivalent of one year's revenue for any system. The benchmark was based on our own experience that it took about a year to earn back the cost of installing service to an area. (We reasoned that the vendor had already earned back some of his investment.) It should have been simple arithmetic: X number of subscribers times Y dollars per month each in subscription revenue.

But after buying a few of these systems and integrating their subscribers with our own, we came on a surprise: many were phantom viewers. The "entrepreneur" selling us the system had included the names of many people who had been receiving the service on a no-commitment, "free trial" basis—he had padded the rolls to enhance his selling price. When we sent those "subscribers" their first bill, they informed us that they had never signed up and, moreover, they didn't want the service!

This forced us to add wording to our purchase contracts to make it clear that only "paying" customers of at least three months' standing would be counted in calculating the company's acquisition value.

Even that was not enough to completely foil one cunning fraudster. Knowing that our rule of thumb was to pay the equivalent of *twelve* months' subscription revenue for each "paying" customer, he simply "paid" the bills for his phantom subscribers himself for three months in order to qualify them, anticipating that he would get back that "investment" plus profit.

We soon stiffened our due diligence of these companies' subscription lists, but stopped expecting to save any money by using the networks they installed. Most of the time they were so sloppy we had to rip them out and reinstall them.

ONE DAY I HAPPENED to walk past a theatre whose marquee I remembered well. I had visited it regularly back in the early days of Melody House, delivering records there for them to play in their lobby and snack bar areas. It was one of the many United Amusements properties in the city. United Amusements, in turn, was owned by Famous Players, one of North America's biggest movie distributors.

I forget what movie they were showing. It may have been *Tom Jones* or the Burton-Taylor epic *Cleopatra*—they were both out at the time. But it gave me one of those crazy thoughts: wouldn't it be neat to add *movies* to the list of Cable TV exclusives?

Back at the office, I got in touch with United Amusements and put the idea to them. Again, remember the era: The movie and television industries still tended to see each other as their respective worst enemies. Film studios relied almost exclusively on big-screen theatre exhibition for their return. Today's enormously lucrative so-called secondary windows of film exhibition—videos, DVDs, airlines and hotels, pay-TV, specialty and cable channels—did not yet exist. Even movies on broadcast television were a novelty for the ABC television network, whose Mount Washington, Maine, affiliate we carried on Channel Eight.

It turned out that at least one executive at Famous Players was thinking ahead. That company had acquired a technology called "Telemeter" that would enable the equivalent of pay-TV.

Famous Players had tried the Telemeter system on a small scale in Toronto. Now they were interested in scaling up the experiment. Cable TV's several thousand subscribers, a mix of private homes and apartments, were a perfect test group for the wider national audience.

At the same time, Famous Players wanted to keep inside the corporate "family" whatever advantage its new technology might offer. Before we went any further, the company informed me, it wanted United Amusements to take an investment position in Cable TV!

Once again I sought out A.L. Lawes' advice. And once again he advised me to seize the opportunity to take out profit. "Dave," he said, "there are times in life when you should think about liquidity."

Early in 1964, United Amusements acquired 20 per cent of the company but left Cable TV's management entirely to me. Over the next seven years the Famous Players subsidiary steadily increased its stake, buying out first Lawes' interest and then the Molsons'. Finally they approached me, asking to buy some of my shares.

United Amusements' target was 75 per cent of the company. My share would drop from a little over 50 per cent to 25. I would have to give up control. At the insistence of A.L. Lawes, I put a condition on the sale of my shares.

"Ask for a voting trust," he advised. The arrangement would require both United Amusements and me to vote our respective shares the same way. It was a kind of "Mexican standoff" clause. In the event of a big enough disagreement over a course of action, either of us could veto any decision.

"You know the business," A.L. said. "They don't. If they want you to vote for something that's not in the best interests of the company, you shouldn't do it. You're really protecting your percentage.

"And in any event, they need you to run it," he added. "If they want you badly enough, they'll consider it."

As it turned out, Famous Players did want Cable TV badly enough. I became a minority shareholder in the company I had founded, albeit one armed with a veto against any truly dangerous decisions. In any event, I never had to use it. Once a year or so, Famous Players/United Amusements sent an accountant from PriceWaterhouse to vote their shares at the annual general meeting, and that was generally that. The relationship was an amicable one for the seven years it lasted.

> "Never invest in a business you cannot understand."
>
> **WARREN BUFFETT, CEO, BERKSHIRE HATHAWAY**

IN THAT TIME Cable TV became Montreal's dominant cable company, with more subscribers cabled to a single antenna than any other system in North America. We would continue offering new programs, breaking through the 12-channel limit of conventional television.

During Expo 67, a showcase of the day's most advanced communications technology, we would create a video wall for the Hydro Quebec pavilion. We installed live closed-circuit cameras to record activity at the utility's mammoth Manic 5 dam and powerhouse development in the north. Microwaves brought the picture signal hundreds of kilometres south to Montreal.

But we would not implement pay-TV. Famous Players' Canadian managers, it turned out, were somewhat ambivalent about their new technology. They worried that showing movies on cable would cannibalize their "bricks and mortar" audiences.

"Fine," I said. "Then give us a chance to show your movies after they've left theatres." But still they balked at approving films for Cable to show.

The subject was as sensitive among the studio representatives who distributed films to the theatre chain. But finally I did find someone who grasped the potential: a forward-thinking distribution manager for Twentieth Century-Fox named Charles Chaplin (no relation!). Charlie rightly foresaw that sales to cable represented new revenue from titles that were no longer earning anything at the box office.

Together, we worked up a package of recent movie titles—we wanted movies our subscribers would pay to see—and a formula for determining what Cable TV would pay Twentieth Century-Fox for them. Charlie presented the proposal to his senior executives in Canada and then at every senior level of the company up to Twentieth Century-Fox's board in Los Angeles—where it was turned down.

The studio bosses, heads firmly planted in the desert sand, could not think beyond their "bricks and mortar" upbringing. Pay-TV and cable movie channels would come anyway, about ten years later. But the perfect storm of competitive television, a failure to invest and lack of imagination would reduce movie theatres to shabby, thinly attended money-losers until a new generation of entrepreneurial owners began reinventing them in the 1980s as multiplexes.

Meanwhile, I didn't let disappointment over our failure to consummate pay-TV sour my relations with the company that now owned most of Cable TV's shares. There were plenty of other fish to fry.

Indeed, Famous Players later found another way to make me useful to their corporate plans. The company continued to acquire cable systems across Canada for their investment value and on several occasions hired me to vet potential acquisitions on its behalf, putting to use my hard-won experience with cable speculators' deceptive ingenuity.

MUCH, MUCH LATER, I learned one more significant, and painful, lesson in the minefields of investor relations.

It happened when we were selling a company. To encourage the creative thinking we needed in the engineering department, I had compensated a number of top staff with shares in the company (on top of generous salaries). When the deal went through, many of them would become millionaires. The buyer, however, wanted all the shares in the company turned in to the offer.

When I reported this proposal to the group everybody cheered—except one guy. He came to me later. "I'm not turning my shares in," he told me, "not at that price." He knew we needed to flip 100 per cent of the shares to make the deal.

"You're willing to hold up everybody else because you want more, just for yourself, not for anyone else," I said, stunned. "I could start calling you names, but okay, you put down on a piece of paper how much more you want and I'll show it to everyone else. I'll let you know."

He hesitated, but not for long. He put down a figure; it was about another 10 per cent. I took it around and told the other shareholders, "We have a prostitute in the place. This is what he wants." I also told them that I would make up what he was asking for from my own share in that company; it would not come from them.

The deal went through. That individual didn't stay on. And thereafter, whenever I gave up stock to anybody I insisted on keeping the votes. They get the value of the stock. I don't want the money; I want the vote.

MOST ENTREPRENEURS are inherently independent-minded and heartily dislike working for someone else. I have always liked to make decisions by retiring to the john and looking at myself in the mirror, then emerging to say, "Okay, here's what we're going to do."

My nightmare is having to nudge and cajole a timely idea from one "presentation" to the next, before this working group, that committee, in a slow lobby up the corporate hierarchy until some senior board, paralyzed by fear of entertaining any actual *risk*, rules against anything new, untried or, God forbid, *different*. By which time, of course, the opportunity will have long flown.

That said, Mr. Lawes, the messieurs Molson and even, despite its timidity, Famous Players/United Amusements, were all investors in the most valuable sense of the role. They had been patient with their money, open with their advice when I sought it out and neither second-guessed nor impeded my decisions.

When my investors spoke, I listened. You have to: it's their money too. But it's also wise. You may (you had better) know your business more intimately than anyone else, but you don't know everything. People with enough money to put into your company are, usually, people with wide and varied other interests. They represent valuable opportunities to expose yourself to new information, new perspectives and a wider circle of business contacts.

Partners offer a different relationship than employees. When later on I was the sole owner of my company for many years, with no partners or investors to bounce things off, I missed them.

Private investors are one thing. Accepting investment from the public is another. It was an option I considered later and rejected. I couldn't stomach the extortionate fees that underwriters charged, for one thing (although those have come down somewhat).

Frankly, I also enjoyed the small "perks" that it was easier at the time for private companies to provide than public ones. Of course, that too has changed in the age of financial scandals.

I hated the idea of giving up that much independence, of being obliged to make decisions based on how they would look in the financial pages and be reflected in my stock's price the next day.

Today I might think about the matter differently. I know more than I did then about business finance. And in the light of contemporary corporate standards I would be a good deal more aggressive about valuing myself. Certainly, I would have made a good deal more money by taking one or more of my companies public.

Entrepreneurs like to start companies and make their own mistakes—not put their money into other people's. During most of my career I seldom invested my own money in listed stocks.

By the early 1960s I was already toying with a new passion—an idea even more exotic than Cable, although Cable had brought it to my attention. It would leverage everything I'd been learning about networks and subscription-based businesses. For the first time, my ambitions would have a chance to go beyond the city of Montreal and eventually into a nationwide operation with partner connections around the world.

Best of all, the idea was crazy, unproven and as technically daunting as Cable had been ten years earlier.

GETTING TO A HANDSHAKE

"Gild the farthing if you will,
Yet it is a farthing still."

GILBERT AND SULLIVAN, *HMS* PINAFORE

"GET IN ON THE GROUND FLOOR," the saying goes. I got in below that in the industry that some say is inaugurating an altogether new era in business: the global network economy.

Most people rarely think about it, but the streets we cross from one business appointment to another are hardly "ground level." The space beneath them is honeycombed with tunnels and passages through which run all the "plumbing" essential to the modern metropolis. Even where there are not subway tunnels or underground parking, there are certain to be criss-crossing conduits encasing telephone, data and video cables, dedicated fire and police lines, electric power mains, gas and water lines, storm and sanitary sewers. Not all the traffic jams at intersections are on the surface!

The multiplication of means of communication in the past half century has complicated the routing and accommodation of all these competing demands on the limited public "space" between the footings of office towers. But even with nothing underfoot but gas, power and telephone lines, things get complicated enough.

Like many large cities, the centre of Montreal is also penetrated by an extensive system of underground service tunnels shared by numerous utilities and municipal departments. This public space is administered by a civic commission whose members represent the various agencies and companies whose wires, cables or pipes run through it. When television cable became a significant presence in the tunnels under Montreal's streets, I joined the city's Underground Conduit Commission.

In 1961, the Montreal Stock Exchange began planning a move out of its magnificent but inefficient old home on St. Francis Xavier Street to a new tower at Place Victoria. Along with the move, the exchange wanted to institute some new system for transmitting share prices, in real time, from its new trading floor to brokers' offices, most of them clustered around its historic former address.

As incredible as it must sound from the perspective of the twenty-first century, the exchange at the time posted the fluctuating prices of shares using technology with which Tom Sawyer would have been familiar. The "board" was just that: a wall-size blackboard with the issues listed on it. Whenever a trader called out a new bid or asking price for a particular stock from the trading floor, a clerk armed with an eraser and a piece of chalk dashed along below the board to erase the old price and chalk in the new figure. When brokers in distant offices wanted to know the price of a stock, they would telephone one of the brokerage's own clerks stationed at the exchange, who read them the price marked on the chalkboard.

The exchange directors had heard about closed-circuit television and its use in home and office security. They reasoned that if it could show you who was at the front door, it could also send a picture of its blackboard to its member brokers' offices. This idea seemed very revolutionary and "high-tech" to them. The exchange envisioned a dozen cameras, focussed on different parts of the board, so that brokers in their offices could follow the action of any issue by choosing among the twelve channels available at that time on a conventional TV dial.

The exchange distributed an outline of its idea, with voluminous specifications, to all the company members of the Underground Conduit

Commission and invited us to quote on any part of the project we felt competent to handle. As a member of the commission, and the only one with any knowledge of closed-circuit television, Cable TV was included.

We circulated the specs around the company and thought about the exchange's idea. All our engineers and I quickly reached the same conclusion: it wouldn't work. Three smudges of the eraser and the numerals on the board would lose all definition. What was left would be a grey-on-grey illegible blur on any distant black-and-white screen.

I called the exchange and met the fellow in charge of the project.

"We've read this closely," I told him. "And the judgement of our people is that this is not going to work."

He looked at me for a moment, then reacted: "You were asked to quote, not to criticize."

I shrugged, thanked him for his time and left. We quoted anyway. If they really didn't care whether it worked or not, we would be happy to be paid to put it in for them if we got the order.

As it turned out, we lost the bid—but came out far better off. The exchange awarded the cameras-and-TV-set part of the contract to RCA. It gave the job of running underground cables between them to another member of the conduit commission, CN Telecommunications.

Forty-eight hours after the winning bids were announced, my phone at Cable TV rang. It was CN's project manager. He wanted to know if we'd take a subcontract to install the necessary cable and amplifiers underground to carry the exchange's "video" board information to brokers' TV sets. Essentially, he was offering me the very same work his company had just won.

"Why?" I asked in amazement. "You got the contract!"

"Well, yeah," he huffed a little. "But you know more about how RF [radio frequency] signals travel than we do."

We wound up supplying the video cable, installing it and handing over each end to RCA technicians to hook up to their cameras and TV sets—all for the same price we had originally quoted to the exchange. CN, which had won the job with a lower quote, swallowed its dollar loss and took the credit for the technical "breakthrough."

Three years later the exchange gave up on its closed-circuit black-boards. No one at the brokers' offices could read the smudged, indistinct numbers on the screen.

We pocketed a very satisfactory profit and something much, much better. Written clear as day in the hazy grey blurs showing up on the brokers' TVs, for someone with the Type E vision to read, one word stood out in bold relief: NEED.

An equity dealer's day can go up or down by millions of dollars over the difference of an eighth of a cent and one minute's notice. For them, getting real-time, accurate market information from the exchange floor was a matter of business life or death. This was the kind of information that gets into a Type E brain and refuses to leave, like one of those fragments of a song you can't stop humming for the whole day. I began turning the problem over in my mind, keeping it at the forefront of my thoughts whenever I trolled the electronic and technical journals.

"Nothing average ever stood as a monument to progress. If we seek the average level we cannot hope to achieve a high level of success. Our only hope is to avoid being a failure."

A. LOU VICKERY, U.S. BUSINESSMAN AND SPORTS-WORLD AUTHOR

IT WAS 1961, and we were entering a decade that seemed full of new promise. A charismatic young president named John Kennedy was in the White House. Man was in space. In Quebec a new premier, Jean Lesage, was shaking off the church-bound practices and attitudes of the Duplessis years. French Quebecers were expressing a new self-confidence as well as fresh anger over old grievances. The emerging catchphrase to describe the era captured both ideas: *la révolution tranquille*—the quiet revolution.

The decade would not remain quiet for long. Disillusioning events would come: Kennedy's assassination; America's disastrous war in Vietnam; social upheaval in the streets. But for the moment those were in the future, unimagined.

By now I had been in business for myself for sixteen years. With Melody House, I had happily ridden the wave of postwar demand and innovation in domestic electronics. I had been equally happy to dispose of the store, for a useful sum of capital, as both forces ebbed and the retail appliance trade began a race to the bottom on price and margin.

Cable TV kept me more than just "busy." We would never reach a stage when our network was finished, when we could simply sit back and cash the cheques; many neighbourhoods and apartment buildings remained to be cabled, for one thing. Natural extensions into areas adjoining our existing networks demanded constant investment. And Montreal was growing; there were always new houses to reach.

The technology was continuing to advance, as well. Colour broadcasts had arrived in the United States and would soon come to Canada. Our coaxial cables could handle all the new advances, but other components of the network needed regular upgrading. Every eighteen months or so, it seemed, we had to replace every amplifier that boosted the video signal to usable strength along our cables.

The older amplifiers didn't wear out, but new ones became available that could handle many more channels. We went from three channels to eight and then to twelve. It was clear that even bigger capacities were coming; visionaries already talked about a 100-channel universe. Each advance gave our customers more reasons to install or stay with cable, but each one still cost a lot of money.

Watching cash flow in from subscriptions and back out to these nonstop investments (for which I still signed every cheque); scheduling more than twenty service crews;* booking production staff for our live hockey and football broadcasts on Channel Nine; scouting for other closed-circuit programming; overseeing the paperwork demanded by a growing tribe of regulators; planning and executing extensive radio and newspaper ad campaigns; managing the office staff administering tens of thousands of customer accounts: all these tasks and more occupied my days even more fully than had the counter at Melody House.

---

* I discovered one day that as soon as they left each morning many of our servicemen drove no farther than the nearest coffee shop. Rather than discipline them, the next day I waited five minutes for them to get settled, then dropped into the shop myself. That put an end to the practice—at least at that shop!

And now I planned to add to my workload in pursuit of another new idea, one that would leverage everything I had learned and accomplished thus far. It would demand not only all the financial assets I had accumulated in Cable TV Limited and from selling Melody House but much more. The campaign to come would call on everything I had ever learned, not only about network switches and amplifiers but about the wider front of new technologies and the tides at work on the business world.

I would also need to deploy everything I thought I knew about "closing the deal." By that I do not mean simply signing you up to a cable account or the time-purchase of a television. *Every* negotiation is the pursuit of a deal of some kind. It may be a purchase; it may be a sale; the stakes may or may not be strictly financial; it may be a "mano-a-mano" duel or a multi-party, round-robin negotiation. But whatever the form, in every case you will have *your* objective and the other guy (or guys, or gals) will have *theirs*.

"Winning" the deal isn't, in my mind, a matter of making off with everything on the table. Successful negotiation lies in reaching an agreement that leaves *both* sides at least somewhat satisfied.

Some of what I had learned about playing my hand in negotiations had come almost reflexively. The moment I walked into the office of the man whose space I wished to rent for my first store, I noted his crude attempt to score psychological points by forcing visitors to look up at his elevated desk. I elected to remain standing. I understood instinctively that to do otherwise would concede weakness at the outset and almost invite him to take advantage of me.

Never show weakness, especially at the start of a negotiation. Twice during the course of that meeting I had turned for the door. Twice the man behind the desk called me back into the room—with a concession. Another lesson took root and bolstered me in many a subsequent negotiation. Whenever possible, *be ready to walk away* from the deal. To the extent a successful conclusion matters more to the other guy than it does to you, you carry an edge into negotiation.

Sometimes, though, you can't walk away—as I was to find out.

Since that first rental negotiation I had done dozens, if not hundreds, of smaller deals and at least a few more significant ones. Each novel appliance Melody House introduced meant working out supply, pricing and terms with a manufacturer or distributor. The deals I reached with ALL underpinned a very promising enterprise I exited at a substantial profit. For Cable TV, I had secured viable terms for us to run our cable through private rights-of-way, across public spaces above and below ground, into apartment buildings and out of performance sites like the Forum. After a few bruising errors, I had learned how to buy smaller cable systems without getting too badly stung by "rollover specialists."

Some of those deals had been done on very little more than a word and a handshake. From here on in, the deals would become more complex, the negotiations more involved and multiple players more often at the table, as was the case at the Underground Conduit Commission. But I had gained some insights that would remain relevant.

CN Telecommunications had been willing to lose money by subcontracting Cable TV to install the Montreal Stock Exchange's ill-fated chalkboard-images network. Its backer was a giant of the Canadian corporate scene, Canadian National Railway. It considered the loss on the contract a small "investment" to secure for itself the image value of being associated with such new technology.

When you're on the buying end of the deal, you can sometimes get value without expending cash. A seller may want to join your organization, might have a tax or estate problem or be embroiled in a family feud. Circumstances like those all soften the price points.

Ask! The worst anyone can say is no. Neither Detergent Incorporated nor the H.H. Scott hi-fi company had the time, resources or staff to develop an export market in Canada (a somewhat more complicated undertaking in those pre–North American Free Trade Agreement days). Both companies were happy to give me exclusive Canadian rights to their products literally for the asking and then to take their profit on the units they shipped me for resale.

To bring the idea forming in my mind to reality would call on those insights and more. Once again, if I had known the challenges ahead I might have turned back, but that entrepreneurial instinct to "just do it" carried me forward.

I had no idea how big the idea would eventually become, or that we would help pioneer a new age of round-the-clock, round-the-globe, non-stop and increasingly borderless business transactions.

> "It is change, continuing change, inevitable change, that is the dominant factor in society today. No sensible decision can be made any longer without taking into account not only the world as it is, but the world as it will be....This, in turn, means that our statesmen, our businessmen, our everyman must take on a science fictional way of thinking." ISAAC ASIMOV, SCIENTIST AND WRITER

THE WINTER OF 1962 relaxed its grip on Montreal reluctantly. I wasn't thinking about globe-straddling networks, only about closing the distance between the Montreal Stock Exchange trading floor and the offices of its member brokers. If I could come up with a new, effective solution to that need, the members of the exchange could afford to pay a great deal for the information. Visions of *"monopoly premium" margins* danced in my head. If the brokers also came to rely on that information for every trade, their ongoing *need* would be my *recurring revenue.*

One day I spotted a small notice in a trade magazine. Someone named Robert Sinn, from a company I had never heard of, announced that he had just received a patent for a system of "information retrieval"—a new phrase to me. Sinn indicated in the write-up that his system had been designed for and would be marketed to the stock-brokerage fraternity. Could it do the trick for the MSE?

It took me three months to track down the elusive Mr. Sinn and his mysterious Ultronics Systems. I eventually found them in Pennsauken, New Jersey.

The town was in an area that was to the early sixties what Silicon Valley later became to the high-tech industry. Miles and miles of single-storey, garage-type buildings between Camden and Philadelphia sheltered dozens of tiny start-up companies, most of them hoping to transform some new idea in the burgeoning field of electronics into the next new thing.

Bob Sinn and three pals had worked for RCA. They had struck out on their own to commercialize an idea they had for storing and retrieving information, and their highest hope for its application lay with members of stock exchanges. Sinn told me that traders on the exchange floors would be able to enter the prices at which equity issues traded into one part of the system and brokers in another office—indeed, in another building or another city—would be able to retrieve those prices by entering the equity's stock symbol elsewhere in the system.

Sinn took me back into the workshop area of the building to show off their brainchild. It didn't look like much. The system was laid out on a "breadboard" (the perforated non-conductive sheets that electronic hobbyists and professionals still use to try out circuitry). It was dotted with tubes and colour-coded capacitors and resistors. When they had the circuit proven, Ultronics planned to miniaturize it on a new-generation silicon "chip."

A terminal held a wheel marked with the letters of the alphabet. To retrieve information about any stock, you turned the wheel to each letter in its stock-trading symbol in sequence (first "G," then "E," for General Electric, for instance) and then pressed one of several buttons marked "Quote" or "Last Sale" or "Volume." The terminal displayed the desired information on what were called "Nixie" tubes: essentially small light bulbs with multiple elements shaped like the figures "o" to "9". As the tubes lit up, the numbers of the selected price appeared in glowing numerals.

They showed me how stock information could be recorded or entered at one end of the system and selectively called up at the other. Sinn assured me that the system could handle large numbers of different requests simultaneously.

I asked them for Canadian rights to the technology. Their answer wasn't what I expected: "Why don't you buy some stock in our company?"

This probably should not have come as much of a surprise. Ultronics was a start-up, still struggling to prove its technology. It did not yet have a single paying customer. And like every technology start-up before or since, it was desperate for cash. Bob and his friends had US$1 million from investors and secured a small-business loan for another million, but ongoing development costs had already burned through most of that funding. They figured they needed another $300,000 to $500,000 (equivalent, at the high end, to about $3 million in inflation-adjusted dollars today) to get their system to market.

But I wasn't interested in their company, only their engineering. "I only came here to get the rights to Canada," I insisted.

"That makes no sense," Sinn countered. "There's only six members of the New York Stock Exchange in all of Canada. How can you consider running a business on that?"

He seemed unaware that Canada had stock exchanges of its own. I tried to explain my plan, but he and his partners could not get beyond their fixation on selling me Ultronics stock. We talked back and forth for more than two hours. At last I broke off the conversation; having flown down from Montreal, I was tired. We agreed to resume in the morning. A cab came to take me back to my motel.

As I sat in the back seat of the taxi and reflected on the afternoon's events, the truth struck me. We had *both* been talking past each other and not listening—or at least not hearing.

The next morning I walked back in to Ultronics and announced, "Okay, I'll buy some stock. But I want Canadian rights along with the stock."

"You've got the rights," Sinn answered, instantly. "How much stock do you want?"

I put US$25,000 into the company, the equivalent of $150,000 today and a lot of cash for me at the time. For that I got rights "outside the United States" to Ultronics' technology. Despite the sweeping nature of the rights, I still viewed this as likely to be a philanthropic contribution: Sinn's technology had yet to prove itself in action. The whole thing was a huge leap of faith. Their system *was* for real, but would it perform as promised under operational conditions? What would happen during a day when trading volumes were high—would the system stand up or crash? And if it worked, would it be accurate?

Later, as Ultronics expanded and needed additional capital, I put in more money. The gamble did pay off, and I filed away another lesson in negotiating: *keep your mind open!* Don't get so narrowly focussed on your own objective (rights, in my case) that you overlook a greater opportunity that arises unexpectedly in the course of bargaining (rights *plus* stock).

IT WASN'T UNTIL I HAD acquired the rights to Ultronics' technology, at the price of a stake in the company, that a new requirement dawned on me. Bob Sinn's equipment would (I hoped) work, but it wasn't inexpensive. A single installation at one broker's office was going to cost a minimum of US$6,000 ($36,000 in current terms). If I wanted stockbrokers to pay a rental sufficient to cover that kind of expenditure, our system would need to supply data from more than just the Montreal Stock Exchange.

Yes, I always prefer a negotiation where the other guy needs the deal more than I do, but that can't always be the case. Sometimes you simply *must* get the deal or an entire plan falls apart.

In this case, if I wanted any other stock exchange to sign on to our untested system, I first had to plead my case before an organization that Sinn and his pals called simply "God." I needed the approval of the New York Stock Exchange.

This proved less difficult than my imagination at first made it out to be. Ultronics had already demonstrated its system to the NYSE, whose managers had been cautiously impressed. But before the exchange would entrust its proprietary price data to the revolutionary new system, it insisted that Ultronics prove its technology would produce accurate results "99.9 per cent of the time." My investment had gone largely to that end.

Now the exchange provided me with an application document that asked dozens of detailed questions. They wanted to know not only about our technology but also about the new company I had incorporated in

Canada, Combined Market Quotations Incorporated, my other business interests and even my personal background.

I took pains over my response, answering each query at length. It was a bracing vindication of a Boy Scouts principle that every entrepreneur ought to inscribe on his or her desk: Be prepared! You need to know your subject—your product, market, customer base, your potential revenues and costs—*before* you walk into the room.

I flew down to New York and delivered the application in person. Then I came home and worried. Did I say the right things? Did I answer everything exactly as they wanted? Was my tie on straight?

Eventually I was summoned back to Wall Street. I presented myself and was ushered into the office of the vice-president of the New York Stock Exchange. "We've considered your application," he said, "and analyzed your answers and looked into your background."

My stomach churned.

"And we have decided to give you a contract to disseminate the NYSE stock quotations." He reached across his desk to hand me an envelope. "Here is your contract."

I believe my hands trembled a little as I opened it. This may not really have been an edict from "God," but it was certainly one of the most important business verdicts I would ever face. The contract was far shorter and simpler than I had anticipated, just three typed pages. I scanned it quickly. Then the blood drained from my face.

The vice-president must have noticed my expression, because he asked, "Is there something you don't understand?"

I said: "This contract is for thirty days. I don't see how I can base the investment I need to make on a commitment of only thirty days."

"Let me explain," he said, with some patience. "It may read that way. But what you hold in your hand is a contract for life—if you live up to its terms. Have you heard of the Dow Jones ticker?"

Of course I had.

"They have the same contract," he explained. "The most important rule is this: *We* own the information you will distribute and *we* determine who can receive it. If we ever tell you to turn off the information to Mr. X for any reason, then *you must turn it off!* If you fail to do so, then this contract *is* for thirty days. Do as we say and it continues, for all purposes, for life."

My blood was beginning to circulate again.

"You shouldn't have any problem with your subscribers on account of this," he added. "They are all fully aware of our rules."

I walked back out into the sun of Wall Street six feet off the ground. I had just "sold" our idea to "God"! My careful preparation had paid off. But I had also learned yet another lesson in the art of the deal: Sometimes the most important things are those that are *not* spelled out in black and white.

Back in Canada, I still needed other exchanges' approvals. I was soon reminded of my earlier experiences with shellac records and access to utility poles: In each of those cases, the moment I secured a concession from one player, others dropped their resistance. Now I set up a meeting with Eric Kierans, president of the Montreal exchange.

I explained to Kierans that I wanted to distribute share quotations from the exchange to brokers' offices. The MSE would get a monthly fee for each of our subscribers who used its information (the same arrangement we had with New York).

"Have you applied anywhere else?" he asked.

"Yes," I told him, "the NYSE."

"And did they approve you?"

"Yes."

"Then so do we," Kierans said. And that was that.

For many months after that I was away from home, travelling to Europe to secure similar rights to trading information from the world's other major equity exchanges.

For most, New York's prior approval would turn out to be decisive— and another lasting lesson in the power of leverage. If the NYSE accepted us, then so did the Vancouver and Alberta stock exchanges as well as the more senior exchanges in London, Paris, Milan, Tokyo and elsewhere;

everybody, in fact, except the Toronto Stock Exchange, whose reluctance (as recounted in chapter 6) had nothing whatsoever to do with the quality or reliability of our service.

> · Don't let people who set themselves up as "authorities" intimidate you. They all put their pants on one leg at a time, just like you.
> · Your thoughts are who and what you are. If others cannot convince you to adopt their point of view, hold your position.
> · If you win, you win.
> · If you lose, you at least end up defending what you believe in, not something others want you to do.
>
> **ANON.**

WITH THE RIGHTS TO DISTRIBUTE quotations from New York, Montreal and other major world stock exchanges in hand, I felt ready at last to try to sign up a first customer. But bringing new technology to market is inherently unpredictable: Just as I was thinking about how to introduce our service to city brokers, I received a phone call from New Jersey.

Someone had invented a way to enter requests for information into a data system like ours using a typewriter-style keyboard! This innovation made our crude letter-wheel terminal seem stone-age. Ultronics needed more money and more time to integrate the new keyboard technology into the rest of its engineering.

I grimaced and wrote another cheque (for which, in fairness, I later got an unexpected bonus: Not all of Ultronics' minority shareholders were able to answer the call for more cash; their interests were eventually offered, at a price, to those of us who stayed in).

At last Sinn phoned to say the system was ready to roll out. I ordered six terminals from Ultronics and began to set up a demonstration. We booked a long-distance data line from the New York Stock Exchange via Boston to a hotel room in Montreal. Then we ordered some sandwiches, set up a bar and invited the city's most influential brokers for lunch and to look over the new system.

Several showed up. They drank our liquor, ate our sandwiches and asked a few questions that made it clear they thought the whole thing was a joke. Then they left. And that was it. Not a single expression of interest.

I poured a drink for myself and stared glumly around the room. Had all my months of work, all my trips to New Jersey and New York, to Europe and Asia, to say nothing of all my money, been wasted? By 2:45 PM I was on the verge of ripping the lines out of the walls and packing up the whole affair when a broker from one of the French-Canadian trading houses walked in.

He had run into some colleagues who had told him he ought to drop by "to see this con game" we were pulling, "just for a laugh." According to his buddies, the wire from the terminal we claimed was connected to New York really just went to a backroom somewhere. The whole deal was really a scam.

"But show me anyhow," he said.

"Certainly," I said. "Is there any particular stock you're interested in?"

"Yes, Jersey Oil," he said, naming the giant corporation now called Exxon.

"Do you know the stock symbol?"

"Yes."

"Then enter the symbol on the keyboard yourself," I told him. He did. "Now press where it says 'Quote.'"

He pressed the key and a figure flashed up on the display. The broker grinned like the proverbial cat with a mouthful of canary. "I knew it was a fake," he said.

"Why's that?" I asked.

"Because I just sold 10,000 shares of Jersey at half a point below that number."

"Well, I'm sorry," I said, "but that's the price right now." I handed him a telephone. "This is connected directly to the floor of the exchange. Why don't you ask the specialist in Jersey Oil directly?"

He took the phone and asked for the specialist. Then he asked for the price of Jersey Oil. His face went pale. He put down the phone and stalked out without another word. Even when we were right, it seemed, we weren't going to be believed. More than a little crestfallen, we struck our demonstration set-up and went home to lick our wounds.

The following day we conducted a post-mortem of the previous afternoon's disaster. Was there something we had missed? Should we have tried some other approach? Our self-examination was interrupted by a phone call.

It was the broker who had sold his position in Jersey Oil too soon. "You'd better get that damn machine over here," he said.

Two lessons came from that experience. One was the power of a well-timed demonstration. The other was this: Never count yourself out of the game too soon!

> A man dies and leaves a collection of French Impressionist art to his son.
>
> The son wants to turn his inheritance into cash and so decides to sell the valuable paintings. But he's also grown attached to them. In search of a solution, he calls a skilled forger.
>
> "I want you to make exact copies of all of these paintings," he tells the forger.
>
> To his astonishment, the forger declines the work. "I can't do that for you," he says.
>
> "Why not?" the son asks.
>
> "Because I already did that for your father."

THE SIXTIES WERE IN full swing. The papers and television news were full of radical young activists demanding equal civil rights for blacks in the United States and for French-speaking Canadians in Quebec. In April 1963, Quebec separatists set off a bomb in Montreal. It did not kill anyone but it would not be the last, and not all the others would explode harmlessly.

That June Henry, our oldest son, graduated from high school. In the fall he began classes at Nova Scotia's Acadia University.

Two months later, an assassin's bullet shattered John F. Kennedy's "Camelot" promise on an afternoon in Dallas. Whatever innocence there had ever been in the decade ended there. But Canada managed to stay clear of the United States' entanglement in Vietnam, while at the same time negotiating a free trade deal in automobiles that was a tonic to the economy. On the world stage, a prime minister who was a Nobel Prize winner—Lester Pearson—was something new for Canadians.

At the midpoint of the decade, the country would assert its expanding self-confidence by adopting a new flag. In 1967 Canada celebrated its centennial as an independent nation, no small accomplishment in the modern world, with the world's fair in Montreal.

TWO DECADES EARLIER, I had leveraged the (near) promise of records from Decca into a firm commitment from RCA. Later, gaining access to Hydro Quebec poles for cable had provided the leverage to access Bell's poles as well. Most recently, the NYSE's leading approval of my application to distribute its market data had tilted the decision our way at other, lesser exchanges.

Now, it took only one of Montreal's more aggressive brokerages to begin serving their clients better with the most current market information for everyone else to clamour for Combined Market Quotations' system. We soon had interest in our equipment from most of the city's stock-trading houses.

My deal with Ultronics required me to pay cash on delivery for all the equipment we ordered, at a price that fully reflected the equipment's cost plus a profit for them. Cable TV was running flat out keeping up with the growth and upgrading of its network. The balance on my credit line was already up to my neck, so I approached my banker.

"Can you guarantee us these things will work as you expect?" he wanted to know.

I had to be honest: "No. And I can't guarantee that I'll live past tomorrow. But I've done my homework. These should work."

"*Should*," he said darkly. But this banker knew my other businesses. "Well, looking at what you've done with Cable—and *only* because of that—here is what we can do...." The bank, he said, could give me 10 per cent of the value of each contract I signed. Those contracts were for twenty-four months, at $2,000 a month. Fully executed, each one would deliver $48,000 in revenue over its lifetime. The bank would give me one-tenth of that amount: $4,800.

It didn't pay for an entire installation, which cost at least $6,000, but it very much lightened the load. The $2,000 monthly subscription fee we charged brokers would repay the loan for each installation within three months. Another month's fee should repay the balance of the equipment cost for each location. Thereafter, most of the monthly income for each installation would be booked as free cash flow. Anything remaining after our overhead would be profit. (Subscribers themselves were responsible for paying the fees each exchange demanded for access to its data. We did, however, collect these payments and pass them on to the exchanges.)

As we installed more terminals, and met our obligations on the credit we had already received, the bank slowly increased the amount it would agree to lend on each additional contract. It first raised the amount to 15 per cent of the contract's value, then 20 and finally to 33 $\frac{1}{3}$. By then, however, we were able to finance most new installations out of the cash flow being generated by early ones.

At that point I received another phone call from my bank. The credit manager wanted to know why I wasn't using any more of their money!

Banks only want to sell you ice cubes in winter, but the incident illustrates another more general truth about negotiating anything: When you need something from the other guy, *he* is in the driver's seat. When he needs something from you (performing loans, for example), then *you* are at the wheel. A case in point was the Toronto exchange: It bobbed and weaved for years and when the real reason for its refusal of our service finally emerged, quite apart from the personal insult and the matter of principle, it handed me an ace in our protracted negotiation. In the fervid social atmosphere of the late sixties, the last thing the Toronto Stock Exchange wished to bring on itself was a public charge of bias.

On that occasion and some others, I had what curlers call "the hammer" and a clear shot at the other guy's rocks. With the TSE, I took it without hesitation. On other occasions I did not. I believe "winner take all" is a poor philosophy in business. "Don't be a pig," my father used to say, "or you'll end up in a pigsty." As well as preferring to leave something on the table for the other guy and allowing him self-respect, I know we may meet again in some future deal. I'd prefer he not be harbouring a grudge when we do.

So we didn't always get the last nickel. Does it really matter?

IT WAS A RELATIVELY short step from winning over Montreal's stock-trading community to approaching their counterparts in Toronto. The intercity portion of the network ran on regular telephone company lines; it was not difficult to reach out to brokers in Ottawa, Halifax, Calgary and Vancouver, as well.

Soon we were reaching out even further. I took a call from Robert Sinn one day: Merrill Lynch wanted to install our service in its London offices, but, Sinn reminded me, I had the rights to Ultronics' technology "outside the United States." It was up to me to handle Merrill Lynch's request.

Apart from the legalities of it, his decision to pass the business to CMQ was no altruistic gesture on his part. Setting up equipment at either end of the transatlantic link would cost in the neighbourhood of $250,000 at each end; renting the necessary dedicated undersea cable time would run to another $28,000 *a month.* This was business I could do without.

Sinn called again a few days later with cheerier news. "I may have a solution," he said. "Reuters has a line under the Atlantic that has enough capacity for sixteen teletypes, but they're only using half of them." And, he said, the news agency was expressing interest in getting into the business of distributing financial-market information as well.

I flew down to New York and worked out a deal with a Reuters man named Cy Smith. We assembled at CMQ in Montreal the data streams that Merrill and other European customers wanted; Montreal conveniently was the jumping-off point for the major transatlantic cable that Reuters used. The news agency accepted the information at the other end and distributed it to investment dealers and trading houses in

Europe, and we received a royalty on the information transmitted to European subscribers.

With United Amusements' investment, Cable TV was also expanding its reach. As I negotiated the acquisition of smaller cable systems for both our accounts, I gained a hard-won familiarity with the inventive ways other parties can set out to deceive.

As those lessons sank in, I began to weigh more carefully the worst-case scenario if a deal went sour. I learned to look behind every paragraph in a contract. I insisted on explicit warranties and guarantees—and still held back a quarter of any cash payments until I was certain the facts were as they had been represented.

A.L. Lawes' dictum came often to mind: "Can you afford the loss? If not, can you afford the salvage?"

Presentations to the Board of Broadcast Governors were formal, semi-judicial affairs. At some of these, while Famous Players/United Amusements was assembling its cable holdings, I appeared alongside lawyers. Memorable among them was Willard Estey, who went on to become one of the most admired justices on the Supreme Court of Canada.

Estey was always a brilliant performer, but in general I acquired a deep aversion to bringing lawyers into anything a moment sooner than absolutely necessary. In his play *Henry VI,* Shakespeare has a character rally his peers with the cry, "First thing we do, kill all the lawyers." I won't go quite that far, but there is a lot to be said for the term "KISS"—Keep it simple, Sam. No lawyer ever earned his or her billing-hour quota by keeping it simple.

Lawyers and accountants share one of the sweetest business models in existence. With almost any other product or service, you know the price before you buy. With these people, you're obliged to buy their services without the remotest idea what it will eventually cost. The meter starts running the second you walk into their offices or they pick up the telephone. If the matter is a complicated one, it will keep running as long as they say it should, even while they do all their research and draft and revise their opinions. And whether or not things end to *your* satisfaction, *they* will expect to be satisfied on their bill in full.

Sometimes these experts are worth every penny, but do not use $600-an-hour legal counsel as stenographers! You shouldn't need to pay anyone else to figure out the heart of whatever it is to which you and the other parties are agreeing. Instead of discussing everything in front of a lawyer while the meter is running, sit down and document what you're talking about *first*. Reach an agreement. Put it on paper. Only *then* bring in the lawyers to tell you if you're breaking any laws or taking on any unacceptable liabilities.

And another thing: when they bring a document back to you with their lawyerly changes, *read it closely.* I have had lawyers return contract drafts to me that departed wildly and materially from what the other parties and I originally agreed on. I sent those documents back to the lawyers for correction *on their time*. It was their mistake. Why should I pay them to fix it?

It is not illegal to open a conversation with a lawyer (or an accountant) by asking, "What are your charges?" Nor is it improper to tell either one you will not pay for any research or other side charges that you do not explicitly approve in advance. And it's neither illegal nor impossible to change lawyers or accountants. I've done both.

As both Cable and Combined Market Quotations grew, I spent more of my time participating in bigger meetings with more players. When I was chairman I developed a policy I maintained later: "Criticize anything you want. But you *must have an alternative*. If you don't, we're going with what we have, no matter how much you dislike it."

At the same time, reaching the consensus in a multi-party meeting is no task for brute force. People are people. They have feelings and expect—whether they deserve it or not—respect. You catch more flies with honey than with vinegar.

I've always enjoyed a good joke. It is hardly new, but always worth remembering, how much a little humour can loosen up a meeting and get spirits moving towards a fruitful conclusion.

Some negotiators, I know, play games with psychological dominance of the kind my first landlord tried to use on me. I haven't the interest, the patience or, perhaps, the subtlety for that. I would rather rely on a strong case, on knowing my subject, product or deal through and through.

Two last thoughts on the subject of negotiation:

- At the end of the day, if someone puts enough zeros on the cheque *everything* is for sale.
- When the ink is on the paper, *don't look back.* Now and again, if I caught myself wondering whether I had left money on the table in this or that deal, I started to get a burning stomach and began to duck other decisions. Don't second-guess. *Move on.*

> "Children: tired of being harassed by your parents? ACT NOW! Move out, get a job, pay your own bills, while you still know everything." **ANON.**

IV A STRONG DRIVE TO achieve unambiguous success is a hallmark of the entrepreneurial personality. Someone asked me one day when in my business career I had begun to feel as though I had "made it." The truth is probably "never." A degree of insecurity is doubtless an essential ingredient in the Type E's reserves of ambition.

That said, the Campbell family's circumstances improved materially during the 1960s.

The house in the Town of Mount Royal was frequently the stage for entertainment that Vivian expertly managed. After the many years earlier in our life when socializing meant going "out," it was fun to be able to invite friends "in," whether for Vivian's spectacularly planned theme events or more intimate dinner parties.

The sixties were the decade of our two older sons' adolescence, with the usual attendant anxiety for their parents. Thanks almost entirely to Vivian, however, all three of our boys were growing into strong and independent personalities.

Business days often ran from early breakfast to late evening. Meetings in New York and New Jersey, in Europe or in Toronto and Vancouver took me out of town weekly, often more than once.

When Henry left for Wolfville, Nova Scotia, to attend Acadia University in 1963, Vivian and I both experienced that powerful surge of pride, hope and apprehension that must flow through every parent whose child leaves home for the first time. We felt it again in the fall of 1967, when Barry began his first year at McGill. (The university by then had abandoned its anti-Semitic policies. Not that it would have mattered: unlike his father, Barry's marks would have carried him in anyway.)

Our youngest, Jeffrey, read for his bar mitzvah in 1969. With our improved circumstances, the Campbell clan celebrated with a much more elaborate affair than my own spartan experience!

Although I was no longer a slave to the store counter and I was often away from home, there were diversions. Our trip to Italy had not been our last. There was no time for long, wandering vacations, but we took trips to Europe and Mexico. In 1967 we bought an apartment overlooking the ocean in Palm Beach. The same year we acquired twenty-one undeveloped hectares near the ski hills in northern Vermont, two and one-quarter hours from Montreal; the next summer we had a vacation house built there.

With both my companies able to pay me well, Vivian and I structured much of our travelling around discovering additions to our growing collection of art.

By the end of the decade, I was in Type E heaven: at the centre of two of the most exciting industries of the day. Cable TV enjoyed a licensed monopoly in its territory. Each month its customers sent *recurring revenue.* Ahead of us were promising *new* services: specialty cable-only channels delivered by satellite and (finally) movie channels.

CMQ, meanwhile, was delivering stock quotations from exchanges around the world to brokerages and institutional trading rooms across Canada. It was the beginning of the twenty-four-hour, round-the-planet global trading day. And I was at the centre of the traffic, holding it all together.

Not bad for a peddler's kid from Fredericton.

CHAPTER 10

GOLDEN, BUT **STILL** HANDCUFFS

"Book smart" is not the same as "street wise."

THE YEAR WAS 1969 and I was on top of the world.

Postwar parents who had bought their first washing machine and later their first television at Dave Campbell's Melody House were now watching their kids grow long·hair, don beads and bell-bottoms and march in the streets against Vietnam, the "system" and anyone over thirty. Lots of them were writing us monthly cheques to watch it all unfold on Cable TV.

A puzzling, charismatic, left-wing Montreal lawyer named Pierre Elliott Trudeau had seized Canada's imagination to become prime minister the previous year. With a panache previously unseen in Canadian leaders, he embodied the country's growing emotional distance from both the Cold War superpower to the south and its Britannic "mother country" and wartime ally.

In Quebec, meanwhile, *la révolution* was no longer so *tranquille*. French-speaking young Quebecers identified themselves with the U.S. civil rights battle. In the wake of inflammatory comments by French president Charles de Gaulle, they had rioted in the streets of Montreal during Canada's centennial year. Bombs continued to go off, sporadically claiming innocent lives.

Early in 1969, students at my alma mater staged the country's biggest student riot, occupying several floors of Sir George Williams College and setting a fire that destroyed a $2-million computer facility.

The decade's social promise appeared to have lost its way. The leading edge of technology, however, raced forward as fast as ever. In July, tens of thousands of Montrealers played hooky from work and gathered around their television sets to see Neil Armstrong set foot on the moon.

A series of political assassinations in the United States, an unwinnable war in Asia and rising inflation in the general economy had combined to set a grim bear loose on stock markets. Across Canada, 70 per cent of securities dealers were tracking its rampage on CMQ terminals.

It made little difference to me whether the market was up or down, whether the reports from the war or the counterculture were good or bad. Our monthly recurring revenue from cable and data subscribers continued. Some of CMQ's customers were casualties, as their business dropped off and they had to "downsize," having us remove our equipment from idle workstations in order to save the monthly payments to us.

That year, 1969, Henry graduated from Acadia University with a bachelor's degree in commerce. With high hopes and a little fear on both our parts, he joined the staff of CMQ, involved in its marketing activities.

But it wasn't just demographics and politics washing north from the United States. For the second time in my business life, corporate events south of the border were to disturb the smooth evolution of my own plans.

"It is unfortunate we can't buy many business executives for what they are worth and sell them for what they think they are worth."

MALCOLM FORBES, PUBLISHER, *FORBES* MAGAZINE

ROBERT SINN WAS A brilliant engineer. His company produced wonderful technology, constantly upgrading and improving the software that lay beneath our service to equities dealers. But Ultronics Systems seldom made much money.

One of Sinn's earliest investors had been giant General Telephone and Electronics Corporation (now Verizon, after several mergers). The huge utility had acquired shares in Ultronics as a window on Sinn's technology, much as Famous Players initially invested in Cable TV to buy a test platform for its pay-per-view ambitions. As Sinn needed more and more money, he continued to sell shares to GTE.

In any case, there came a point when GTE moved in and bought the rest of Sinn's company. I received a call from one of its legions of executives.

"Mr. Campbell," he informed me, "we've bought the balance of Ultronics Systems from Robert Sinn. And we'd like to buy your end of the company, too." This meant more than just my stake in Ultronics; the U.S. giant wanted CMQ as well.

Like Monsanto, the company that had acquired my young detergent business, the Connecticut-based telecommunications giant had Canadian subsidiaries. It owned Quebec Tel and B.C. Tel (now Telus, after merging with Alberta Government Telephone). GTE was aware that my contract for Ultronics' technology would expire in six years. If I didn't sell my company to them, the executive pointed out, I would lose it in six years anyway when GTE transferred my rights to its Canadian properties.

Despite its "offer you can't refuse" undertone, the price GTE put on the table was not unreasonable. After a little back-and-forth, we reached an agreement. But then they threw out an unexpected curve.

"And we'd like you to stay on and run it," the GTE vice-president handling the acquisition said. "If you were bright enough to develop it to this point, and we were stupid enough to pay you what we're paying you for it, we would be idiots not to have you continue to run it."

"But I'm running Cable TV," I protested. "I can't give you 100 per cent of my time."

"Just give it what you've been giving it up to now," he said. "We'll give you a salary of $25,000 [Canadian]." This was the equivalent of $120,000 today, for working about one-quarter of my time.

At the age of fifty, I contemplated becoming an employee for the first time in twenty-seven years. It would be the first time in my life that

I had tried to conform to the requirements of corporate America. Could I do it?

The Type E personality is used to standing alone at the wheel and driving outside the lines. His whole character itches to break out of the box, shatter the status quo, ignore the rules. The entrepreneur's instinctive idea of due diligence is to ask the question: "Can I do *that?*"

My reading of business journals and frequent dealings with managers and executives over the years suggested that the corporate climate had only become more "professionalized." Whether the individual parties were actually graduates of a business school or not, as a group they demonstrated what I began to see as "M.B.A.-type" thinking. Instead of being aimed outward at the customer and the environment, all of their interest, attention and creative focus was directed *inward,* at the company.

If you have just spent $100,000 to become an accredited "master" of business administration, I suppose it's only human nature to want to prove your creative chops by inventing some new way to "administer" a company. And, of course, the bigger the canvas on which to display your personal artistic vision of "change management" or "organizational transformation," the better for your ego.

But this narrow focus on the *process* of business risks losing sight of the transactions that keep a company *in* business. The *point* of business may be to make money for its shareholders, but the *reason* for business, why it exists, is the exchange of value with a customer. The M.B.A.-type people I met appeared not to be very interested in making the first dollar by winning the customer.

"Customers don't care how you're organized. Spend time on what they do care about."   RICHARD A. MORAN

CHARLES CHAPLIN AND I had led Twentieth Century-Fox and Famous Players theatres to the pay-TV door. The companies' senior executives dared not cross the threshold; that had been nearly a decade early for them. Only now, in 1970, were U.S. film studios and cable systems getting around to talking about the concept.

My experience with the "professional" business type had likewise been underwhelming. I have mentioned that in 1961 I started a Toronto paging outfit, The Beeper People. I didn't mention that I initially had an M.B.A. as a partner.

He was selling appliances for Philips Company when I met him, but he found the paging idea exciting and told me about his business degree from Harvard. He was extremely bright and could quote chapter and verse on business theory.

He had $35,000 to put into the business and I put in the same. We ordered some pagers and opened a storefront. He was in charge.

But nothing ever seemed to move off the starting line. We signed up a handful of customers, but nowhere near the number of people I thought could be attracted by the convenience and economy of pagers. I tried to get him interested in several ideas for marketing. Putting the focus on the customer, I suggested different occupations and industries we could pursue, as well as the channels to reach them. He gave me back business school jargon.

"But that's not how *people* react!" I would object.

My frustration grew as his elevated "B-school" theory failed to translate into revenue on the ground. After eight months I bought him out and found someone with less learning and more experience to make something of the opportunity. The Harvard man went back to another large company.

Type E personalities, I understood. Seasoned investors with Type E qualities of their own, such as the Molson brothers and A.L. Lawes, had proven to be tremendous teachers. At General Telephone, I was finally going to learn how the "professionals" do business.

CMQ'S SALE TO GENERAL TELEPHONE closed. I became a senior middle-management employee (albeit part-time) of one of America's largest corporations.

Within weeks, Canada plunged into crisis. Radical Quebec separatists kidnapped a British diplomat, James Cross, and murdered a provincial cabinet minister, Pierre Laporte. Prime Minister Trudeau in

Ottawa revealed a steely resolve, declaring martial law. Soldiers appeared on Montreal street corners.

At both Cable and CMQ, I continued to be the one making every necessary day-to-day decision. Both systems were growing, and there was lots of interesting work still to do in both arenas. From a financial point of view I had no complaints, either. Vivian and I had, really, sufficient money for all the things we enjoyed.

Henry was still working at CMQ and had recently become engaged to a delightful young woman. Barry had moved on from McGill's under-graduate program to begin law at the same university. Jeffrey was still with us at home. We saw lots of all the boys, their girlfriends and other pals at the house in Vermont, where the whole family retreated on as many weekends as we could. The place was minutes away from the Sugarbush ski hills. Winter was for skiing, summer for big, sprawling parties and clambakes in the driveway.

The proceeds of selling the company to GTE had financed some addi-tional luxuries. We first planned an addition to the house in Vermont, changed our minds and installed a pool in the excavated foundation hole instead. We roofed it and it became an indoor pool, with an apart-ment above.

There should have been nothing easier for me to do than sit back in a deckchair with a frosted highball, light up a cigar and enjoy the sunlight dancing off the water in the swimming pool. Of course, I couldn't do it. In no time at all I was restless.

GTE was at that time the biggest "telco" outside the Bell system in the United States. It served tens of millions of local-exchange subscribers and commanded a big telecommunications network. Its successor is still the local phone company in Washington, D.C., and twenty-eight states. My little operation, as important as it was to me, was almost an afterthought in the workings of its vast organization.

In principle, the executives in Connecticut left me to run CMQ my way. But there was a corporate rule book, and I was expected to play within its lines. Head office controlled my budget. I was allowed to spend $25,000 a year (around $250,000 in today's dollars) on capital improvements or expenditures. Anything above that needed head-office approval. Every quarter, I would travel to Stanford and report to a vice-president there.

Frequently I would carry with me some new idea to improve our service or increase our revenue. I was always on the lookout for these, encouraging our engineers to develop them on their own or in response to customer feedback. Any idea that looked likely to pay for itself within a year, I was usually eager to put into the field.

Each time, my GTE contact complimented me warmly, then told me to forget about developing the improvement. "Yours is one of the few acquisitions we've made that's earning a profit," he told me on more than one occasion. "Just keep running things the way they are. Don't change *a thing.*"

The Type E individual regards obstacles as challenges to his ability to surmount them. There are ways around everything, even corporate budgets. I managed to find enough money here and there to make some of these improvements anyway, adding new functions that made our data more useful to subscribers.

On my next visit to Stanford I demonstrated the advance to the vice-president.

"How the hell did you do that?" he asked.

"We used some internal funds," I waffled.

"You don't have budget for that," he objected.

"Well, no. But we did it. But if you say you don't want it . . ."

"No, no. Of course it's something we should be doing."

" . . . we can always toss it out."

"No!" The vp held up a hand to arrest that thought. "But don't do it again. It's against corporate policy."

There you have it: corporate policy on innovation—"Don't do it again"! To my Type E mind, standing still is the same thing as falling behind. If *I* don't get to the next new and needed idea first, some other guy will. And soon he will be eating my lunch.

In this part of corporate America at least, the idea of innovation was in no one's business jargon. Nor, it seemed, was "risk."

Some time after GTE acquired CMQ, my new corporate parent noted that the deal I had struck with Reuters to assemble financial-news streams in Montreal and transmit the aggregated data over Reuters' lines for the news agency to resell in Europe for a period of ten years was nearing expiry. GTE would need to decide what to do then: try to strike a new deal with Reuters or take back the rights and go into competition for the European financial-news market. My vice-president commissioned me to investigate the market opportunity and report back.

I spent weeks visiting all the major accounts and exchanges in Europe and then wrote a detailed report. I suggested that there was a substantial business to be developed by taking back the rights to our *unique* information and going after European subscribers ourselves.

Instead, the corporation opted to renew the deal with Reuters. Perhaps that was the right choice. But in doing so, the M.B.A.-thinkers at GTE walked away from business generating a minimum of $80 million a year.

At other times I could hardly believe some of the follow-the-leader ideas on which these guys were ready to "spend money to make money." On one occasion I called the vice-president I reported to, only to find him too busy to talk to me and in a very agitated state. "I don't have time," he apologized. "I have to spend two and a half million dollars today."

"*Have* to spend it?" I was incredulous.

"It's the end of my budget period," he explained. "If I don't spend it, I lose it."

I shook my head. To my frugal, Depression-scarred, Type E soul, this attitude to money was not just misguided, it was offensive!

On one of my regular visits, GTE's president asked me to sit in on a meeting of his senior acquisitions and new ventures committee. The subject was a proposed new product. New, that is, to GTE: Several other companies already had something like it in the marketplace.

A senior vice-president representing a division stood up and spent the better part of an hour at a podium with flip charts and overheads and statistical tables—today it would all be PowerPoint bullets. For a

$38-million investment (roughly $200 million in current dollars), his division would develop a product that would take a 1.2-per-cent share of the market away from Westinghouse, 0.75-per-cent share from General Electric, and so on. In this way, they thought, GTE could manage to get as much as 4.8 per cent of the worldwide market for the product. Not even 5 per cent; 4.8.

The presentation came to a rousing close. The meeting now had to decide whether to approve the $38-million investment. Before he called a vote, however, the president introduced me and asked for my thoughts on the proposal.

I thanked him, but demurred. "I was invited here as an observer," I said. "I don't really think I should offer an opinion."

"But you've started companies," the president said. "You have an entrepreneurial approach to things. We'd like to hear your views."

Not everyone at the table will, I thought. But when at last I felt I could delay no longer, I said, "Okay...I think it's the most ridiculous and unnecessary waste of money I've ever seen proposed."

There was a shocked silence, but I warmed to my theme. "Where are all the brains in this company? Why would you commit $38 million and develop a 'me too' product so you can get, if you're lucky, *4.8* per cent of the market?

"Why wouldn't you take 10 per cent of that amount, $3.8 million, and put six or eight people in a research area and have them come up with a truly *new* product? A product that is different, unique, novel and needed *and takes 100 per cent* of the market?

"Even if you fail, at least you tried and you didn't blow $38 million. But I believe your engineers have the smarts to do it."

No one spoke for quite a while, until the president suggested the meeting break for lunch. Over the meal he observed, "You know, Dave, I think you're the only person who has ever come to one of these meetings and said no."

"It's very simple," I reminded him. "I don't need this job. I have another one and I can afford to say no. You don't need yes-men, you need people who say no—or at least question."

That $38-million project did not proceed, and GTE directed more of its efforts into developing new products. But several former senior vice-presidents at the company do not speak to me to this day.

· Be warm.
· Put people first.
· Have fun.
· Be bold enough to say, "Let's try it!"

I DON'T WISH TO SUGGEST that the many schools charging their students big money today to learn how to do business provide nothing of value. I expect (I hope, certainly) that they explain the basics of bookkeeping and accounting procedures, what banks expect, how to draw up a balance sheet—the kinds of things I absorbed by osmosis or took an occasional night class to learn. Never having benefited from one their programs, any criticism I might make of business school curricula or standards would be out of place.

I can only speak of what I have seen of business school graduates outside the academy. Many emerge with their sheepskin without having met a payroll or made a sale. Most of those who have applied for jobs with my companies have asked immediately about the benefits and perks, the compensation and the stock packages we offer. Only later, if pressed, are they willing to talk about what they can do to earn them.

Many M.B.A. types approach business problems in a detached, academic way; they are not instinctive. They may know what the book says, not necessarily what experience teaches. That tends to make their thinking rigid and actions timid. Maybe because M.B.A.s know how much money they could lose, their formal training makes them risk-averse. Whatever the origin of the timidity, they become fearful of doing anything original, of departing from "the book."

This may make them poor entrepreneurs. Like many other untutored Type Es, I was never inhibited by what I had learned in a textbook. I flew by the seat of my pants and whatever I picked up from talking with customers and other people.

The M.B.A.-type thinker's fascination with the *process* of business seems to me often to disregard and ignore the essential prerequisite of business: *the customer.* Is it mere coincidence that so many of the big enterprises they manage fail to pay adequate attention to the customer?

THE MOOD OF THE PRESENT bears some similarities to the early 1970s. Then, as now, the new decade seemed headed into deep yogourt and there was an early nostalgia for the turbulent optimism of the one just past.

That same year, 1971, United Amusements made me an offer for the remaining share of Cable TV that the company did not yet own. This was a serious decision. Cable TV was something *I* had created. Its entrepreneurial cycle had been ignited on that day Melody House began taking down more television antennas than we were putting up. Cable TV now had 85,000 customers, 1,300 kilometres of cable and nearly three dozen service trucks. We were still adding subscribers every week, but the company was no longer growing at breakneck speed.

The city itself wasn't growing the way it once had. The War Measures Act had been lifted long ago, but the openly separatist Parti Québécois was poised to become the official Opposition in the next provincial election. As uncertainty over the future gnawed at the confidence of business investors, Quebec's economy was beginning to sputter.

At the same time, some very big expenses loomed in Cable TV's immediate future. The company continued to generate recurring revenue in gratifying amounts, but we were about to confront equipment upgrades to meet the demand and potential of new technologies.

By the mid-seventies, satellite-fed specialty channels would become available. Distributing them would mean replacing all our video amplifiers once again and subsidizing our customers' acquisitions of a new generation of set-top decoder boxes. These devices would make it possible to address services to individual households and generate a host of premium-price channels, but they would also cost millions of dollars to deploy.

Television-through-a-cable was no longer new. We had increasingly become a commodity utility with a regulated map of monopoly territories. It was clear that, from here on, growth for any cable player could come only at another's expense. Consolidation was inevitable. The winners in that consolidation would have the size that would be needed to implement the new technologies.

There were other considerations. I was spending much of my time preparing for and appearing before the national regulator (CRTC). Now that we were making money, they wanted to tell us how much we could make. I often thought that I would have welcomed their interventions when we were starting out in the business and Bell Canada was trying to keep us out.

The Trudeau government had also passed legislation to introduce a capital-gains tax, to come into effect the following year. After that I would have to share any profit I made from the sale of shares in Cable with the taxman. If I chose not to sell to United Amusements now and instead waited for my Cable shares to become more valuable, I needed to discount that expected gain by the amount of the anticipated tax, to say nothing of all the investment we would need to make between now and then.

I did some sums. By my calculation, it would take *twelve years* for my shares to grow enough in value to outweigh the tax and new capital-cost investments and be worth again what was being offered to me now.

As A.L. Lawes had said more than once: "Dave, there are times when you need to take something off the table."

Just ahead of the capital-gains tax I brought Cable TV's entrepreneurial cycle to its conclusion. I relinquished the balance of the company to United Amusements.

The cheque I received was for $1.5 million, worth about $6.5 million in today's currency. My father was still alive at the time, and I thought this figure might impress him.

Before cashing the payment, I invited my father to lunch. While we were enjoying an excellent meal, I told him that I had sold my remaining interest in Cable TV and slipped the cheque across the white linen tablecloth for his inspection.

My father glanced at it. His expression didn't change. "That's nice," he said, and went back to his meal. He could not comprehend the figure.

EARLY IN 1973 the new Organization of Petroleum Exporting Countries (OPEC) cartel sent oil prices up a wall. The shock sent a wave of inflation rippling through the rest of the economy and within thirty months Pierre Trudeau, whose government had been reduced to a minority in an election in 1972, would win a renewed majority by campaigning against wage and price controls—and then impose them.

The internal workings of big business were going through their own sea change. A decade of emerging-market investments had made the leading U.S. corporations more "transnational" than ever before. As their operations became global, so did their need for communications and data management. It was the era of back-office conversions to first-generation, big-box mainframe computing.

The first recognizable "personal" computer would not appear for another two years, when International Business Machines (IBM) would release a machine (its 5100 model) with sixteen kilobytes of memory and priced at $11,000 (for $20,000 you could get sixty-four kilobytes of memory, enough to hold a document the length of this chapter). The idea that executives might need to know how to run a computer was as far-fetched as suggesting they collect their own mail.

In some areas, business practices hadn't changed all that much since the Depression, or perhaps earlier. In his autobiography, information mogul and now mayor of New York Michael Bloomberg recalls his earliest encounter with how Wall Street stored and retrieved financial data. During the same period when I was reporting in person to GTE's vice-president in Stanford, Connecticut, Bloomberg was a junior stockbroker at Salomon Brothers on Wall Street in New York. He remembers:

> [S]tacks of *Wall Street Journals*... were our source of historical stock prices. Nearby, dozens of loose-leaf notebooks contained public stock ownership lists. Piles of papers crammed with facts about the companies behind those securities littered our desks. Each night, a

clerk would painstakingly go through the day's transactions and, like Bob Cratchit, manually update all of our trade history records.*

Salomon agreed to let Bloomberg look, in his spare time, into automating its access to company data. An irrepressible Type E, Bloomberg would turn that assignment into a knowledge base from which he eventually leveraged a fortune in business-news and data distribution. To do so, however, he would also need to break free of the corporation where he had incubated his ideas.

Meanwhile, the state of the art in business-data automation was represented by the Ultronics-GTE terminal already on every Salomon equity trader's desk. But these, as Bloomberg fairly points out, "were just sophisticated successors to the old ticker-tape," and "technologically impossible to employ for the data-distribution we contemplated."

I had warned Bob Sinn against betting his company on proprietary terminals. Now that GTE owned it, the Ultronics brand was to pay a further price for Sinn's decision. One of Bloomberg's first moves was to "remove Ultronics" from Salomon desks and install a competing terminal with greater capabilities.

I, too, could not restrain myself (or the highly capable engineers I had working for me) from developing new and better ways to present the financial data CMQ distributed, addressing some of the very defects Bloomberg would later write about in his memoir. I took these ideas to Stanford and presented them for approval.

Once more I heard: "No, just keep doing things as you have been."

It was once too often. I returned to Montreal and drafted my resignation. My letter informed GTE that since the company was unwilling to introduce any of my suggestions, I was going to quit and try them on my own.

A couple of days later the phone rang. "You can't quit," GTE's president said. "You have a non-competition contract."

"That's years old," I said. "I'll take my chances in court."

---

* *Bloomberg by Bloomberg.* J. Wiley, 1997.

"Well, we don't want to compete with you."

"Then implement some of the things I suggest."

"We *can't* implement them."

"Why not?"

"It would compete with our partners," he admitted. "Quebec Telephone and B.C. Tel will eventually want to do what you're talking about. We don't want to get in their way."

"By the time they think about it, study it, analyze it, I'll have done it," I said.

"Well, what do you suggest?"

"Sell me back my company."

> "To spot the expert, pick the one who predicts the job will take the longest and cost the most." ANON.

YOU NEVER KNOW what you'll get by asking. GTE agreed to sell CMQ back to me.

It was 1973 and there was a significant amount of cash sitting in CMQ by then, retained income from our operations since being acquired by the Connecticut giant. If GTE took that money out as regular income, it would be fully taxable in the United States. If, instead, I bought the company's stock from its parent, the sale would be recorded on GTE's books as a capital gain on the shares, with less U.S. tax exposure. And, of course, once I owned the company stock I also owned the company's cash. The money sitting in the company would help me pay for it. We didn't haggle over the price. I wanted control back. GTE wanted its money.

As a lifelong entrepreneur I have seldom enjoyed the benefit of close confidants. Proprietors find there are some things—fears, possibilities, wild-blue-sky ideas—they simply do not wish to share with even the most senior employees. Once my early mentors passed into retirement, I often wished for a sounding board to bounce things off.

But whatever collegiality comes with the corporate arena, it has always seemed to me to be undercut by the infection of M.B.A.-type thinking, bogged down in "process," "policy" and earnest, inside-the-box claptrap. At the end of the day, personality rules. M.B.A. types demonstrate the prowess of their academic mastery by rearranging the company "org" chart; Type Es are more visceral: we seek gratification—for our customers and for ourselves.

The representatives of GTE and I signed the documents transferring ownership of CMQ back into my hands at the corporation's Stanford head-quarters. I returned one last time on the now-familiar flight to Montreal.

The next day I walked into my office on Beaver Hall Hill and looked around. Visibly, everything was exactly as it had been when I had left for Connecticut forty-eight hours earlier. Nothing had changed, apart from a few tiny words on the company letterhead.

But everything had changed.

TOP OF THE GAME

"Money isn't everything, but it sure keeps the kids in touch."

ANON.

BETWEEN 1963 AND 1970, Quebec's radical separatists set off no fewer than 200 bombs and killed seven people. Several of those bombs went off in our Town of Mount Royal neighbourhood, another in the Montreal Stock Exchange, which I often visited. The murder of Pierre Laporte and kidnapping of James Cross demonstrated that the radicals' tactics were escalating. In October 1970, Pierre Trudeau ordered in troops and Quebec premier Robert Bourassa authorized a police roundup of perceived political extremists. The violence ended.

But the political sentiment for Quebec independence did not die away. The sweeping arrests confirmed many French Quebecers' worst suspicions of *les anglais,* and many who had been wavering on independence as a goal now embraced it.

I could understand some of their historic resentment: I had certainly felt the sting of Anglo disdain. But at least with regard to CMQ the separatists' rhetoric of "oppression" by "English bosses" was truly misdirected. Our office was functionally and largely effortlessly bilingual. I had hired some of the earliest and brightest of Quebec's engineering graduates. Meetings went on in whatever language most participants wanted to speak. My own French was perhaps not pretty, but it was functional.

However, as a Maritimer transplanted to Montreal I had observed over forty years a thing or two about Quebec. I agreed with the views of Gerard Filion, president of giant shipbuilder Marine Industries Limited. A francophone Quebecer and former editor of the influential Establishment daily *Le Devoir,* he bluntly told the Montreal Chamber of Commerce in 1969:

> The caricature of Yvon Deschamps, '*un boss et une job steady,*' is unfortunately the ideal of the whole of French-Canadian society at all levels.
>
> Quebec reserves the place of honour for professionals above all, the next place for that vaguely defined category of those who are generally termed intellectuals, university or college professors, economists, sociologists or writers, in short anyone with sharp tongues and clean fingernails. To workers we grant a sympathetic tip of the hat . . . to agents of economic life, a frown.
>
> While English-Canadians and Americans were building factories, we were flushed with pride at the thought of erecting more luxurious [church] sanctuaries.

QUEBECERS AT THE TIME paid Canada's highest provincial taxes. Despite also receiving hundreds of millions of dollars in federal "equalization" payments, the province was unable to balance its books. It would be twenty years before a new generation began to think with a more entrepreneurial spirit, and for much of that time intractable unions, soaring unemployment, xenophobic language laws, political insecurity and the threat of secession placed a steep "risk premium" on anyone doing business in Quebec. Many of the province's brightest and most ambitious young people concluded that opportunity lay elsewhere.

Daily, it seemed, I opened the paper to read of another company that also had decided the costs and lost opportunities of staying in Quebec were too great. RCA Victor, for example, pulled out. Hawker Siddeley, a big maker of vehicle and railroad parts, did the same. Others followed. When the province's public servants went on strike, I read that conditions in Quebec were "causing local financial consultants to advise their clients seeking long-term investment to place their money outside the province."

> "Once we realize that imperfect understanding is the human condition, there is no shame in being wrong, only in failing to correct our mistakes."
>
> **GEORGE SOROS, FINANCIER**

WITH THE SALE OF Cable TV in 1972 and my reacquisition of CMQ the following year, my family's material situation was better than it had ever been. The round-the-clock financial market of today was then just dawning and CMQ was in the thick of it, connecting Canadian traders and investors with an increasingly global network of markets. Now that I owned the company outright again there were plenty of opportunities to take something off the table.

Vivian and I travelled to Europe and indulged our attraction to art with an increasing pace of purchases, even if we did not yet think of it as "collecting."

But more and more often as the decade wore on, when I went to call at a securities-trading house the decision makers had moved. I began spending a great deal of time in airplanes, visiting clients and dealing with issues at our office in Toronto, then coming home to Montreal for the night or the weekend.

Our customers were in every Canadian city large enough to support a stockbroker. CMQ leased communication lines from public carriers— telcos and data-network companies. In turn, we leased terminals connected to those lines to our clients. But our company's "assets" were mainly in its management and engineers. Decades ahead of most other businesses in Canada at the time, CMQ was a "dispersed" and largely "virtual" enterprise.

Our customers came increasingly from points west of Montreal and, unlike companies whose mills, mines and factories still dominated Canada's economy, it would take very little for us to move headquarters from Montreal to Toronto.

"Home" was not quite what it had been, either. The house had become quieter after first Henry and then Barry left the nest. By 1976 Jeffrey, our youngest, had finished high school and moved out on his own.

That year, Liberal premier Bourassa's mandate to govern expired. It was increasingly certain that the separatist Parti Québécois would win the ensuing election. Its popular, chain-smoking leader, René Lévesque, was already promising to crack down on the use in business and education of any language but French—and to take Quebec out of Canada.

Doing business in French was no problem; we had been doing that for years. But Vivian, though not quite as fluent in French as I, deeply resented being *forced* to speak it. You cannot legislate culture. And neither of us wanted to be there if the Quebec government really did try to secede.

One day early in the year I got off yet another Air Canada shuttle, picked up my car from the Dorval Airport parking lot and drove home to our lovely red-brick corner house in the Town of Mount Royal. As always after these trips, I pulled into the driveway drained and exhausted. Vivian met me at the door.

"I have to get an apartment in Toronto," I said wearily. "I'm tired of these trips."

She gave me a concerned look.

"Or else we have to move," I said. "Or I have to get a mistress."

"You can stop after number 2!" Vivian said.

We moved to Toronto that April. For me, it was a deeply emotional departure. With my own hands I had turned the basement of our Montreal house into a recreation room. Vivian, much more magnificently, had made the house a home.

No matter how stressful the endeavours and decisions at work had been, it was always a solace to come home and find her smiling (living with me, I often wondered how). When we moved in, Jeffrey was still in a bassinet. Now all three of our children were living independent lives on their own.

The day we were to leave the house for the last time, I woke up at three in the morning. I got up and paced the silent, empty rooms, remembering the past and looking forward. With Henry's marriage and the recent birth of our first grandchild, Jonathan, the Campbell clan was still growing.

|| WHILE I WAS delighted to shake off the corporate M.B.A.-type thinking that had restrained CMQ while GTE owned the company, it was now up to me to decide what CMQ should do with its reclaimed freedom.

One choice was instinctive.

There are two strategies for profit. One strategy accepts that competitors will appear and margins eke away, that the only way to preserve profit, let alone increase it, is to relentlessly squeeze down every cost. This strategy takes the market as established and basically static. It relies for its advantage on possessing better business procedures than the next guy: a better *process*, that is, rather than a better *product*. It is classic M.B.A.-type thinking.

That isn't the strategy of the Type E individual, who isn't interested in fighting incumbents for a share of a stale market. The Type E wants to create altogether *new* markets, with different, unique products that command high prices and monopoly-premium profits.

My challenge now was to maintain the pace and urgency of innovation in a company that was already dominant in its market. Could I get the engineers and sales staff at CMQ to run fast enough to stay in that position?

One of the first manifestations of our new freedom to innovate came by way of another alumnus of Robert Sinn's now-dispersed Ultronics crew. His name was Neil Hirsch. One day when I was visiting New York he said he wanted to show me something he was working on. He escorted me to a building near his office and up to the tenth floor. There he opened a door to reveal a room all of six by six metres in size, with four people at desks, gazing into monitors, telephones at their ears.

"I'll take fifty," one said into his phone.

"Give me seventy-five," barked another.

"You can have one-twenty-five," a third said.

I turned to Neil and was about to say something when he put his finger to his lips and nodded me back out to the hall. When the door was closed behind us, I asked him what I'd been looking at.

"That was a currency trading room," he explained. "Every time you heard 'Give me fifty' or 'You can take seventy-five,' they were talking in millions. There is not a day goes by when they don't trade a minimum of one billion dollars."

I was impressed. The B-word wasn't tossed around so freely in those days. The new service Neil was working on was soon to become another centrepiece technology of the 24-7 global trading system.

CMQ's initial service had been built around equities: we distributed bid, ask, high, low, latest trade, volume and other data for corporate shares, options and warrants. As major corporations globalized their business, however, foreign exchange had become more central to their operations, hence the growth of currency-trading floors like the one I had just visited. These transactions, moreover, were increasingly complex. If a company operating in Germany was doing business with a Dutch supplier (in those pre-"Euro" days), someone needed to figure out the exchange between the two currencies and, quite possibly, their relationships to the United States dollar.

Neil's new "Telerate" system incorporated that and other capabilities. He had arranged to access market information, worked out the software needed to perform the kinds of calculations and comparisons that traders needed, and formatted the presentation layout.

It was immediately evident that currency data like this was a perfect complement to our existing equity-data offerings. CMQ became one of the earliest distributors of Telerate's currency information.

Over time, Telerate extended its coverage to U.S. Treasury, corporate bond and other fixed-income securities. Its present owners, Dow Jones, boast that the service is the "preeminent global provider of benchmark content for the capital markets covering fixed income, foreign exchange, money market and OTC derivatives asset classes." On our own at CMQ we also added coverage of commodities, metals and futures markets, as well as steadily expanding the overseas stock markets we tracked.

Our pricing model was essentially straightforward. Ever working to ensure that price was no barrier to a sale, we charged a flat monthly rate for our basic data feeds, regardless of how often the customer accessed the data to which it subscribed. Our strategy was then to leverage our customers' loyalty to this monthly usage to "up-sell" them to further services for relatively modest additional monthly charges.

||| CMQ WAS NOW, by a large margin, the Canadian market leader in real-time, comprehensive financial market data. Eight out of ten securities dealers considered their CMQ account as important a tool in doing business as their telephone.

But with CMQ operating comfortably in the black on its existing portfolio of service offerings, it was an ongoing challenge to ensure that our sales and engineering staff preserved a spirit of urgency about developing "the next new thing."

This inertia was not something I suffered from personally. I was always on the lookout for emerging market *needs* and the technologies to meet them in *new* ways capable of supporting sustained high margins. I had maintained my practice of reading widely in the business and electronic press.

Shortly after moving to Toronto, I went further. In a decade when many people at the executive level were still asking what computers were *for,* I enrolled in a number of computer-programming courses that IBM and other manufacturers offered.

A side effect of this constant immersion in the evolving technology was that I knew very well how many smart, inventive, motivated people were out there. I never shed the entrepreneur's reflexive fear that someone faster and sharper might come along with a better idea.

To drive the point home, I posted a large sign in our Toronto offices. It read: REMEMBER: WE OBSOLETE OURSELVES EVERY MONDAY MORNING. I wanted every employee to share my own fear of the unknown competitor and his better idea.

A common protest at the planning and operations meetings I chaired was "But Mr. Campbell, we've always done it that way."

"And that's exactly why we need to re-examine it," was my insistent response. In fact, I eventually instituted a policy that every routine business practice at CMQ be re-evaluated every three months.

When our engineers did come to me with a better idea of their own, they faced the discipline of two critical questions: How much will this cost? When will I get my money back?

Engineers, like all creative people, are easily romanced by the attraction of what they *can* do. I wanted to focus their minds on that subset of all possible innovations that would also turn a profit for CMQ within a reasonable time. Given the pace of technological innovation, I wanted to see my investment paid back within six to twelve months. If they could not answer my two questions, they went back to the drawing board until they could.

More than once engineers came back to me, as the deadline loomed to implement some promised innovation, to beg for additional time to add another feature. With very rare exceptions, my response was "Hold on! Finish product number 1 first. When it's made the first dollar and is earning some revenue, we'll talk again."

> "If you don't constantly monitor how people are operating, not only will they tend to wander off track but they also will begin to believe you weren't serious about the plan in the first place."   **JOHN DOYLE**

DRIVING INNOVATION in our products was one thing. Introducing those new services to our customers in a way that made them salivate with desire was another. Happily, I developed an approach that worked well while also eliciting regular, unedited feedback about our overall service.

We hired three smart, attractive and personable young women and dressed them in professional but stylish fashion. (Today I would add a good-looking man or two to the team.) We trained them on our expanding data system until they knew its every capability backwards.

Three times each year, one member of this team would visit every one of our customers. They normally appeared unannounced, explaining that they were simply there to check and test the installed equipment and make sure it was functioning properly. This, indeed, they did, visibly demonstrating CMQ's strong commitment to maintaining the highest standard of service. But our "Trojan" servicewomen also had other, less overt missions.

We encouraged them to engage subscribers and their office staff in conversation and to make careful note of any suggestions or complaints that surfaced during the "casual" exchange.

Then, as they came to the end of their standard series of test commands, we had them throw in one or two additional commands that called up new functions we were just introducing. When these failed to produce a result, the women would exclaim, "Oh, your equipment must be inhibited for that."

Invariably, the trader using the equipment would want to know, "What do you mean, my terminal is 'inhibited' for that program?"

Our helpful "equipment checker" would then demonstrate the new function—calling up overseas exchanges or comparing prices for the same security across several exchanges, whatever it might be.

The trader would say, "Hey, I like that. I can use it. Put it into my system."

At that point the young woman would excuse herself, saying, "I'm sorry, I'm only here to check the equipment. But I can have someone from sales contact you."

When CMQ's salesperson later did make a call and present the new service, it was to a receptive audience that had already indicated an eagerness for the capability.

Our advance troops were all intelligent young women and they kept an eye and ear out for how our customers were using our service and what they liked or disliked. Their reports on these visits gave us invaluable insights into our customers' needs and the associated opportunities to meet them in new ways.

At one point, rules came in that allowed brokers to discount their trading commissions. Up to that point, flat-rate regulated commissions had made it easy for both investors and brokers to figure out what part of a charge for the transaction was going to the broker. With discounting, however, each broker was free to reduce his or her commission by an individual amount, leading to a range of trading commissions.

Our service team began to report back that the brokers they visited all had electronic calculators cluttering their desks. With each trade they were laboriously calculating the amount of their discounted commission.

"Why can't we do that?" I asked the engineering team. Why couldn't there be a function of our service that allowed every broker to enter his commission discount rate, then apply that rate to every subsequent transaction report onscreen?

"We *can* do that," the engineers replied.

I asked my two questions: How much will this cost? When will I get my money back? I gave them a couple of weeks to work out the answers.

They came back and reported that we could institute the new facility within four and a half months. Their study indicated that customers could afford $100 a month for the extra service. They estimated we would get 40 to 50 per cent of the market and earn back our investment in seven months.

I thought about that for a moment. Then I said: "Let's do it at $75. If we do it at $100, it's easy for someone to come in at $75. If we do it at $75, it's a lot harder for them to come in at $65."

It took a couple more months to get our money back that way, but we got more than 80 per cent of the market and held it for years.

That's Type E thinking.

IV BY THE 1980s, CMQ was distributing information from twenty-two stock exchanges around the world, covering *60,000* securities. Standard market information on each of those securities was updated in "real time," every second of every minute of every day of the trading year. Other streams covered additional trading arenas: oil, precious and base metals, farm commodities. Through Telerate, we had comprehensive live coverage of foreign-currency trading as well as all the major government and corporate bond markets.

Two decades ahead of today's popular Internet-based market "wires," our service provided the same 24-hour data streams. Market traders in every province based trading decisions worth billions of dollars every working day on the information they received through our terminals. CMQ's revenue and profits went up.

Some of the innovations we developed at CMQ required significant new investments, but most did not. Our operations were spinning more than enough cash to cover those requirements and still leave me with opportunity to "take some money off the table" as we went along.

With the extra income, Vivian and I began to enjoy some of the more frivolous indulgences that became available to us. We visited both our Vermont property and the Florida condominium regularly.

Our acquisitions of art picked up. We were not "educated" collectors who followed a theme. We had only one rule: we both had to like a piece before we bought it. Now and again we found works we liked in commercial galleries; more often we bought through one or two dealers whom we came to trust, or occasionally directly from artists.

People have often asked me, "How do decide what is worth buying?" My answer is one I once heard actor and art collector Vincent Price give: "If your eye likes it, and your pocket can afford it, it's worth it."

We continued to enjoy our getaways to resorts. On one of these, soon after we had moved to Toronto, we found ourselves on a beach in Jamaica. A couple next to us was playing Scrabble and became embroiled in a debate over the meaning of a word; as one sometimes does in casual circumstances, I volunteered the correct answer. An acquaintance sprang up.

Mickey Gold turned out to be chief assistant to the legendary impresario and talent agent Sol Hurok. Hurok represented many of the international stars of classical music who appeared with the Toronto Symphony Orchestra as well as with the city's ballet and opera companies. (He had played a pivotal role in Mikhail Baryshnikov's defection.) As we got to know each other better, Mickey suggested that Vivian and I consider becoming patrons to the non-profit Toronto Symphony.

When we all returned north Mickey followed up by introducing us to Walter Homburger, the general manager of the TSO. He soon nominated me for membership in the symphony society and then to its board of directors.

Over the years our companies, and Vivian and I as individuals, had routinely supported a variety of charities. But the invitation to become involved with the symphony elevated my engagement with philanthropy to a new level.

> "Always go after the eighty per cent, and don't worry about the remaining twenty per cent, which is seldom worth the effort."   RICHARD A. MORAN

WITHIN A VERY FEW years of our own move to Toronto our sons joined us there. All three were married now, to intelligent and supportive women, with families coming along. The obvious love reflected in their family circles and our pleasantly lengthening list of grandchildren's birthdays to remember brought us joy and delight.

I knew very well the gulf of an empty pocket. When she was a child, Vivian's family had been better off than mine, but our newlywed years in a "studio" flat and cramped lower duplex had been far from grand. We had put off buying luxuries that many of our friends had been quicker to acquire, walking and taking buses through most of the 1940s and early '50s before buying a car.

Now we were enjoying the fruits of our labour. A central pleasure of the resources now at our disposal was being able to make sure our children did not experience the same privations we had.

Each of our three sons spent time in the business with me. Henry, who knows more about computers and other sophisticated technology than I will ever know, joined CMQ shortly after we moved to Toronto. His expertise greatly strengthened our technological base. Jeffrey joined the company shortly after finishing university, working at a variety of management assignments. (Barry would also work with me for a period in the late 1980s, after graduating in law from Harvard, working briefly at the International Monetary Fund in Washington and then returning to earn a partnership in the Toronto law firm McCarthys.)

V A DOZEN GIANT conglomerates dominate global media today. Forces like Time-Warner, Viacom and News Corporation/Fox are the result of a period of industry consolidation that began in the mid-eighties. Australian Rupert Murdoch's News Corporation first acquired Twentieth Century-Fox in 1985. Over the years that followed, Murdoch, Viacom's Sumner Redstone and other like-minded empire builders assembled stables of "content" and their means of delivery. The first included libraries and producers of movies, music, books, magazines, newspapers and TV shows, both popular titles and more esoteric journals and directories. The delivery channels being acquired similarly ran the gamut: old-fashioned printed directories, radio and television stations, cable networks. Soon many of the media conglomerates would be adding Internet service to their delivery stables and Web portals to their content.

As a very successful, consistently profitable, market-dominant distributor of exclusive, high-margin, specialized content, CMQ was an obvious and attractive acquisition for *someone*.

On May 23, 1985, I turned sixty-five. It would be wonderful—in theory—to be able to build a business, retire and have your family run it afterwards, with or without a continuing role for the founder. In fact, examples of such smooth successions—the dynastic Molson family, New Brunswick's Irvings—are exceptional. The predominant lesson of business history is that most of the time it doesn't work out.

In our case, it was a luxury I did not have. Succession would not be an issue. The first intimation of this was a call in 1986 from IBM. The technology company was interested in CMQ as much for our experience in building, maintaining and enhancing interactive networks as for our exclusive content rights. In addition, IBM made much of the equipment and associated software that our clients used in their "back office" operations: executing transactions and maintaining account records. These operations already used information that came into clients' offices via CMQ.

We agreed to meet, and my son Barry, a lawyer, accompanied me to IBM's Toronto offices.

"We already use your information," the IBM man began. "It would be a very interesting fit if we had both ends in this equation. Is your company for sale?"

"We haven't given it any thought," I answered. "We're very happy. But what are you thinking?"

"We'd like to acquire your company and put your operation together with ours," he said. "We've done some numbers...." Even though we were a private company and released very little financial detail about our affairs, he had a good grasp of our scale and operations.

He finally came to the point. "We'd be interested in making an offer of $50 million," he said. "Plus assumption of the debt." That would add about $6.5 million to their cost.

Our debt was very much less than the limit of our $10-million credit line. It was being comfortably serviced from cash flow. I was not under the slightest pressure to sell, and their figure was not what I had in mind.

"Thank you," I said, feeling entirely calm. "But I think your research is flawed somewhere. This company is worth considerably more than that, and you know it. Thank you, but no thanks."

Beside me, Barry's face changed colour. IBM had just held out $50 million and I had turned it down. He interjected, diplomatically trying to suggest to me that I take some time to think it over.

"I will think it over," I said. "But I'm sure my answer will be the same." I suggested IBM re-examine their research, take another look at their numbers and get back to me. Although IBM's wasn't the offer I was looking for, it was undeniable that CMQ was now, as the financial crowd says, "in play." Even before IBM had a chance to make a reconsidered offer we heard from another big technology company, this time a pure software giant.

Automatic Data Processing Incorporated (ADP) makes industrial-strength process software for big business. Its products include customized desktops for securities brokers that link to ADP's back-office transaction, order-management and accounting engines—products in direct competition with IBM's in the field. CMQ's real-time, live market data, and our own presentation software, would make a very natural fit here, too, and significantly enhance what ADP had to sell.

Once again we settled into chairs and the small talk narrowed down to the point. The ADP executive said that he thought his company and ours would fit well and ADP also wished to make an offer for CMQ. He was going to name a figure. It was what ADP thought CMQ was worth and, if it was acceptable, they would enter into a "due diligence" review of representations and assumptions.

"Hold on," I said. "Stop right there. Back up. You probably know, but if you don't I'll tell you, that IBM has been here with the same approach."

The ADP man nodded. "Yes, we know."

"And we did not proceed with IBM," I said firmly. One, we were not for sale. And two, if we were, the price they suggested was not acceptable.

"What do you think the business we do is worth to you," I asked him, "knowing what it would do for you in relation to your competition? [Among them, of course, IBM.] I know you can replicate what we do, but by that time we'll have moved on and enhanced the system and our information. You'll be playing catch-up all the time.

"I'm sure you've done your homework. So tell me the figure you have in mind and I'll tell you whether we are interested."

Whether he had intended to name a figure then and there, or thought better of it, I don't know. But by the time we adjourned the ADP representative had not put a number on the table.

It came a couple of days later. And it was $20 million north of IBM's. I thanked ADP for its interest and suggested it go back and check its figures.

With IBM and ADP intermittently on lines 1 and 2, a third line lit up. Thomson Corporation's Web site today describes itself as "The world's leading information source." Although its name is not as familiar to many everyday media consumers as those of Time-Warner or Fox, Thomson's boast may not be far off the mark. Its "content" assets include many of the world's most important law, tax, medical and scientific libraries, journals and databases.

Their approach was the opposite of the others'. The initiative came directly from Ken Thomson, founder Roy Thomson's son, chairman of the company and a personal acquaintance through our common interest in the Toronto Symphony.

Thomson's operational head opened the conversation by explaining that the company was restructuring some of its operations. It was considering easing out of daily mass-market periodicals and getting involved with information service providers on which financial-specialist professionals relied. The company wanted to add financial-market data to its menu, but realized it would be faster and easier to acquire the dominant player in the field than to try to compete with him.

"I'm sure you've been approached by others. IBM. ADP. Maybe some others," he said. "We're not going to suggest a price for your business. We'd like you to tell us what you'd consider selling the business for. If the number's reasonable and acceptable, we'll go forward. If not, we'll thank you for your time and end the discussion."

This was a much more intelligent approach.

"Yes, I have a number in mind. If that number is acceptable to you, we can keep talking." I breathed deeply, then went on. "My number is $100 million, and you take over the bank debt."

Truthfully, I had not based the figure on any deep analysis of our balance sheet or revenue projections. I just had a gut feeling it was the right number.

They nodded and said something like, "We can work with that."

The Thomson people began their due diligence review of CMQ's business, books and assets. After several weeks they were satisfied with everything and wanted to proceed—except for one little thing. Along the way, their reviewers had run across our contract with Dow Jones for Telerate.

The U.S. business-information company competed directly against Thomson, then as now. Dow Jones had long ago acquired the master rights underlying Neil Hirsch's bond and currency market streams. Our contract, however, was simple. It specified that CMQ had the rights in Canada to the Telerate information *and* that those rights would endure in the event of a change in CMQ's ownership.

But the good folks at Thomson wanted to make sure. They wanted to contact Dow Jones/Telerate and get its blessing on the sale.

"Don't do it," I told them. "You don't have to. You've seen the contracts. There is no requirement for Dow's approval. The rights go with the company. The contract would continue with a new owner."

"Well, yes, we see that," they said. "But we still feel we should tell them and make sure this isn't going to be a problem for them."

"You'll blow the deal," I said. "Tell them you're buying CMQ and they'll just put in a bid against you."

They did it anyway. And forty-eight hours after I'd talked to Thomson my phone rang.

"Hey, Dave," it was a senior executive at Dow. "What's this we hear, you're selling CMQ?"

"I'm not *selling*. Someone wants to *buy* CMQ. There's a difference."

"Doesn't matter. *We* want to buy it."

"Well, that's a problem," I said. "Why don't you discuss this with Thomson? Because right now I'm in the middle."

"We already have. Thomson's agreed to step back if we want to proceed." Then he got to the nub. "We also know how much Thomson was willing to pay. We're willing to pay that and a small premium for you to come to us."

BY NOW IT WAS 1987. I had become more deeply involved in both my community involvements and the pleasures of caring for, managing and adding to what I had finally to concede was a modest "collection" of art. As the discussions with IBM, ADP, then Thomson and eventually Dow Jones moved forward, I had some opportunity to consider my plans for life after—and without—CMQ.

September turned to October as the last details were squared away for Dow Jones to acquire us. The sale was set to close a week or so after Thanksgiving. Vivian and I had already made plans to take a short holiday after the sale closed. The Israel Museum was sponsoring a tour of the antiquities collections at several leading U.S. museums; we had recently developed an interest in ancient artifacts and were looking forward to the promised chance to meet leading collectors.

Monday, October 19, dawned like any other morning. Then, in stock markets from Wall Street to Bay Street and beyond, from Tokyo and Bombay to Paris and London, panicked investors lost their nerve and ran for the exits. They ran especially hard and fast in New York. Dow Jones's own industrial average index plummeted 508 points, slicing more than 22 per cent off the biggest market's capitalization in a single day—nearly twice the paper wealth that the run in 1929 had destroyed.

It would turn out to be the worst week in Wall Street history. By the end of it, surveys reported that two out of three Americans expected a serious recession, if not a second Depression.

I felt a sting in the stomach. I wondered how firm my $100-million sale was now.

CHAPTER 12

LIFE AS AN ANGEL

"Years wrinkle the skin, but to give up enthusiasm wrinkles the soul."

SAMUEL ULLMAN

I CAME DOWN to breakfast that Tuesday morning with a sense of foreboding. The *Wall Street Journal* lay on the breakfast table. The headlines took away my appetite.

"Market Rout," they blazed. "Free Fall." "Money Managers Are Bewildered by Market's Overwhelming Slide." "A Repeat of '29?"

The second stock-market crash of my sixty-seven years didn't mean very much to me directly; I had no portfolio to speak of in equities. Playing the stock market is like spinning the wheel in a casino—and they serve better drinks in Las Vegas. But I had vivid and painful memories of the aftermath of 1929. I very much hoped not to live through a sequel.

"Depression in '87 Is Not Expected," read another of the *Journal's* headlines. I hoped it was correct, but I could not minimize the gravity of the risk to CMQ's pending sale to the *Journal's* parent, Dow Jones Company. Catching Vivian's eye, I indicated the headlines. "The deal may not go through," I warned her. "They haven't signed anything."

My stomach felt that familiar nausea. In my agitated state I placed a call to the Dow Jones executive handling the negotiations. I opened the conversation with some inane question about the mood in New York.

"Dave, what are you asking?" he cut me off. "Are you worried this deal may not close?"

"It crossed my mind," I admitted.

"Don't worry. We don't buy things for one day. We buy things for the future." What they didn't know, but I did, was that Thomson, one of the other interested buyers, had called us right after the crash to say that if Dow Jones blinked, they would still be a buyer.

And, in fact, despite a certain heightened apprehension I felt over the next forty-eight hours, he was as good as his word. The deal did indeed close two days later on the agreed terms.

One imagines the closing of a multi-million-dollar transaction as somehow dramatic: a handshake across the table of a fancy restaurant, a cheque with a lot of zeros changing hands, the pop of a champagne cork. The reality is more unremarkable, even a little bureaucratic.

Barry and I and several other senior CMQ people trooped over to Toronto's Exchange Tower and on up to the sixteenth floor. This was the office of Weir & Foulds, the law firm representing Dow Jones. Their boardroom table was set at every place with packages of documents.

You don't just hand over the door code to the executive suite, slip a cheque into your wallet and walk out the door. Transferring title to an ongoing business of 250 people, with offices in more than half a dozen cities, together with all of its associated assets, network leases and data-supply contracts, its credit lines and bank accounts; effecting all the financial transfers and dispersals in appropriate sequence; affirming all the various warranties and representations either side is making: all this took dozens of signatures on multiple copies of every document.

We went from one set of papers to the next around the table, scribbling our initials and signatures, like guests at the Mad Hatter's tea party. Finally, we exchanged a last round of handshakes with the Dow Jones team.

As the lead executive from Dow Jones released my hand, he said, "Now we've bought you, what should we do now?"

"You need to buy Bloomberg," I told him,

The former Salomon Brothers stockbroker, future New York mayor and quintessential Type E Michael Bloomberg was doing fresh things, bringing *new* services to a growing subscriber base. His Innovative Market Systems Corporation put company price-to-earnings ratios, debts and dividends at brokers' fingertips. With that information, traders could match the share prices that CMQ's service reported against more detailed knowledge of the companies behind individual listings. Packaged with Dow's long-standing Telerate, the combination of in-depth market and company information could create an irresistible "category killer" in investment information.

Dow's man sniffed. "We'll kill Bloomberg," he said.

"No, you won't," I smiled, and left.

We went back to CMQ—where I had agreed to oversee the transition for up to a year—and finished the day. I may have had an extra scotch that night.

> "Whenever an individual or a business decides that success has been attained, progress stops."   **THOMAS J. WATSON JR., FORMER CEO OF IBM**

THE "SWEET" ARC of the entrepreneurial cycle is on the early, growth side of the circuit. Somewhere, the entrepreneur identifies a market need and has a crazy idea for meeting it. He risks his time, energy, assets and cash to ignite a new business based on the value he believes his idea has to offer customers. Luck, daring and effort pay off: consumers grasp that value and respond.

Now, because the product is unique, the entrepreneur enjoys an early monopoly. He or she is in the "sweet spot." This advantage endures for just as long as the entrepreneur's product *remains* uniquely responsive to the market, at least one innovation ahead of its competition.

Usually, though, the advantage does not go on forever. The entrepreneur's strong position inevitably attracts competitors. Several things can happen then.

A company's growth may stabilize and its profits shrink, as competitors join an increasingly mature market for commodified products. The management advantage in that kind of situation goes to the sharp administrator who can expand margins on the bottom end, by driving costs down. That is not the forte of the entrepreneur, who is temperamentally always in pursuit of the next source of monopoly margins by innovating.

The company may even lose its ability to innovate; if that happens, the market passes it by. It will go the way of resistant buggy-whip makers in 1910 and typewriter manufacturers in 1985.

Or another company may decide it is more efficient to *buy* market share or unique technical competency than *build* it—and make you an offer.

The business press is full of examples of companies that failed to make the first transition, from the intuitive executive style of an entrepreneurial founder to the standardized, academic style of professional managers. Bankruptcy courts and liquidation sales process the remains of companies that lost (or never found) their footing in the marketplace.

Entrepreneurial companies invariably rest on the spirit, ambitions, vision and energy of their founders. As these individuals get older (yes, it happens), their interest and priorities may change, even if their energy does not begin to ebb. At some point, a prudent entrepreneur begins to consider his exit strategy.

Staying on with CMQ or its new owners in any permanent way was out of the question. I was too accustomed to running things my way. I had felt the friction and poor fit of the corporate bridle on my impulses during my unhappy period as a part-time employee of GTE. I had no wish to relive it, let alone wear that bridle off into the proverbial sunset.

I was already two years past the age when convention says Canadians should begin collecting pensions and take up golfing five days a week. It was certainly time to step away from the day-to-day intensity and drain of fielding every executive decision that needed to be made. Was it time to "retire"?

As a final score summing up my business career, the figure $100 million makes a nice round number. All the more so when it is set alongside what Vivian and I started with, forty-two years earlier: a $2,000 debt. For the very first time, that hungry, eager, Depression-era boy inside me began to relax, just a little, into the unfamiliar feeling of financial security.

Not that I received all of that money. The value of the transaction included payouts that made millionaires of several engineers who had held shares in the company. And a distastefully long list of other fees, charges and deductions, including a substantial tax bill, further reduced what was due to my account.

That still left me with something more than two-thirds of the transaction value of CMQ's sale in liquid funds. It was enough to support some interesting possibilities.

By the time Vivian and I joined the rest of our fellow travellers for a tour of U.S. museums at the end of that eventful week, I had no detailed vision of the next phase of my business life. I just knew there *would be* a next phase. The capital generated from CMQ's sale would need to go to work.

I no longer had the energy for the exhausting, endless, unconditional commitment required to found a new enterprise from scratch and see it through to maturity. But I never lost the appetite. I had no confidence in the fund managers who invest other people's money in investment pools; they must necessarily limit their investment choices to whatever is acceptable to the average of their unitholders.

But I could no more become some other kind of man than I could change my sense of humour. I could see the world only one way, through the eyes of an entrepreneurial personality. Opportunity would not stop leaping out at me just because I no longer had a driving need to chase it down.

In general terms, I was determined to use at least some of the proceeds of CMQ's sale to back some of these opportunities. Now, however, it would be someone else, someone younger, out on the ice. I would coach from the bench. But I hated it.

▌▌ JUST AS EVERYTHING changed, and nothing changed, when I walked back into our offices (then in Montreal) after buying back CMQ, so nothing and everything changed after its sale in Toronto to Dow Jones.

The shift was apparent within days of my return from our brief holiday. I was still, nominally, in charge, but most people in the organization understood they no longer needed to come to me for permission or advice.

The sense of personal loss ran deeper than this erosion of power and authority. An entrepreneur must invest inordinate amounts of himself in his business in order to bring it from dream to fruition. Inevitably, the two identities become bound up. CMQ was mine, yes, but it was also *me,* and *I* was CMQ.

Just as inevitably, the rupture of this happy union of self and enterprise takes some adjustment. I had the money, but I no longer had a professional identity. What do you say to a casual acquaintance who asks, "And what do *you* do?" You can hardly go on long saying, "I used to be president of a big company." It took many months for me to entirely get used to the idea that I was merely David M. Campbell, ordinary citizen.

Most substantially, we had to vacate the Royal Bank Tower quarters we had occupied for over a decade. Before the transition year ended I would need to find another office for at least myself and any of my staff who stayed with me.

With the help of my friend and long-time legal counsel, George Whelan, I developed a plan for disposition of the returns from CMQ's sale.

Among the things Vivian and I did was to endow a foundation. Subject to Canadian law, the David and Vivian Campbell Family Foundation would donate 80 per cent of the annual return earned on the principal to charitable projects, while adding to that base from other funds over time.

I still owned The Beeper People, and I put some of what I had received into portfolio investments. With most of what was left we capitalized a brand new company. At the age of sixty-seven, with half a dozen entrepreneurial cycles under my belt, I was setting out again on a new beginning.

Tricaster Holdings* would be both old and new to me. For the first time, I planned to invest in existing, operating businesses in whose managements we had confidence and would largely leave alone. I planned, however, to seek these investments in the new and emerging communications technologies that have fascinated me ever since I assembled my first crystal-set AM radio.

As always I would look for ventures in which our investment could help bring to market some *new* product; preferably, one with a potential for *recurring revenue* as well as *"monopoly premium" margins.*

The strategic objective was to protect our capital base while we investigated new opportunities, seizing those with promise. The new company came to life in early 1989.

It was a propitious time for new beginnings. The lethal wall that had encircled Berlin since 1961 was seen coming down on global television. With its fall, the curtain was drawn on a "cold" nuclear standoff that had divided the world even longer. In Russia and China, central planners turned their economies over to entrepreneurs and free enterprise. In the west, most governments embraced a "get out of the way" philosophy that favoured business innovation.

Although almost no one outside the computer community was then aware of it, something called the Internet extended its network past 100,000 hosts in 1989. The next year the first commercial "service provider" would bring the amorphous "cyberscape" to the first retail subscribers. The year after that, Tim Berners-Lee would release software creating something he called the "World Wide Web."

At the end of the Second World War, demographics and technology utterly transformed North America, presenting its citizens with unexpected new threats and immense opportunities. Now these two turn-of- the-twenty-first-century forces—the global triumph of markets and the dawning of the "information" economy—would do the same. Together, they would propel the continent over a decade of scarcely

---

*   George Whelan suggested the name; it plays on our trio of sons (Tri-) and the French (*castor*) for "beaver," not only Canada's national animal but the name of the street, Beaver Hall Hill, where CMQ had been headquartered in Montreal.

interrupted growth until "irrational exuberance" for the "new paradigm" began to erode judgements, and investors began mistaking tulips for real wealth assets.

THERE MUST BE A jungle telegraph among businesses that are looking for those relatively rare individuals willing to put their personal wealth behind someone else's ambitions with no guarantees. It did not take long after Tricaster hung out its shingle for deals to emerge.

My judgements had changed since the days when I was new to business. Then, decisions seemed easy. I had nothing to lose, except perhaps my credit rating—and even that I had needed to establish before it could be lost.

I still had the Type E individual's ability to become enthused by an idea. Just as I had done as a salesman-buyer at Melody House all those years ago, and had learned to do with art, I now had to learn to say no to a deal that, in my mind, was ill-conceived.

And now that there was real money on the table, it was also often much harder to make a risk decision. I knew exactly what I could lose. I needed to develop new criteria for making a commitment.

Inspired by the discipline I had observed in the Molson brothers long ago, we set a limit on Tricaster's involvement in any single venture. This would contain our risk should any one play fail; it protected the capital base. But it also obliged us to take a pass on a number of attractive propositions. One we let go of only reluctantly would have placed us at the helm of the world's leading duplicator of music CDs—at the cost of $23 million.

We turned down countless other proposals that failed the test of "new, different, *unique*." An office-supply company sought our investment to move into refilling printer cartridges; they wanted to acquire a running concern doing $2 million in business. But there was nothing proprietary about the device used to refill the cartridges. Anyone with $100,000 could buy one of them and join the party. Pass.

In other cases we didn't like the approach or priorities of the management. Business ideas with potential outnumbered the available entrepreneurial individuals we could find to develop them. Nobody, it seemed, felt it necessary to start modestly, to *make the first dollar* for their company before it began paying them gold-plated CEO salaries.

We also met many deals we liked. Not all turned out to be home runs. But the essence of the entrepreneur's way is risk. Things don't break your way all the time.

IV TWO GREAT NETWORKS, both unknown to all but a very few Canadians as recently as 1990, have since come to define the new century's communications landscape: *wireless telephony* and the *Internet*. It was the cost of building out the infrastructure for these two networks that drove most of the "tech" frenzy of the late 1990s. The madness that seized stock markets in that era was really over "telecommunications" more than technologies in general. Companies like WorldCom, 360 Networks and America Online became insanely overvalued.

Some of the more fanciful expectations proved ill-founded, but many technologies that still seemed like science fiction a decade and a half ago are now on the hips of every teenager (camera-phones that E-mail pictures to pals). And if the great "new paradigm" of "E-business" did not, in fact, mean that profit no longer mattered, it did truly open up immense new opportunities to create customer value and entrepreneurial wealth (eBay, Amazon, Expedia).

My reading, still voracious, kept me abreast of developments in both fields. When the Canadian government issued a call in 1992 for proposals to establish cellular telephone services in the country, on what was called the "PCST" standard, Tricaster leaped at the opportunity.

We created a new company called Telezone Corporation. To provide cash flow and expertise in a related technology, we vended The Beeper People, the paging company I had begun thirty years earlier, into the new company. Late that year, we were one of four Canadian companies granted licences to launch the country's first cellular phone services. With little difficulty we secured firm commitments from equipment vendors, financiers, landlords and strategic service partners. With everything in place, we began to implement our build-out plan in Toronto, Montreal and Vancouver.

Then Ottawa changed the rules. Responsibility for cellphones was shifted to a new federal department. Industry Canada, after reviewing the file, decided that PCST format wireless was becoming the international Betamax of cellphones. It was to be abandoned in favour of a new format, "PCS."

Industry Canada indicated that it might issue as many as six licences for the new standard. Preference would go to proponents that could demonstrate "experience" in the industry. How this experience was to be gained, given that the industry did not yet exist in Canada, was not explained.

Undeterred, and still keen to play a role in this new generation of communications, Tricaster recruited a gold-plated team of partners for the Telezone bid. U.S. giants Bell Atlantic Corporation and AirTouch Communications—both with experience in PCS technology—came in as minority participants.

With the work we had already done, everything was in place for a quick rollout of service. We had addressed every criterion the government had set for its selection of the winning bids. According to the handicappers in the trade press and business pages, Telezone's mix of technology, backers and experience made it the bid to beat.

Then Ottawa changed the rules again. First, Industry Canada limited the number of licences it was going to grant to four—holding two in escrow. Word leaked out that the criteria for selection among the bidders were being revised. "Experience" was no longer considered so critical. Being Canadian was suddenly the make-or-break quality. Competing bidders, we learned, were calling the regulator's attention to our *American* minority partners.

Was it for that reason alone that Telezone did not end up among the final four in the winners' circle when the licences were handed out? I cannot say. It was certainly a major disappointment to us (although our expertise continued to be validated by the number of large financial, hardware and telecommunications companies that subsequently sought our advice on subjects ranging from rolling out PCs to business strategies for new wireless product).

With our progress blocked, we decided to exit the wireless business entirely and in 1996 we closed Telezone at a substantial loss and sold The Beeper People (which continued to the end to operate at a profit) to Bell Mobility.

The experience only deepened my distaste, since disposing of my remaining shares in Cable TV, for the unpredictable and opaque operating environment of a regulated industry. Given a choice, I would always prefer to do business in an arena not tightly overseen by bureaucrats. When it hangs by the thread of a regulator's decision, you never know how secure your franchise really is.

When it rests on strong customer demand for your—and specifically *your*—product, you have less to worry about.

THE SAME CANADIAN telecom regulators gave a green light to another new industry in the 1990s: what they called, in bureaucratic jargon, "Competitive Local Exchange Carriers" (CLECs). The 'C' in their name distinguished these from so-called Incumbent Local Exchange Carriers, or ILECs.

Behind the acronym soup, the decision really meant that independent companies with new approaches (CLECs) were allowed for the first time to compete with traditional regional-monopoly phone companies (ILECs), to sell local and long-distance voice, data and Internet service to organizations large enough to need them.

With our background in data networks and the work we had been doing in wireless, satellite and market-data networking, we thought we saw opportunity here. In 1998 we created Combined Telecom Incorporated (CTI) to go after medium-to-large organizations that are heavy users of the entire mix of telecommunications services: universities, health centres and hospitals, and the financial-services sector we knew well. To run it, we recruited an executive who had led Lucent Technologies Canada (a networking spinoff formerly part of AT&T) to 600-per-cent growth over six years.

At a sales presentation one day, I ran into someone I knew from Bell. We started talking and I described Tricaster's latest venture.

"You guys have expertise we don't," he conceded. "You know, there's business we know we won't get. But there's business we don't want to lose, either. Maybe we should do something together."

As a result of the conversation, CTI entered into what the Bell people referred to as a "channel partnership" with Bell's Nexxia unit (a marketing ploy in which the old monopoly was hoping to behave like a C-LEC rather than an I-LEC). CTI was supposed to get preferred access to Bell's networks and expertise, as well as sales referrals, in return for dividing up the market between it and Nexxia. Nexxia wanted to go after the "whale" accounts—provincial government departments and the very largest enterprises. CTI was to have a clear run at the rest.

True to our expectations, CTI quickly began to find a footing. The University of Toronto, whose academics and administrators log millions of phone calls, data transfers and Internet transactions a year, took CTI's service for a pilot of 100 lines. That number quickly grew to 1,400. Down the street, Mount Sinai Hospital was looking at Combined Telecom for a system of nearly 5,000 lines. This was beginning to look good.

Then it began to look even better. The University of Toronto informed CTI that it was invited to bid on the entire campus—all 19,000 lines!

That was when the people at Bell blew a gasket. "You're moving too fast!" Bell objected. Only to a corporation could that be a bad thing. Evidently Nexxia had not been faring quite as well in its pursuit of "whales." Forty-eight hours later Bell called again. Its unit was going to violate the "channel partnership" agreement with CTI and move down the food chain: "We're going to quote against you."

There was no escaping Bell's intention to win the bid, at any cost. We consulted legal counsel but the consensus was disheartening. CTI had a strong case for breach of contract; Bell had much, much more money. We might well win—if we wanted to spend a decade or so in court. We didn't.

In the end, we abandoned that field to the "incumbent." Sometimes it is just too difficult to take on the big boys, unless you have something they need and cannot replicate.

V MY ATTITUDE REMAINED at all times proprietary—and active. I thought of companies we invested in as *our* companies, at least in part. They were all still in their start-up phases. They were shooting for that sweet arc on the high side of the entrepreneurial cycle where they might hope to reap monopoly-premium margins. When their managers missed opportunities that stood out in neon to a Type E observer, I wanted to wade in and correct them.

AS ENGAGED AS I was in Tricaster's activities, I no longer needed to be around the office every day. There was more time than I had ever had in my life before for outside interests. Of these, two absorbed most of my energies and ultimately went hand in hand. And does it surprise you to learn that when they did, they also brought my Type E instincts back into high alert?

Buying art, placing works in one of our homes, appreciating and occasionally selling them were long-standing passions for both Vivian and myself. Since being invited into the Toronto Symphony family, we had also expanded our involvement in other active philanthropy.

Vivian and I like people; we always have. Our involvement in amateur theatre in Montreal, the lively exchange of parties thrown and attended during our Vermont summers: these had always been at the centre of our lives away from my work. Now we often found the same social pleasure and unexpectedly interesting encounters at benefits for the symphony or at meetings of the board of the Canadian Stage Company. Often, we made our home available for events in support of those or other organizations.

Not everyone at these events was another wealthy donor being courted for a contribution. We met all kinds of interesting people: professional artists, international performers, people who care deeply about things.

The David and Vivian Campbell Family Foundation responded to projects in areas where *we* cared. Sometimes that was for personal reasons. We knew someone who had died of cancer and we helped fund a palliative-care facility in his name. Yo-Yo Ma, whom we met through the symphony, recruited us to join other donors in realizing his dream of a music garden on the Toronto waterfront. Many of our opportunities to donate arose from connections in the art, museum and university communities.

Those had deepened greatly during the 1980s. We became life members of the Royal Ontario Museum. I served on the board of the Art Gallery of Ontario and as its chairman. As my business schedule lightened, I joined the board of the University of Toronto's Art Centre. Vivian and I became senior fellows at Massey College and I chaired the advisory council to the U. of T. School of Graduate Studies.

Entrepreneurial thinking can be applied beyond business. Our foundation employed its *leverage* at every opportunity to amplify the effect of its contributions.

As a result of my involvement with University of Toronto graduate studies, the dean of that program approached me one day. Knowing my interest in collecting, he thought I might be receptive to the university's desire to extend its graduate-level museum studies program. The university was looking for as close to $1 million as it could find. The interest on this sum, $40,000 or $50,000 a year, would allow aspiring scholars in art and antiquities to intern at any museum in the world for a couple of months after graduation.

Wisely, the dean was not seeking the entire million from our foundation. The provincial government of the day was willing to match any private contribution; the university itself would do the same. Thus, our $300,000 donation would trigger a fund totalling $900,000—close enough to the million, in the dean's eye.

The time-payment principle that brought the very first piece of art, that vivid Robert Pilot seascape, into our home more than fifty years ago now has been just as effective extending our philanthropic reach.

After nearly suffocating through a summer conference at Massey College, one day I cornered its master, John Fraser, and said, "This place should be air-conditioned!" He sighed his agreement. Then I said: "Let me know what it would cost."

Fraser did some investigating and gave me a call a few days later. Air conditioning the college would cost $350,000 plus. That was significantly more than the foundation's yearly income, but by breaking the project into parts and spreading our contributions over several months—in a word, *leveraging* our contribution over time—we managed it.

There is a hazard to becoming identified as a donor. Fundraisers are nearly as ruthless as the barracudas of the stock market. Just as with the deals that walked in the door daily at Tricaster, I had to learn to say no, with a polite explanation. I quickly developed a reply that effectively forestalled the frivolous and impatient: I informed them that the foundation was fully committed for the next X number of months and that we would not be able to look at their project until our current obligations were met. It was always true, too.

There is a tremendous satisfaction in being in a position to make significant contributions to your community. Given my insatiable curiosity and interest in new ideas, there is the considerable fringe benefit of meeting so many people at the top of their respective fields in the arts, sciences and business. But let us be honest, there is also a dimension of ego gratification to philanthropy. Vivian and I prefer to associate our names with projects that are especially close to our hearts.

The Vivian and David Campbell Conference Facility is a room off the courtyard at the University of Toronto's Munk Centre for International Studies, just across the street from Massey College. Natural panelling and light lend the place a contemplative tranquillity, but to call this a "room" is like calling a personal computer a "box." The modular, movable desks conceal state-of-the-art microphones, recording, video-conference and satellite feeds. Leather armchairs can be arranged to accommodate confidential negotiators in a close circle, or a public audience of 150 in theatre format.

Scientists and social activists from around the globe used the facility to talk about saving the planet. Academics from Europe, North America and Australia met there to examine how globalism is affecting cultures. International historians and archaeologists met and video-conferenced there to assess how much damage various wars and postwar looting have done to the store of antiquities lodged in the Persian Gulf.

The Vivian and David Campbell Gallery at the Art Gallery of Ontario is a quite different room. Where the conference facility is a space waiting for people, the cool chamber deep within the art gallery meets its visitors through the changing exhibitions to which its intimate space is dedicated. In 2003, for example, it was home to a collection of portraiture: the bold glance and flaming red hair of the millionaire Marchesa Casati, captured by Jacob Epstein's brush in 1918; the French poet Baudelaire, sculpted in marble and looking a little like that oval-eyed "alien" character.

Art and philanthropy intersected in other ways, as well. Over the years we had assembled a respectable number of woodblock prints by Edvard Munch, best known for his famous *The Scream*. In 1997 we placed that collection on loan to the Art Gallery of Ontario and helped it arrange the additional loan of one of only four known oil versions of *The Scream*. One reviewer rhapsodized that the exhibition the gallery mounted of the Norwegian's work was a critic's "fantasy come true." This show travelled later to several other North American museums.

Another artist whose work we liked and accumulated was the English silversmith Omar Ramsden. Our collection of his silver travelled the States as part of an exhibition mounted by the Smithsonian Institution.

We also met some fascinating people. The opportunity to mix with professional museum managers, curators and acquisitions officers both broadened and deepened our half-century love affair with art. Sooner or later, it was bound to trigger my entrepreneurial reflexes.

People who know I have bought a lot of art often ask me, "If I pay this much money for a work of art, is there a guarantee I will get my money back?"
I tell them, "No. There is never a guarantee. If you buy it, it will be three years, at least, before you can expect to see the price come back to what you paid.

"If you hold on to it, it may be worth more in twenty years' time and you may make something." Or again, you may not. Markets change.

But if you chose it in the first place because you liked it, you will always enjoy it over the years.

If the market determines that your choice deserves a premium many years later, then you will receive an added bonus.

VIVIAN AND I HAD, by the early 1990s, acquired hundreds of individual works. As well as a major collection of Ettore Sottsass's Italian glasswork, majolica porcelain and antiquities, we had many drawings and paintings bought simply on their individual merit. Apart from special occasions such as the Munch or Ramsden exhibitions, we kept most of these where we could enjoy them—with us in Toronto, at the Vermont house or the place in Florida.

As the value and number of the pieces we were buying grew, it became necessary to think more seriously about them. My understanding of the fickleness and unreliability of the art market became more sophisticated. Once again I learned the truth that *Things are seldom what they seem.*

Gilbert and Sullivan's warning is especially worth noting for connoisseurs of art. Not every great artist signed every one of his or her works. Even experts have changed their minds about which unsigned oils are really Rembrandt's and which not. Honest errors apart, plenty of out-and-out forgeries are almost indistinguishable from authentic works. (I stopped collecting Russian enamels when I discovered there was a jeweller in Brooklyn turning out eggs better than Fabergé's.) And even when a work is truly by the attributed artist, it may or may not be the legal property of the vendor. Robbing graves for artifacts and black markets in stolen art are as old as civilization.

Since 1969 the International Foundation of Art Research (IFAR), a non-profit organization based in New York, has worked to call attention to these problems. In the 1980s I was invited to join its board to further its efforts to contain and deter the circulation of forged, misattributed or misappropriated art. It left me aghast to learn that thousands of known, identifiable works of art were still missing around the world. Most of them, in all likelihood, are in the hands of unscrupulous collectors.

In 1991 IFAR was encouraged to associate itself with the London-based Art Loss Register, which records reports of stolen art and maintains a database where buyers can check the status of a prospective purchase. It also works with law enforcement officers investigating art thefts or seeking the legitimate owners of seized art. IFAR turned its database over to the Art Loss Register, sharply enhancing the resources at its disposal. Since then the register has identified more than US$100 million in recovered stolen artworks. Still, it continues to register an average of 10,000 newly stolen items yearly!

AS THE TURN OF the millennium approached, I faced my eightieth birthday. With Tricaster, yet another entrepreneurial cycle had been added to the chain begun on that day when I first realized I could buy scribblers from the supplier and sell them to my classmates for less than the corner store.

I had been twelve then. Television was still an experiment in someone's lab. Detergent didn't exist, nor automatic washing machines. Cable television was not yet even a wild idea; nor was the Internet. My bedroom was the hallway of our apartment over Mother's beauty salon, where I slept ready for a quick getaway at 4:30 each morning to my paper route.

Now we had Picassos on our walls.

It had been a wonderful, amazing, unlikely ride. But perhaps it was time to look ahead. Realism, too, is an entrepreneurial attribute.

CHAPTER 13

STILL **CRAZY**
(AFTER ALL THESE YEARS)

"Birthdays are good for you. The more you have, the longer you live."

ANON.

I RAN INTO A woman at a reception recently. "Mr. Campbell," she said, "I recognize you." I didn't recognize her. "And I've got a bone to pick with you."

My guard went up. I searched my memory for some link to this woman, who seemed nearly as old as I am. She fixed a determined look on me. "You sold me a stove fifty years ago."

Good Lord. "Really?"

"Yes. And just the other day... I had to *throw it out!*"

The woman finally broke into a merry smile. I relaxed. Funny, at age eighty-four I can still be thrown off-balance by the idea that a customer might not be entirely satisfied. One interpretation might be that my focus on the customer forty years ago is still earning returns in goodwill today, long after that business passed out of existence.

It is now almost sixty years since we opened the door for our first day of business at Dave Campbell's Melody House. In reviewing the decades since, from a vantage point inevitably closer to the end than the beginning, it is impossible to avoid regret entirely.

Are there deals I would do differently in retrospect? Of course. I would never have given my engineers at CMQ the opportunity to hold up its sale by declining to tender their employee shares, for one thing. But that's one of the funny things about how a Type E thinks: We don't remember our failures very well.

We do try to learn from our mistakes, not to repeat whatever went wrong. But we don't think of them as any reason why the *next* venture shouldn't be a success. Indeed, we're likely to think the very opposite. Knowing what I do now, my chances next time should be even better.

It's the same natural optimism that encourages a Type E individual to seize an untried "crazy idea" and run with it, even when other types around us find ample reasons why it shouldn't work.

Plenty of businesses fail, including some of mine. But those of my crazy ideas that *did* work turned a borrowed $2,000 into a company worth millions.

Initiative is necessary, but it's not everything. I had also chosen good businesses to be in. The entrepreneur has an economic principle in his corner. Give people a solution to a problem and they will try it. If the solution is effective, the product will find a market. If it is also *unique,* the vendor will reap "monopoly premium" margins—for as long as the product remains unique.

After Melody House, I chose always to be in businesses where I could introduce improvements to our products at minimal cost. Certainly there were costs to maintaining and improving our networks at both Cable TV and Combined Market Quotations. But, unlike the retail trade, I could introduce service upgrades—closed-circuit hockey games, embedded commission calculations—and not be stuck with a bunch of obsolete appliances to sell at a discount.

That these businesses shared the capacity to dominate their respective markets was one attraction. Cable TV acquired a geographic monopoly territory backed by a government licence. CMQ won 82 per cent of its market by delivering exclusive market data and user functions.

A further attraction was that both enterprises produced *recurring revenue.* Once our networks were largely in place, we enjoyed high margins, reliable cash flow and regular opportunity with each billing cycle to contact our customers with offers of new services or to solicit feedback.

Certainly, money has meant security to me since my childhood. Then, *lack* of money meant chronic *in*security, even for a ten-year-old. Since disposing of cmq I have, almost, shaken off the fear that drives many Type Es, that somehow someone or something will take it all away and I will find myself once again scrambling for *the first dollar.*

> "I don't want to achieve immortality through my work. I want to achieve immortality through not dying." **WOODY ALLEN, FILMMAKER AND WRITER**

NEVER BE SHY to take profit. But wouldn't life's satisfactions be dry if they ended with a number followed by a lot of zeros? Cash may provide the score at the end of the game, but it's not the reason most of us play.

For the entrepreneur, no hobby is more thrilling or compelling than seizing upon a business opportunity and making it real. The talents demanded are so varied, the unexpected challenge from left field so routine, the scope of the enterprise so open and the chances of failure or success so directly in one's own hands—what is not to like?

Perhaps, for some people, a lot. There are timid individuals who find it frightening to take responsibility. They may actively prefer to earn less, doing a more limited task but leaving decisions to others. And of course many people have passions as powerful as the Type E's for creating value in other ways: repairing injured bodies; painting (be it pictures or houses); awakening young minds in a classroom; erecting bridges.

The entrepreneur is less of a specialist. I was in business for most of my life in the fields of electronics and communications. Other entrepreneurs never strayed far from selling hamburgers, growing hothouse flowers or cleaning drapes and carpets. Yet it is rare to hear an entrepreneur say that any specific knowledge of their product leads the reasons for their success.

Of course, you do need to know your business—intimately. But knowledge alone is never as powerful as knowing what to do with it and *having the initiative to use it.* Successful entrepreneurship is a matter of what *you* bring to the party, not what's on the buffet table.

Quite a few sources have sought to enumerate the attributes of the winning Type E.* Many of these lists start with "drive" or "ambition."

Some of my own motivation doubtless came from the deprivations of a Depression childhood, yet not everyone who went through the Dirty Thirties emerged an entrepreneur. I credit my parents. They strove constantly for a better life. My father's perseverance and my mother's initiative imbued me with those basic values. I learned the all-important first principle that *I* am responsible for making my own way—and no one else is—from a schoolyard gang on a long-ago afternoon in a Fredericton alley.

The long, bare decade of the thirties ingrained other qualities that people who study these things associate with self-made Type Es. Frugality heads that list. There is nothing like the memory of literally counting pennies to see if you have enough to join the other fellows for a fountain soda to make you attentive to the little leaks and wastages that can later sink a company.

In my adolescence, many of my friends' families enjoyed much more money than my own. I associated the easy acquisition of enviable possessions, the peace of mind and unrestricted opportunity these friends enjoyed, with financial wealth. That link between money, success and security became forged and fixed in my thinking.

The fundamental concept of profit came to me at an early age. Whatever I failed to absorb in class, I understood that if I bought a scribbler from the wholesaler for two cents and sold it for five, I was coming out ahead. Thereafter, I was always looking for that gap between what it cost me to do something and what someone else would pay me to do it. The desperate urgency to *make the first dollar* at every chance strongly encouraged my antennae for opportunity, another essential facet of the Type E.

---

* For one example, see Elena Fawkner's article "Entrepreneurship," reproduced with permission in the appendix to this book.

A lack of money is no reason to neglect your curiosity. Both my parents and my faith insisted on the value of learning. I not only delivered newspapers, I also read them. The money I earned from my teenage enterprises bought me sodas, but also the crystal, wires, resistors and other "breadboard" parts to make my own "ham" radio, as well as magazines and books.

I remain a sponge for new information to this day. I don't care where it comes from: Forbes, the Internet, a magazine at the dentist, a chance acquaintance over canapés at a cocktail reception, the woman who serves soup in the mall below my office. Everybody knows something of interest, certainly something new to me.

Is it new? Is it true? Does it fit with something else I know? These are the questions that go through the Type E mind relentlessly and reflexively. Does some tidbit of information over *here* marry up with some critical gap over *there* and provide a *unique* answer to some *need?* Thinking this way led me to the technology that much later made possible Cable TV Limited and Combined Market Quotations Incorporated.

Wartime experience knocked home other entrepreneurial attitudes that experts have come to identify with success in founding a business. From high school I stepped into the thick of an arms, technology and production race between Allied aircraft builders and those in Germany. Innovation was more than a motivational motto. The "competition" was racing for its life as hard as we were—and it really *did* want to kill us.

Discovering and implementing new, better and faster ways of building faster, more powerful bombers, fighters and trainer aircraft was a matter of life and death for our flyers—and freedom for all of us. No idea was too "crazy" to consider. No brilliant idea was worth a second thought if it couldn't be put into action "pronto."

The experience reinforced both my forward-looking instincts and real-world pragmatism. It drove home the instinctive sense that whatever we are doing *today* is not good enough. There is never a moment to lose in finding some way to improve on it. At the same time, pouring too many resources into too distant a goal may deprive you of a more achievable opportunity.

The same years confronted us with the reality that *risk is everyday.* Not every airplane that takes off comes gliding back to a three-point landing. Don Quinn's marvellous wit would not be returning to Montreal for another curtain call.

Risk isn't something unique to the entrepreneur. Risk is getting up in the morning. It is, again, a question of what you *do* with the risk. Some people spend their lives dodging and minimizing it. The Type E embraces it. He regards risk as the Chinese regard crisis in their calligraphy: it is the presence of danger with the presence of opportunity.

By the time Vivian and I plunged into Melody House, I had had plenty of practice working hard and not watching the clock. Another oft-noted entrepreneurial attribute is a high energy level. That's another way of saying you'd better be willing to work as hard as it takes, for as many hours as it takes, for as many days in a row as it takes, to get your venture off the ground. My experience was anything but unique: *most* businesses begin to prosper only after their founder has put in many years of unpaid work.

You will only do that, of course, if your passion for the undertaking matches your general drive for success. If it felt like "working" all day, every day, you would never stick with it. What would be the point? For that kind of drudgery, a fellow might as well skip the risk and get a "job."

To the Type E, of course, juggling all these balls at once is what you'd do in your spare time even if you *weren't* being paid for it. "Work, to entrepreneurs," it has been observed, "is play."

Vivian and I were babes in the woods with that first business; we knew nothing. We tried things. Some of them worked, some didn't. Any that worked went down as a success; anything that didn't was taken as a lesson. Some people let their mistakes weigh them down. "*Failure, to an entrepreneur,*" says one list of qualities, "*is nothing more than an opportunity waiting to be discovered.*"

The same list notes that Type Es are adept at "resource utilization," meaning they "utilize ALL their available resources." The emphasis, present in the original, is striking. My mother's insurance policy;

Decca's veiled semi-serious promise of shellac records; Melody House's inventory; cable access to Quebec Hydro poles; the Molson brothers' connections with the Montreal Canadiens; my own knowledge of networks; the installed base of CMQ terminals in dozens of traders' offices across the country: over the years I leveraged all of these and more to extend the reach of what I could accomplish in business.

Risk is everyday. So is change. And, like risk, change is an alloy of danger and opportunity. The Type E embraces both for the same reason: they represent potential profit. Stockbrokers are discounting their commissions all of a sudden? Make it easy for them, and charge them a few cents for the facility.

The entrepreneur bridles at the word "can't." Confined in the straitjacket of GTE's corporate supervision, I chafed mightily until I finally bought back my freedom of executive action.

Rash impulsivity, on the other hand, can lead to disaster. Nursing an idea from spark to flame demands realism about the circumstances and environment. Do the research. Prepare for the obvious contingencies; that will give you more time and resources to deal with the inevitable *unexpected* ones.

Deadlines, goals and targets, routine reviews of every process: these aren't just for rule-bound corporations. I signed *every* cheque, questioned *every* unjustified charge and rewarded *performance,* not hours on the clock. Thinking outside the box doesn't mean you let chaos reign *inside* it.

Some founders manage to stay afloat, for a little while at least, without paying regular attention to their receivables and payables. They can usually do this only so long as their business generates such profuse margins that they can afford the running drain of inevitable waste. That kind of luck seldom lasts. Most entrepreneurs will find they need their bookkeeping to be rigorously businesslike or they will quickly no longer be in business at all.

Still, the Type E is the maverick loner of the business family. I prized being able to hold executive committee meetings with the mirror in the office john. I never regretted it, but autonomy, like everything else, comes with a price. Sometimes the loner also feels a little lonely. The singular responsibility of making a big decision entirely on your own, with scores of other people's livelihoods on the line, can weigh heavily. The habit of making all the tough calls yourself can also invite a misplaced arrogance, especially if you make more than half of them somewhere near right.

Some Type Es who keep their moral bearings through the difficult uncertainties of establishing a new enterprise are brought down by the temptations that become available once it is a roaring success. I was fortunate to enjoy the company of sociable people and to have found early in life a compatible woman who shared that enjoyment. It took a weight crisis to remind me that fitness, a more balanced life and sustainable pace are all important to one's productivity. It took somewhat longer to implement all those lessons in my activities.

Corporations are beginning to revise their enthusiasm for the professionalizing of management. "In the 1990s," one technology recruiter said, "our typical client wanted its CEO to be a bright, young up-and-comer with an M.B.A. from a good school. Today, real-world experience is far more important."

One thing about an M.B.A., of course: it's easy enough to acquire. If you can pass the entrance requirements, raise the $60,000 and devote two years to the project you, too, can have one.

The same cannot be said for an entrepreneurial temperament. In the last fifteen to twenty years, academies and researchers have begun to recognize and try to isolate the Type E essence, the entrepreneurial "spirit." Many M.B.A. curricula, I notice, include sections on "entrepreneurship." But the academics are frustrated in their efforts to replicate the entrepreneur. I recently ran into a professor from a leading graduate business school at lunch. He recognized my name, but it seemed to provoke his dismay. "I know you're an entrepreneur," he said. Then he confided: "I teach in the business school, and one of our biggest problems is, how does one *teach* entrepreneurship?"

Do not look in the genes. My father was no Type E. Yet entrepreneurs arise in Nature all the time. The world is full of them. Walk down any commercial street in any country you choose outside North Korea and you will find legions of Type Es selling cellphones and hot noodles, doughnuts and sea cruises, tax shelters and packaged liquor.

And, like other personality types: once a Type E, always one.

IN THE PAST YEAR, I have brought the latest of my businesses to the conclusion of its entrepreneurial cycle, disposing of Tricaster Holdings' remaining assets. It is a reflection of the entrepreneurial temperament perhaps, that I have found it much harder to downsize than to build.

The "latest" business. I won't yet say "the last." I am an optimist but not, I hope, a fool. Eighty-four is eighty-four. Sooner or later there are some eventualities more inevitable than taxes that must be contemplated.

A New Yorker named William Zabel made some interesting observations about men and their "last will and testament":

> Fear of death, inability to quantify loving relationships in terms of one's property and repression of anger over loss of power and control are but a few of the many reasons why men do not make wills. . . . The will-making experience should be a healthy and open confrontation with a man's true feelings about himself, his death, his property and the persons and causes he loves.

Death is just another change. It presents its own opportunities. A will is one prudent way of taking advantage of them, but there are others.

I am still a voracious reader, although lately I have given up the electronic journals and even most of the art catalogues for the Income Tax Act. Its provisions for handling the transfer of assets are worth understanding.

In Canada, unlike the United States, you can give anyone any amount of money, or an asset worth any amount of money, at any time, without confronting the *recipient* with an automatic tax bill. *You,* on the other hand, *may* face such a bill. If the gift is contained in your will, the tax due will be charged to your estate before it is disbursed.

That won't happen if the gift is cash: the Canada Revenue Agency presumes you have already paid tax on the money at its source. But if the gift is a non-cash *asset*—stock certificates, a vacation property, a vintage

Mustang, a Matisse—the law treats it as though you sold the asset when you gave it away. If it is worth more on the day you gave it away than on the day you acquired it, you have experienced a capital gain (even if you did not realize it) and the agency wants the tax due on that gain.

Many assets can be expected to appreciate in value over the years. For that reason, it may save your estate (and your inheritors) substantial tax liabilities to give a bequest to someone *before* you die, rather than in your will. Even if you don't own a Matisse or a vintage Mustang, this is something more people should think about.

Why? First, because the actuaries tell us that Canada is about to go through one of the most massive transfers of wealth from one generation to the next in its history. A wider understanding of the foregoing facts could keep billions of dollars' worth of "inheritance" in the hands of families instead of government.

And, secondly, there's a business here for the individual with the entrepreneurial vision to see it.

If a gift is a *financial* asset—a stock, bond, foreign currency or other security—its value, either when you acquired it or on the day you give it to someone else, is easy to establish. Just check the market prices for the security on the two dates; the difference is the taxable gain (or loss).

Things get trickier when assets are real and valuable but not traded on well-reported markets like those for stocks or bonds. A collection of comic books, acquired for dimes and nickels over the years at lawn sales, may now be worth many thousands of dollars—but how do you prove it? If you, or your estate, cannot establish, with supporting evidence, how much you paid for an asset and how much it was worth when you gave (or willed) it away, Canada Revenue will require independent valuations and calculate the tax accordingly!

Almost everybody collects something: if not art then cars, books, stamps, coins, dolls, salt-and-pepper shakers. I know one man who has a corkscrew collection, several who collect wine and cigars, and even one who collects hotel keys now that they have all been replaced by plastic cards. Many of those collections are worth a substantial amount of money. *But how much? And how do their owners prove it?*

A Type E, even an eighty-four-year-old one, can't help sniffing an unmet *need* in those two questions. To the bred-in-the-bone entrepreneur, *every* problem is a new opportunity to provide a service that creates a lucrative business.

And every new circumstance, even death, creates its own opportunities.

> "Growing old is no more than a bad habit which a busy man has no time to form."   ANDRÉ MAUROIS, FRENCH BIOGRAPHER AND NOVELIST

IF YOU HAVE stayed with me to this page, there is a risk you may be thinking, "Well yeah, but all of that was in another century. Things are done differently today. Those kinds of tactics just wouldn't cut it in the twenty-first century."

I think the phrase my grandkids would use here is, "Well, duh." *Of course* the circumstances of business today and next year will be different from all those that went before, just as the world after August 1945 was not the world that preceded it. September 12, 2001, was not like the world before September 11 that year. Things change.

New products, new networks, new sciences and more people in every region of the limited planet who are trying to do more with their lives than people have ever imagined before: all of these can only mean more problems, more *needs*—and more opportunities.

Lack of opportunity is never the limit on success. New opportunities bloom daily. There is plenty for everyone. What are in short supply are those extraordinary individuals with the vigour, vision and vitality to exploit all the opportunities that events provide in such abundance.

Are *you* an entrepreneur? The answer depends on how *you* approach the day. Do you *see* opportunity at every turn? Do you *seize* the moment when it is ripe? Do you *do whatever it takes* to make the potential real?

The truth is that I could be in two new businesses a week. But then I would have to run them, and I am running out of time for that.

There are other things to do with my time now. I can't wait to get up in the morning. I'm studying Italian. I'm considering going back to school and finishing that university degree at last. I'd like to know more about economics. There are 100 things I would like to know more about—and that's just today.

A business school not long ago asked me to speak to one of its classes. I agreed, but asked for some time alone in the lecture hall before the audience was allowed in. The administrators looked a little perplexed, but agreed.

After the students filed in, I spoke for about thirty minutes. At the end of that time I said, "Ladies and gentlemen, you've sat there very patiently and listened to this old man ramble on. I'm sure you're all ready to stretch your legs. I'd like you all to stand up where you are."

They did, the entire roomful of twenty-something kids getting to their feet, looking a little unsure about it, as though the old guy at the front had maybe not taken his pills that morning.

"Now," I said loudly, recovering their attention, "now if you each look beneath your seat, you'll find an envelope taped there. Retrieve the envelope and open it."

There was a shuffle and murmur as they followed my instructions, then a rising buzz as each envelope was opened to reveal a one-dollar "loonie."

"There now," I said, my voice booming out over the room's loud-speakers. "If you get up off your butt, you can make a buck."

Entrepreneurship: Do YOU Have What It Takes?
© 2001 Elena Fawkner, used with permission.

PERSONAL QUALITIES

Equally important as the common issues shared by all entrepreneurs are the personal qualities of the entrepreneur him or herself. To start you thinking about whether you have the right stuff to make a success of an entrepreneurial venture, here's a list of character traits and work ethics common to successful entrepreneurs. Although it is not necessary that you possess all of them, you should possess most:

Passion—entrepreneurs have a strong passion for their idea or concept, so much so that their work is their play. If you don't like what you do, you won't stick it out when challenges come along, as they inevitably will.

Curiosity—entrepreneurs need to understand how things work. They ask a lot of questions. Curiosity therefore triggers innovation.

Sponges—entrepreneurs are sponges. They devour information about their industry and are always current on new and emerging trends and technologies, not only in their specific industry but in closely related industries. This habit of scanning their environment is a rich source of discovery of new opportunities. Entrepreneurs are

ALWAYS looking for new markets, applications, products or twists on an old concept.

Optimism—entrepreneurs think of problems as opportunities for improvements and new ideas.

Forward looking—entrepreneurs are never satisfied with the status quo and are always proactively carving out their future.

Careful about money—entrepreneurs are careful with money and have a firm grasp on what things cost and their value to the business. This allows them to recognize a true bargain when they see one.

Started earning at a young age—entrepreneurs commonly displayed entrepreneurial leanings as a teenager seeking out entrepreneurial activities such as babysitting, lawnmowing and lemonade stands.

Competitive—entrepreneurs are naturally competitive and don't let the grass grow under their feet.

Time conscious—entrepreneurs know the value of time and how to make the best use of it. You won't find entrepreneurs spending much time on nonproductive activities. That said, entrepreneurs typically also recognize the value of downtime and time with family and will factor these activities into their schedule.

Risk takers—entrepreneurs are not afraid of taking calculated risks. They typically trust their hunches and act on them.

Usually loners—entrepreneurs generally prefer a solitary work environment as opposed to teamwork.

Professional—entrepreneurs are professional in their approach to work. They operate as they would in a corporate environment and don't allow themselves to be distracted by outside influences.

High energy—entrepreneurs have a plan and a vision and they work it. Entrepreneurs are often health-conscious too, recognizing that the fitter they are, the better their minds work. So entrepreneurs will take time from their schedule to work out and eat well.

Flexible—entrepreneurs are nothing if not responsive to change. Although they appreciate the importance of having a plan and working that plan, they allow themselves room to react and respond to opportunities that may suddenly reveal themselves.

Nurture entrepreneurial spirit—entrepreneurs seek out and nurture the entrepreneurial spirit in their employees and reward them accordingly.

Confident goal-setters—entrepreneurs are confident and set long-term goals, both for themselves personally and their businesses. They view money and financial security as a measure of accomplishment and a source of peace of mind.

Persistent—entrepreneurs never give up. They persist until they succeed.

Learn from failure—entrepreneurs learn from their failures and those of others. Failure to an entrepreneur is nothing more than an opportunity waiting to be discovered.

Self responsibility—entrepreneurs take the initiative and personal responsibility for their success or failure (which is always a merely temporary state).

Resource utilization—entrepreneurs utilize ALL of their available resources.

Internal locus of control—entrepreneurs don't believe in luck. They firmly believe that success and failure lie within their personal control or influence.